The Experimental Approach to Free Will

Recently, psychologists and neurobiologists have conducted experiments taken to show that human beings do not have free will. Many, including a number of philosophers, assume that, even if science has not decided the free will question yet, it is just a matter of time. In *The Experimental Approach to Free Will*, Katherin A. Rogers accomplishes several tasks. First, canvasing the literature critical of these recent experiments (or of conclusions drawn from them) and adding new criticisms of her own, she shows why these experiments should not undermine belief in human freedom – even robust, libertarian freedom. Indeed, many of the experiments do not even connect with any philosophical understanding of free will. Through this discussion, she generates a long list of problems – ethical as well as practical – facing the attempt to study free will experimentally. With these problems highlighted, she shows that even in the distant future, supposing the brain sciences to have advanced far beyond where they are today, it will likely be impossible to settle the question of free will experimentally. She concludes that, since philosophy has not, and science *cannot*, settle the question of free will, it is more reasonable to suppose that humans do indeed have freedom.

Katherin A. Rogers is Professor in the Philosophy Department at the University of Delaware. Her publications include *Perfect Being Theology* (2000), *Anselm on Freedom* (2008), *Freedom and Self-Creation: Anselmian Libertarianism* (2015), and numerous articles in the philosophy of religion, medieval philosophy, and ethics, including such topics as freedom and foreknowledge, time and eternity, the moral status of abortion, and the justification of punishment.

The Experimental Approach to Free Will

Freedom in the Laboratory

Katherin A. Rogers

NEW YORK AND LONDON

First published 2022
by Routledge
605 Third Avenue, New York, NY 10158, USA

and by Routledge
4 Park Square, Milton Park, Abingdon, Oxon, OX14 4RN, UK

Routledge is an imprint of the Taylor & Francis Group, an informa business.

© 2022 Katherin A. Rogers

The right of Katherin A. Rogers to be identified as author of this work has been asserted in accordance with sections 77 and 78 of the Copyright, Designs and Patents Act 1988.

All rights reserved. No part of this book may be reprinted or reproduced or utilised in any form or by any electronic, mechanical, or other means, now known or hereafter invented, including photocopying and recording, or in any information storage or retrieval system, without permission in writing from the publishers.

Trademark notice: Product or corporate names may be trademarks or registered trademarks, and are used only for identification and explanation without intent to infringe.

Library of Congress Cataloging-in-Publication Data
A catalog record for this title has been requested.

ISBN: 978-1-032-19402-8 (hbk)
ISBN: 978-1-032-19403-5 (pbk)
ISBN: 978-1-003-25898-8 (ebk)

DOI: 10.4324/9781003258988

Typeset in Times New Roman
by SPi Technologies India Pvt Ltd (Straive)

Printed in the United Kingdom
by Henry Ling Limited

Contents

Acknowledgements viii

Introduction 1
Outline of the Book 8

1 Reasons for and against Free Will 12
*Introduction 12
Part I. Reasons to Commit to Free Will 13
  Freedom and Human Dignity 13
  More Pragmatic Arguments 20
  Evidence from Introspection 23
Part II. Presuppositions against Free Will 26
  Problematic Descriptions of Free Will 26
  Determinism 31
  Physicalism, the Self, and Epiphenomenalism 35*

2 A Paradigmatic Free Choice 42
*Introduction 42
A Paradigmatic, Libertarian Free, Morally Significant
  Choice 44
Other Kinds of Choice and Decision 55*

3 The Libet Experiments 61
*Introduction 61
Problems of Description and Translation 64
The Timing Problem 67*

Post Hoc ergo Propter Hoc 71
The Soon et al. Experiment 73

4   Conscious Will is an Illusion   79

Introduction 79
The "Illusion" Thesis 81
Evidence for the Illusion of Conscious Will 89
Responses to the "Illusion" Claims 96

5   Situationism   104

Introduction 104
Evidence for Situationism 108
The Challenge to Reasons-responsiveness 115
The Challenge to Character Building and Virtue Ethics 131

6   Ethical Issues in Experiments with Human Subjects   140

Introduction 140
Deception and Informed Consent 141
Harms to Subjects 146
Wrongs to Subjects 157
Harms and Wrongs to Researchers and Beyond 163
Expected Benefits 170
Uncharitable Interpretation 180

7   The Future Study of Human Freedom: Setting the Stage and Ethical Issues   183

Introduction 183
A Possible Future: The Brainiometer 184
The Future Study of Human Freedom: Harms and Wrongs 187
The Future Study of Human Freedom: Benefits 199
Alternative Methods and Charitable Interpretation 202

8   The Future Study of Human Freedom: Practical Problems   204

Introduction 204
The Need for a Brainiometer 204
Problems with Developing the Brainiometer 207
Studying Free Will 216
Conclusion 228

Appendix	229
Bibliography	232
Index	245

Acknowledgements

I would like to thank the students in my Senior Seminar class on "Freedom and Science" for their enthusiasm and insightful suggestions at the beginning of this project. I would also like to thank anonymous reviewers of earlier versions of the manuscript, especially the reviewer for Routledge. Their comments have led to significant improvements.

The Experimental Approach to Free Will

Introduction

For over two thousand years, philosophers have debated the question of whether or not human beings have free will. There are powerful philosophical arguments on both sides of the issue. Although many philosophers have come to firm and well-reasoned conclusions with which they are fully satisfied, the long debate has not rendered a consensus. In recent decades, a new approach has been added to this age-old discussion: Philosophers, psychologists, and neuroscientists have begun to assess empirical evidence that is held to bear on the question of free will. For example, there have been experiments showing that certain sorts of brain activity may precede choices. There is research showing that people's behavior can be influenced by factors of which they are unaware and research showing that people are often mistaken about what they are doing or have done. Thus, there is often a disconnect between people's intentions and beliefs about their actions and the actions themselves. Some experiments have been taken to show that people simply respond to the situation in which they find themselves and that character and considered reasons play little (if any) role in producing behavior. This body of evidence has led some to hold that the empirical evidence provides good reason to deny that human beings have free will.

Scholars debate the importance of free will and what the consequences would be if human freedom were shown to be an illusion, but a significant number – following a tradition that goes back at least to St. Augustine of Hippo – hold that one of the most valuable traits ascribed to human beings is our ability to choose freely. According to this tradition, free will grounds moral responsibility and, at least in part, explains our obligation to treat one another with a special respect which we do not owe to other animals. The issue is not just that we may properly reward or punish you if you are free, it is that you are the *kind of thing* that can properly be praised and blamed. As free, you have a special value, a special status, often labelled

DOI: 10.4324/9781003258988-1

"human dignity". In the Western world, our social and legal systems are rooted in this tradition and intertwined with belief in free will. If belief in free will is generally undermined, we cannot know what the result would be, but a case can be made that there would be serious upheaval of which the results could be decidedly negative.[1]

In the present work, I examine the philosophical debate over these recent free will experiments – a debate in which many brain scientists have actively participated – with two goals in mind. The more modest goal is to bring together, and sometimes add to, the various arguments showing that the experimental evidence to date leaves the question of human free will open. This is a useful project for two reasons. First, some, even in the philosophical community, hold that the experiments provide reason to doubt human freedom.[2] I argue that the debate so far demonstrates that this is a mistake. Second, in reviewing, and adding to, the criticisms leveled at the empirical anti–free will claim, I will develop a catalogue of problems facing attempts to study free will experimentally – problems both practical and ethical. (It is important to note the ethical problems since some of the moral issues attached to the study of human subjects are magnified when the question is the very private, and personally significant, matter of choice.) Some problems are more serious than others, and some seem more likely to admit of solutions than others, but the list is long and the problems are weighty. The list can be found in the Appendix at the end of this book. Establishing this catalogue of problems allows me to address my more ambitious goal: I will argue that experimental science will probably *never* be able to settle the question of free will.

This is a controversial claim. Although many philosophers hold that contemporary science leaves the reality of free will an open question, a common assumption is that, in the future, science will settle the issue. This is the thesis of Mark Balaguer's *Free Will as an Open Scientific Problem* (2010). According to Balaguer, "the libertarian question reduces to a straightforward empirical question about the physical world".[3] And Peter Simons writes,

---

[1] Other cultures may not share the Western conception of free will (Heidi M. Raven, "Putting Free Will in Context and Beyond", AJOB *Neuroscience* 6:2 (2015): 1–2, at 2). But this would not undermine the value of human freedom nor of "our" belief in free will. Nor would it establish the truth of whether or not free will as "we" understand it actually exists.

[2] Gregg D. Caruso, Elizabeth Shaw, and Derk Pereboom, "Free Will Skepticism in Law and Society: An Overview", Chapter 1 of *Free Will Skepticism in Law and Society: Challenging Retributive Justice*, edited by Elizabeth Shaw, Derk Pereboom, and Gregg D. Caruso (Cambridge, UK: Cambridge University Press, 2019): 5–6.

[3] Mark Balaguer, *Free Will as an Open Scientific Problem* (Cambridge, MA: MIT Press, 2010): 21.

We are discovering new facts about the workings of the brain at an unprecedented rate, which hold out the promise that some or all of the mysteries surrounding the operation of free will can be resolved, and the [free will] controversy resolved.[4]

I call this assumption into question.

In assessing the experimental evidence regarding free will, I will take it that the main concern is morally significant freedom – the freedom to choose well or badly, the freedom that can ground moral responsibility and hence underlie our special value, our human dignity. (I am understanding "morally significant" broadly such that what some philosophers might distinguish as "prudential" falls under the heading of "moral". More on this in Chapter 2.) There are many other sorts of choices – some trivial (like chocolate or pistachio) and some very important (like what career to choose). If human beings do have free will, it may well be that many of these non-moral choices are made freely. And various kinds of actions not involving deliberate choices may – on the assumption that human beings have free will – be appropriately considered free and in a way that grounds moral responsibility. For example, it could be argued that certain automatic actions and actions consequent on culpable forgetfulness are done freely and are subject to praise and blame. I bracket discussion of these issues for present purposes in order to focus on what I take to be the most pressing worry: whether or not human agents can ever make deliberate free choices in a way that grounds moral responsibility and the sort of dignity that has traditionally been associated with free will.

There are many philosophical theories regarding what constitutes human freedom. For the purposes of this book, I will focus on the libertarian theory of free will. The question is: What do the experiments tell us, and what might they tell us in the future, about the ability of a human being to make a libertarian free moral choice (LFMC)? There are several species of libertarianism, but the differences can largely be set aside for purposes of the present work. In Chapter 2, in the hope of getting clear on the object to be studied, I will sketch the general outlines of an LFMC, taking the core requirements to be the agent's capacity to deliberate rationally between options, a robust "ability to choose otherwise", and the agent's being the ultimate source of the choice. Focusing on an LFMC might appear to be an idiosyncratic way to proceed in that many, perhaps most, philosophers today who ascribe free will to human beings reject libertarianism in favor of compatibilism. Elsewhere, I have argued that it is libertarianism that best grounds moral responsibility and our human

---

4 Peter Simons, "Forward". In *Free Will and Modern Science* edited by Richard Swinburne, (Oxford: Oxford University Press, 2011): vii–xv, at xv.

dignity, and I have attempted to respond to criticisms of libertarianism.[5] A review of the philosophical debate over free will lies outside the scope of the present work. My main reason for focusing on libertarianism is that it is, at least prima facie, *harder* to square with popular scientific attitudes than is compatibilism.

Here a brief detour into terminology and basic concepts is in order. This is a work of philosophy, but it is about the brain sciences and many of the players are brain scientists rather than philosophers. Thus, it is perspicuous to explain and employ terms, definitions, and concepts that connect with the project at hand. In recent years, in philosophy, "causal determinism" is usually defined (roughly) as the claim that the events at any moment of time, plus the laws of nature, entail the events at any other moment in time. For reasons that will become clear shortly, it is best, for our purposes, to think of this view as *universal* causal determinism (UCD). It is difficult to square UCD with robust human freedom. A recent and well-known expression of the problem is Peter van Inwagen's "Consequence Argument". van Inwagen, explaining his "basic argument", writes,

> If determinism is true, then our acts are the consequences of laws of nature and events in the remote past. But it's not up to us what went on before we were born, and neither is it up to us what the laws of nature are. Therefore, the consequences of these things (including our present acts) are not up to us.[6]

And – according to the libertarian, at least – our choices must be "up to us" if we are to have the freedom associated with human dignity. Some brain scientists seem to accept a version of UCD, but when studying human agency experimentally, they (by and large) are not interested in "the remote past". It is almost always events in the recent past of a choice or action that concerns them. Many argue that experiments provide evidence to deny free will because they show that all of our choices and acts are produced by events in the recent history of those choices and acts, events over which we have no control. Although different scientists point to different sorts of determining events, we can call this general claim *local* causal determinism (LCD). UCD is widely disputed today, and were it somehow *shown* to be false, that would have very little impact on the actual experimental work concerning free will. A "local" version of the consequence argument – mutatis mutandis – seems to underlie the denial of free will for which some experimenters claim to have found empirical evidence. To paraphrase:

---

5 Katherin Rogers, *Freedom and Self-Creation: Anselmian Libertarianism* (Oxford: Oxford University Press, 2015).
6 Peter van Inwagen, *An Essay on Free Will* (Oxford: Clarendon Press, 1983): 56.

If local causal determinism is true, then our acts are the consequences of laws of nature and events in the recent past over which (as our experiments show us) we have no control. But events over which we have no control are not up to us, and neither is it up to us what the laws of nature are. Therefore, the consequences of these things (including our present acts) are not up to us.

Philosophers (focusing on UCD) have tended to divide into compatibilists and incompatibilists. The incompatibilists hold (roughly) that the existence of free will or *meaningful* free will or *responsibility-grounding* free will cannot be reconciled with UCD. In that case, the three main options are embrace UCD and reject free will (a position sometimes labelled "hard" determinism), embrace free will and reject UCD (the libertarian move), or recognize the incompatibility but suspend judgement on how the world is vis-à-vis free will. One could equally be an incompatibilist regarding LCD. Many of those doing experiments involving human agency seem to assume incompatibilism and, understanding their experiments as evidence of LCD, many deny free will (often seeming to think of free will along libertarian lines.)

Compatibilist philosophers hold (roughly) that free will or *meaningful* free will or *responsibility-grounding* free will can be reconciled with UCD. One popular approach is to argue (*pace* van Inwagen) that, even if UCD is the case, our choices and actions can be "up to us" in a way that allows for free will (or, if not free will, still moral responsibility). The theories usually distinguish between preceding factors that figure in the history of a choice and would undermine free will – for example, an uncontrollable phobia – and preceding factors that figure in the history of a choice but do not undermine free will or are even requisite for free will. For example, one standard move holds (very roughly) that an agent's choices and actions are free (or at least done responsibly) if they follow upon the agent's considered reasons and desires.

The psychologists and neuroscientists working on human agency often seem unaware that in philosophy there is another way besides "hard" determinism or libertarian free will. One reason for this lack of interest may be that the versions of LCD defended by many of the experimenters would conflict with many compatibilist theories as well as with libertarianism. The versions of LCD proposed by experimenters often do not allow the standard compatibilist moves (e.g., that a choice can be free or responsible when it follows in the right way from the agent's reasons and desires). The sorts of events which some neuroscientists and psychologists take to produce our choices and actions (along with the laws of nature) might be, for example, brain events over which we have no control. Or perhaps our choices are caused by elements in our environment of which we are unaware. Thus, some argue that we never choose what we choose and do what we do based on rational deliberation. So, although in principle compatibilism could reconcile some analyses of freedom and responsibility with some species of LCD, the actual kinds of LCD for which experimenters say they have found evidence are often *in*compatible with many versions of compatibilism as well as with libertarianism.

Most libertarians – in company with most compatibilists – will insist that the agent be able to rationally assess his options and choose on the basis of his reasons and desires. Libertarianism (at least the version I am working with as set out in Chapter 2) adds two more requirements: the agent must confront genuinely open options and he must choose "on his own"; that is, he must be the ultimate source of his choice. Libertarianism, then, is incompatible with both UCD and *any version* of LCD. If it can be shown that the experimental evidence does not – and probably never can – disprove *libertarian* free will, then it is extremely unlikely that it could disprove compatibilist free will. So, if I can make my case that the question of whether or not human beings make LFMCs probably cannot be settled empirically, I have defended free will in general, under both libertarian and compatibilist views.

Another reason for focusing on LFMCs is that, as mentioned above, many of the psychologists and neuroscientists who hold that human beings do not have free will seem to assume a libertarian account.[7] In the editorial leading a 2015 number of American Journal of Bioethics (AJOB) *Neuroscience* devoted to the empirical study of free will, Heidi M. Ravven writes, "Let's clarify a bit what is meant by free will.... [a] choice is 'free' because we could have done otherwise in the present, and in identical conditions we could do otherwise in the future". She adds that this involves an "implicit attribution to human beings of characteristics beyond nature and the natural".[8]

Whether or not the "folk" assume a libertarian view of free will is an open question. Indeed, it is not clear that there is one, common understanding, nor that the views of non-philosophers are metaphysically informed or coherent.[9] (It should be noted that many of the studies have

---

7 Eddy Nahmias, "Why 'Willusionism' Leads to 'Bad Results': Comments on Baumeister, Crescioni, and Alquist", *Neuroethics* 4 (2011): 17–24, at 18–19.
8 Ravven (2015): 2.
9 For some recent studies coming to differing views on the question of the folk understanding of free will, see Tim Bayne, "Libet and the case for free will skepticism", in *Free Will and Modern Science* edited by Richard Swinburne (Oxford: Oxford University Press, 2011): 25–46; Esthelle Ewusi-Boisvert and Eric Racine, "A Critical Review of Methodologies and Results in Recent Research on Belief in Free Will", *Neuroethics* 11 (2018): 97–110; O. Deery, T. Davis, and J. Carey, "The Free-Will Intuitions Scale and the Question of Natural Compatibilism", *Philosophical Psychology* 28 (6) (2015): 776–801; Andrew E. Monroe and Bertram F. Malle, "Free Will Without Metaphysics", in *Surrounding Free Will: Philosophy, Psychology, Neuroscience* edited by Alfred R. Mele (Oxford: Oxford University Press, 2015): 25–8; Myrto I. Mylopoulos and Hakwan Lau, "Naturalizing Free Will: Paths and Pitfalls", in Mele (2015): 123–44; Eddy Nahmias, J. Shepard, and S. Reuter, "It's OK if 'My Brain Made Me Do It': People's Intuitions about

been done on undergraduates.) That non-philosophers may have muddled concepts concerning human freedom does not conflict with the claim that free will, under some description, is valuable and valued, nor does it conflict with the worry that the denial of free will on the part of some scientists – a well-respected caste in our society – could have harmful consequences.[10] The connection which our tradition, and our society, makes between free will and human dignity suggests that it is demeaning to a human agent to deny that they have free will. Of course, that does not settle the question of whether or not people actually do have free will. However, it is wrong to demean people without good reason; so, with an unsettled issue like free will, it seems appropriate to place the burden of proof on those who would deny human freedom. (I will argue this case in Chapter 1 against those who assign the burden of proof to those who defend free will.) The experimental evidence should be strong before it is claimed that human agents never exercise free choice, and my argument will be that we cannot expect such evidence, even in a distant future where the brain sciences have advanced far, far beyond what they are capable of today. (The last chapters of this book construct a thought experiment in which the brain sciences do not suffer under current limitations.) There are further issues related to this prescription to avoid demeaning people. One is that ethical considerations must be taken seriously in the attempt to study human freedom experimentally. Another is that, where multiple interpretations fit the data equally well, interpretations that respect the participants should be preferred or, at least, not rejected.

There are deep, perennial philosophical questions associated with how to assess the free will experiments. For example, there are questions about the nature of causation: What is a cause? How do we discover causes? What constitutes an adequate explanation? Should questions concerning causation be dealt with purely conceptually as a metaphysical issue, or should the actual practice of the various sciences be invoked? Another question related to the free will experiments has to do with the relationship of the mental to the physical, mind to matter, soul to body. The neuroscientist studies goings-on in the brain, but a free choice, if there is such a thing, is a conscious action on the part of an agent. How are these prima facie very different sorts of things to be associated? Volumes and volumes have been written on these thorny and recalcitrant topics, and multiple

---

Free Will and Neuroscientific Prediction", *Cognition* 133 (2) (2014): 502–16; Jonathan Schooler, Thomas Nadelhoffer, Eddy Nahmias, and Kathleen D. Vohs, "Measuring and Manipulating Beliefs and Behaviors Associated with Free Will", in Mele (2015): 72–94; Jason Shepard and Shane Reuter, "Neuroscience, Choice and the Free Will Debate", AJOB *Neuroscience* 3 (3) (2012): 7–11.

10 Eddy Nahmias, Stephen Morris, Thomas Nadelhoffer, and Jason Turner, "Surveying Freedom: Folk Intuitions about Free Will and Moral Responsibility", *Philosophical Psychology* 18:5 (2005): 561–84.

theories advanced. Although I will have a little bit to say about each of these issues and about a few other hard, perennial philosophical questions, delving deeply into the extensive literature on such questions is too ambitious a task for the present work. I believe I can amass my list of problems for the experimental study of free will without expressing and defending a position on these complex and currently debated philosophical issues.

Although I aim to point out numerous problems concerning research on free will and on the conclusion that denies human freedom, my criticisms will be narrowly focused on specific elements of particular experiments and interpretations. There is an enormous literature in the relevant fields which looks to *advance* the cause of human autonomy. I will take it that the capacity for making LFMCs is an "either-you-have-it-or-you-don't" sort of property, but if we assume that people are capable of LFMCs (and even on many compatibilist theories), it seems plausible that an agent can have more or less autonomy (i.e., more or less control over their situation and character). A great deal of neuroscientific research aims to help us understand how the brain functions when the agent is making choices and decisions. This, in turn, will help us as a species to work toward averting the *mal*functions. And, as will be discussed in Chapter 4, there are psychological studies galore on how people make mistakes about what they have done and are doing. Awareness of this tendency to misunderstand our choices and actions could give us better control in the future. Moreover, the findings of psychological studies have been used to help people conquer internal stumbling blocks and so to take more control of their own psychological landscape. This progress often occurs within the context of studies which will advance even more this aim of helping people to pursue, in more productive ways, the goals that they choose.[11] So, although I point to problems within various experiments in neuroscience and psychology, these sciences should not be seen as the enemies of freedom. Rather, allowing the possibility of morally significant freedom, they will, I believe, prove to be among the best friends of human autonomy.

Outline of the Book

Chapter 1: Reasons for and against Free Will

In Part 1, I discuss reasons for believing in free will in the absence of empirical evidence. The main reason is that belief in human freedom is connected to belief in moral responsibility and human dignity. Other practical

---

11 See, for example, Peter M. Gollwitzer, Ute C. Bayer, and Kathleen C. McCulloch, "The Control of the Unwanted". In *The New Unconscious* edited by Ron R. Hassin, James S. Uleman, and John A. Bargh (New York: Oxford University Press, 2005: 485–515); Yaacov Trope and Ayelet Fishback, "Going Beyond the Motivation Given: Self-Control and Situational Control Over Behavior". In Hassin, Ron R. et al. (2005): 537–65.

benefits of believing in freedom are discussed, as is the evidence from introspection. I offer brief responses to recent arguments that denying free will may not prove harmful overall. Part 2 deals with problems in how "free will" has been understood in the free will and science debate and with controversial metaphysical assumptions, such as the assumption of determinism (either UCD or what I am calling LCD), that some bring to the analysis of experiments purporting to provide information concerning freedom.

Chapter 2: A Paradigmatic Free Choice

In order to deal with the various Problems of Translation – issues concerning whether the data from the experiments can be applied to morally significant choices – it is useful to see what such a choice might involve. It is also helpful to appreciate that elements often associated with free choice are not among the criteria necessary for a choice to be free. The sketch I offer of an LFMC is general and simplified enough to satisfy most libertarians. The main elements are that the agent be torn between moral options, be able to choose either one, and make the choice *a se* – from himself or on his own. I then discuss some other sorts of choice in order to pinpoint the differences between these choices and the LFMC.

Chapter 3: The Libet Experiments

In the early 1980s, Benjamin Libet conducted experiments which he took to show that brain activity precedes, and produces, the urge or decision to move. Libet himself did not take this to conflict with free will since he believed he had found evidence of an ability to "veto" the urge or decision and not make the movement. Many others, though, cite the Libet experiments as evidence that human agents do not have free will. There are many problems with Libet's interpretation of his experiments, including that the "choice" he was studying is nothing like a morally significant choice, the situation in which his subjects were observed was highly artificial, the problem of how to isolate an individual "urge" or brain event is not addressed, the subjects are asked to observe their own mental states, which may interfere with the system under observation, and Libet and many who cite him commit the post hoc fallacy. Later experiments by Soon et al. (also cited as evidence against freedom) are subject to many of the same problems.

Chapter 4: Conscious Will Is an Illusion

Daniel Wegner and Michael Gazzaniga provide evidence that there is a disconnect between our intentions and our actions such that the former are not among the causes of the latter. Among the problems that arise is the Problem of Generalization: moving from "some" to "all" without sufficient justification. Another issue is the Problem of Focus: experimenters mistakenly concentrate on an event that is not directly relevant to the study of free will or to the conclusions they draw. For example, the *feeling* that one is deliberately intending an action is taken to be the same thing as deliberately intending an action. And failing to correctly remember what one has done is taken to show that one's action did not follow upon conscious intentions. This "illusion" thesis also raises the Problem of Self-Refutation. For example, performing experiments, by definition, is purposive activity, so if one's conscious goals do not figure in the causal history of one's actions, one cannot have performed an experiment.

Chapter 5: Situationism

Situationism holds that people do not have robust character traits but rather act on the basis of trivial elements in their situation. This poses a problem for free will in that it appears to entail that people do not act for reasons. As I describe an LFMC, it must be preceded by the torn condition where the agent rationally deliberates concerning his options. Moreover, many who defend free will see one of its great values as allowing the agent to help in the construction of his own character, but the situationist calls into question the existence of character itself. The situationist interpretation of the relevant experiments is open to serious doubt, especially because of the Problem of Perspective. What appear to the situationists to be trivial elements may very well be extremely powerful motivators from the perspective of the subjects in the experiments. The Problem of Focus arises because the situationists focus on the character trait of compassion but that proves to be an especially problematic trait when seeking evidence about character in general. The situationist experiments are particularly interesting for my purposes because they do *not* bring up the Problem of Translation Regarding the Object of Study. They often involve subjects (at least apparently) making moral choices.

Chapter 6: Ethical Issues in Experiments with Human Subjects

Experiments with human subjects inevitably involve moral issues. To introduce ethical questions that will be relevant to the future study of free will, I look at some recent debate, focused mainly on deceptive experiments, using the Milgram experiments as an illustration. The discussion proceeds within the framework of the Ethics Code of the American Psychological Association (APA) noting especially harms and wrongs that the APA code does not emphasize, such as ongoing psychological distress to subjects, putting the subjects at moral risk, violation of privacy, and harms to the characters of researchers. It is not clear that the benefits in terms of knowledge gained from the Milgram experiments are worth the cost. I conclude by noting that interpretations that demean subjects should not be preferred to more charitable interpretations when the data support both equally well.

Chapter 7: The Future Study of Human Freedom: Setting the Stage and Ethical Issues

I imagine a scientist of the future, Dr. F, who hopes to settle the question of human free will and has access to a Brainiometer. With it he can observe brain activity that correlates to mental events and read minds with great accuracy. The Brainiometer can solve some of the most recalcitrant problems that brain scientists have faced, most notably the Problem of Translation Regarding the Object of Study. Dr. F can study the systems and processes that constitute (what appear to be) morally significant choices. But ethical problems are exacerbated. The Problem of Privacy is especially worrisome, so that informed consent is crucial, but finding a representative pool of subjects willing to be monitored by the invasive Brainiometer while they make moral choices may prove daunting. And it is not clear that the benefits of information gained from Dr. F's experiments are worth the cost.

Chapter 8: The Future Study of Human Freedom: Practical Problems

The best bet for Dr. F to study free will is to observe human beings making what appear to be morally significant free choices. But in order to do that, he will need to observe what goes on in the agent's brain/mind with great specificity. And he will need to grasp not only the content of the agent's beliefs but also the nature of the agent's desires. Thus, he will have to have the Brainiometer or something like it. But it is unlikely that humanity will ever be able to construct such an instrument. A review of a recent experiment which correlated concepts with brain activity in a very general way demonstrates the difficulties with the sort of fine-tuning that the Brainiometer would require. Finally, human choices are complex and absolutely unique. Even if Dr. F, using the Brainiometer, were able to detect a particular pattern of brain activity before the agent made a choice of one option over another, he could not prove that that activity caused the preference since a single instance does not make that case. Science will probably never settle the free will question. That being the case, it is better to commit to belief in human freedom.

Chapter 1

Reasons for and against Free Will

Introduction

My thesis is that science will likely never be able to settle the question of free will experimentally. In Part I of this chapter, I offer a brief outline of why it is reasonable to commit to belief in free will when the empirical evidence leaves the question open. Although I will mention introspection, the most important reason to accept free will is the connection between freedom and human dignity. Also very important is the evidence for harmful consequences that might follow upon widespread, popular denial of free will. These pragmatic reasons place the burden of proof on those who hold that science does (or can) show that we do not have free will. I dispute the recent attempt by "free will skeptics" to argue that belief in free will has overall harmful consequences and that the burden of proof is on the defender of free will.

In Part II, I look at a number of philosophical presuppositions that lead some scientists involved in the debate to deny free will, or at least lean strongly toward denying it, even before they engage in the various free will experiments. First, I note that some scientists offer a description of "free will" that is far from any typical, philosophical understanding – libertarian or compatibilist. Furthermore, many scientists presuppose metaphysical positions that they take to conflict with belief in free will. Some assume universal causal determinism (UCD), a metaphysical stance that would indeed conflict with free will. Often the assumption of UCD is justified by the supposition that belief in UCD – or at least LCD – is required in order to do the science in question. I argue that this is obviously false. Some scientists accept physicalism and assume that physicalism entails the denial of free will. I say just a little about physicalism (and the related issues of dualism and epiphenomenalism) since a developed discussion is beyond the scope of the present work, but I will note that the assumed entailment is not a necessary one.

Part I. Reasons to Commit to Free Will

Freedom and Human Dignity

If (as I will argue) science cannot settle the question either for or against the existence of human free will, is the most rational position to sit on the fence? I think not. We have to act in the world, and embracing or rejecting belief in robust free will can have a significant impact on how we go about the business of our lives. That science does not provide a conclusion does not entail that agnosticism regarding free will is the most rational position. I will argue that those who aim to show that human beings do not have free will bear the burden of proof and, in the absence of powerful evidence against free will, it is more reasonable to commit to the view that human agents are free.

It is a standard claim in the Western tradition that free will is necessary for the agent to bear moral responsibility to be capable of being morally blameworthy or praiseworthy for individual choices. But coupled with that value (and even more fundamental) is the thought that freedom is a core aspect of human dignity – the value that accrues to us in virtue of our being the very impressive kind of beings who can (to some degree) exercise control over how our lives go and hence contribute to the sorts of people we become. I will take it that this is the most important reason for committing to the claim that we are free; it is demeaning to people to deny that they possess what has traditionally been considered such a significant value-bestowing property. Participants in the science and free will debate often note – sometimes with disapproval – that belief in the value of free will has been handed down to us from within the Christian tradition. I take it that this is correct. (Belief in the universal dignity and basic, metaphysical equality of all human beings can also be credited to that tradition.) Evidence of the traditional importance of free will is apparent in the fact that philosophers within the Christian tradition for the last two thousand years have consistently insisted that God (that being than which a greater cannot be conceived) must be free – on the grounds that a being is a better kind of thing if it is capable of free choice than if it is not. An actor who lacks freedom cannot be good on his own, lacks power, and must depend on beings outside himself to do what he does.

Christian philosophers have traditionally applied the same principle to human beings. Augustine, one of the main architects of Christian philosophy, argues that being a free agent makes one a better kind of being, even if one abuses one's free will.[1] Since the days of Irenaeus and Augustine,

---

1 *On Free Will* 2.19. Augustine is clearly a compatibilist in his later work, and his early insistence on the value of freedom coupled with this compatibilism generated ongoing debate. The work of Immanuel Kant constitutes the locus classicus in modern times of the connection between free will and human dignity.

Christian philosophers have insisted upon the enormous value of human freedom in proposing versions of the "free will defense" and "free will theodicy"; the former attempts to show that the moral evil in the world is at least consistent with a perfectly good and omnipotent God, whereas the latter attempts to offer an explanation for why a perfectly good and omnipotent God would permit so much moral evil. Both approaches operate on the assumption that human free will is so important that God "stands back" and allows human agents to make free choices, even though this entails the possibility of unleashing significant evil. Free will is worth the cost.

For some contemporary participants in the science and free will debate, the fact that belief in the value of free will originates mainly through the religious tradition makes the ascription of free will to human agents automatically suspect.[2] But others will see it as an obvious truth that the ascription of free will, whatever its origins, is key to belief in human dignity. Robert Kane, the most important proponent of event-causal libertarianism, sets himself the task of defending

> the traditional image of free will... [which] accounts for the association of free will with human dignity, expressed in the religious traditions by saying that humans are made in the image of God – being creators *ab initio* of at least some things in the universe, their own purposes and the actions issuing from those purposes[3]

Timothy O'Connor, introducing his agent-causal libertarian theory, writes,

> Freedom of will is directly connected to the possibility or significance of moral responsibility, autonomy, the uniqueness of persons (involving creativity, originality, and their life histories in general), dignity, love, and friendship. In short, it is connected to everything that fundamentally matters to us in our relationships with one another.[4]

At least some of those who explicitly deny or are deeply skeptical about free will for philosophical reasons agree with this assessment of the traditional connection between freedom and human dignity. Among philosophers, Derk Pereboom, a free will skeptic, holds that "no matter what of value about human life hard [determinist] incompatibilism can legitimately

---

2 Paul Sheldon Davies, "What Kind of Agent are We? A Naturalistic Framework for the Study of Human Agency". In *Distributed Cognition and the Will: Individual Volition and Social Context* edited by Don Ross, David Spurrett, Harold Kincaid, and G. Lynn Stephens (Cambridge, MA: MIT Press, 2007): 39–60, at 44.
3 Robert Kane, *The Significance of Free Will* (New York: Oxford University Press, 1996): 4. Kane devotes Chapter 6, "Significance", to developing the connection between free will and human dignity.
4 Timothy O'Connor, *Persons and Causes* (New York: Oxford University Press, 2000): xii.

retain, it must relinquish a component of the ordinary conception of what sets human beings apart from the rest of the world". If we reject free will, we can retain our concept of moral worth, "but it is more similar to the value we might assign to an automobile or a work of art".[5] Saul Smilansky, though denying the reality of libertarian free will, takes *belief* in free will to be so important that "illusion often has a *large and positive role* [Smilansky's italics] to play in the issue of free will". He writes, "There is a sense in which our notion of moral self-respect, which is intimately connected with our view of our choices, actions, and achievements, withers when we accept [that there is no libertarian free will]."[6] He argues that even if people do not have more robust libertarian free will, compatibilist free will should be defended as grounding respect for others. Why is it important to pay this respect to others? Well, we want to be respected ourselves and so it is just to offer that same respect to our equals. And people do have a special value, which it is important to appreciate.[7]

The traditionally perceived connection between freedom and human dignity is also recognized by scientists, although some apparently find the view benighted. Don Ross labels his introduction to *Distributed Cognition and the Will* "Science Catches the Will" and writes dismissively that "It has been taken as a principal source of human specialness that we are putatively original authors of some events." I take it that he is right about the perceived connection between human "specialness" and our being the authors of some of our behavior. He goes on to paint those who make this association between free will and human dignity as scientifically backwards. "Millions of people around the world deny rationally incontrovertible evidence for evolution because they fear that natural selection threatens the sense of human and divine autonomy."[8]

Although some who grant the connection between free will and human dignity are comfortable rejecting human freedom, the Code of Ethics of the American Psychological Association (APA) states that psychologists are expected to respect people, and part of that respect is coupled with appreciation of the individual's right to self-determination and the individual's autonomy. Thus, the Code seems to embrace human freedom (at least under some description) and to make the connection between freedom and dignity. Under General Principles of the Code of Ethics of the APA, we read "Principle E: Respect for People's Rights and Dignity":

---

5 Derk Pereboom, *Living Without Free Will* (Cambridge, UK: Cambridge University Press, 2001): 153–4.
6 Saul Smilansky, "Free Will, Fundamental Dualism, and the Centrality of Illusion". In *The Oxford Handbook of Free* Will, 1st ed., edited by Robert Kane (Oxford: Oxford University Press, 2002): 489–505, at 500, 499.
7 Saul Smilansky, "Free Will and Respect for Persons", *Midwest Studies* 29 (2005): 248–61, at 249.
8 Don Ross, "Introduction: Science Catches the Will". In Ross (2007): 1–16, at 1, 5.

Psychologists respect the dignity and worth of all people, and the rights of individuals to privacy, confidentiality, and self-determination. Psychologists are aware that special safeguards may be necessary to protect the rights and welfare of persons or communities whose vulnerabilities impair autonomous decision making.[9]

Mark Balaguer, who holds that whether or not human agents have libertarian free will is a straightforward empirical question, argues that even though we may *want* freedom as necessary for responsibility and hence for the human dignity that is associated with it, that desire is irrelevant to a scientific approach to the issue. "There's the job of figuring out which kinds of freedom are worth wanting, and there's the job of figuring out which kinds of freedom we've got, and the former is not relevant to the latter."[10] Granted, these are two different jobs. But if one is concerned about what position to hold on the question of human freedom, then the former job is relevant to the latter in two ways: First, I take it that most of us agree that it is wrong to promote disparaging claims about our fellow human beings unless those claims can be supported. This (as I will argue) places the burden of proof on those who would deny free will. Second, in the absence of proof either for or against free will, we should consider what is the most reasonable attitude to adopt. Balaguer grants that at present the empirical question of "what kinds of freedom we've got" is open, and he holds that "All we can do at the present time is shrug and say, "Who knows?""[11] I suspect that it is not possible to maintain this agnostic attitude in practice, but (in any case) I believe it would be a mistake. As philosophers of such differing views as Kane, O'Connor, Pereboom, and Smilansky agree and as the Code of Ethics of the APA suggests, the ascription of free will and human dignity entails practical consequences regarding how we think of ourselves and how we treat each other. In the absence of philosophical consensus and scientific proof, agnosticism would encourage us to suspend judgment regarding the respect for the dignity of free human beings which has been a cornerstone of our civilization. For those not convinced by the philosophical arguments for determinism (UCD or LCD), it is far better to commit to belief in free will and to the respect for the dignity of our neighbors that has traditionally accompanied that belief.

Sometimes it seems to be supposed that the value that defenders see in belief in freedom is simply that it allows us – society – to punish wrongdoers: "Philosophers have worried that the absence of free will would mean the absence of responsibility and therefore the inability to punish people

---

9 https://www.apa.org/ethics/code/ethics-code-2017.pdf.
10 Balaguer (2010): 44.
11 Balaguer (2010): 69.

for their harmful actions."[12] Psychologist Steven Pinker suggests that the point of assigning responsibility is only to justify punishment to deter harmful behavior and that, deep down, this is the case even for those who *say* that their aim in punishing is to see that the wrongdoer receives his just deserts. We do not hold lower animals responsible, precisely because they cannot be deterred by punishment of others. Deterrence is "the active ingredient that makes responsibility worth keeping".[13] The implication of this supposition that the central concern in the free will debate is the justification of punishment is that being free and responsible would be (on balance) a negative for the free agent.

Scott Sehon, in his *Free Will and Action Explanation*, seems to share this attitude. Proposing a non-causal account of free will, he argues that, unlike his own theory, causal accounts such as Robert Kane's event-causal libertarian theory and John Martin Fischer's and Mark Ravizza's reasons-responsive semicompatibilist theory[14] suffer a serious epistemic problem; on their analyses, it is impossible now, and may be impossible simpliciter, to tell whether or not their theories describe reality. Sehon goes on to conclude that the proper approach for someone adopting such a scientifically unproven (and perhaps unprovable) account of free will is to "accept that, for all practical purposes, we should treat ordinary adults in ordinary circumstances as *not* free and responsible for their actions". This should be the default position since "it would be unfair to hold people responsible under those circumstances."[15] Derk Pereboom seems to share the view that our main lookout in assessing where the burden of proof lies in the free will debate has to do with punishment. The worry about harming the wrongdoer who is not blameworthy in the basic desert sense should encourage free will skepticism, which (for practical purposes) looks (at least to me) to be a denial of free will. Pereboom writes, "if one aims to harm another, then one's justification must meet a high epistemic standard" – a standard free will theories have not met.[16]

12 Carol S. Dweck and Daniel C. Molden, "Self-Theories: The Construction of Free Will". In *Are We Free? Psychology and Free Will* edited by John Baer, James C. Kaufman, and Roy F. Baumeister (Oxford: Oxford University Press, 2008): 44–64, at 44. See also Derk Pereboom, *Free Will, Agency, and Meaning in Life* (Oxford: Oxford University Press, 2014); *Free Will Skepticism* edited by Elizabeth Shaw, Derk Pereboom and Gregg D. Caruso (Cambridge, UK: Cambridge University Press, 2019).
13 Steven Pinker, "The Fear of Determinism". In Baer, et al. (2008): 311–24, at 317–18, 322.
14 This semi-compatibilism combines agnosticism about the compatibility of free will and determinism with the view that human agents can bear moral responsibility even if determinism is true.
15 Scott Sehon, *Free Will and Action Explanation: A Non-Causal, Compatibilist Account* (Oxford: Oxford University Press, 2016): 195–6. Sehon mentions the issue of praise, but it is not clear whether or not he takes it to be *unfair* to praise someone who is not free. In any case, he holds that his own analysis of free will avoids the problem by adopting a teleological account of free will rather than a causal account.
16 Pereboom (2014): 178.

I will be operating with the sort of account of free choice against which Sehon raises his epistemic problem; the *freedom* of the choice lies in how the choice is brought about. The thesis of my work is that science has not (and probably cannot) determine whether or not human beings make free choices. But I take the opposite view from Sehon's and Pereboom's: In the absence of conclusive scientific evidence, we should treat ordinary adults in ordinary circumstances as free and responsible for their actions. Doesn't this mean accepting the risk that – since possibly human agents do not have free will – harm may be inflicted on wrongdoers without the justification of their having the sort of robust, responsibility-grounding freedom that would allow for the wrongdoer to *deserve* the punishment? I fear it does. But there are three points to make here. First, and most importantly, at least in the Western tradition, the ascription of free will to human agents has not been motivated only (or mainly) by a desire to ground deserved punishment. Augustine said, and century after century of Western intellectuals followed him, that one core aspect of human dignity is our ability to choose freely. This, along with rationality, makes us images of God. Even those who deny the existence of God (or bracket theism when they are philosophizing) have made this connection between freedom and dignity. Even the APA makes the connection! Thus, denying freedom to someone demeans them. And failing in respect may have significant harmful consequences. Second, even if we grant that ascribing freedom risks unjust harm to the wrongdoer, there is also a risk of failing to give credit where credit is due. Assigning freedom and responsibility concerns praise as well as blame. If, in the absence of conclusive evidence for free will, we do not hold people free and responsible, we run the risk of failing to praise and reward those who deserve it.

Third, as the quote from Steven Pinker above suggests, denying that human agents possess free will does not entail that wrongdoers will escape punishment. Rather, the harm will be inflicted on the wrongdoer mainly to prevent him from further wrongdoing and to deter others. To put the point uncharitably but not inaccurately: On the denial of freedom, society will (and should) think of the wrongdoer as someone to be used for our benefit.[17] Pinker quotes Oliver Wendell Holmes with approval:

> If I were having a philosophical talk with a man I was going to have hanged (or electrocuted) I should say, 'I don't doubt that your act was

---

17 Some recent philosophers have aimed to minimize the unappetizing connotations of "using" someone by drawing an analogy between inflicting harm on the undeserving, because not free, wrongdoer and quarantining the contagious person in defense of self and society. For example, Gregg D. Caruso, "Free Will Skepticism and Its Implications: An Argument for Optimism" in Shaw et al. (2019): 43–72; Pereboom (2014): 165–74. Pereboom grants that harm to the wrongdoer still constitutes "use" but it is justified use (167).

inevitable for you but to make it more avoidable by others we propose to sacrifice you to the common good. You may regard yourself as a soldier dying for your country if you like. But the law must keep its promises.'[18]

The willingness to "sacrifice" the wrongdoer seems problematic in itself. And abstracting out a notion of what the criminal *deserves* seems to set aside questions of justice. For example, it could undermine the thought that there should be a proportion between the punishment and the crime. The issue becomes what punishment will best serve the ends of society. C.S. Lewis writes, "I urge a return to the traditional or Retributive theory not solely, or even primarily, in the interests of society, but in the interests of the criminal."[19]

Moreover, as critics of purely preventive and deterrence theories of punishment always ask rhetorically: If some are to be "sacrificed" in this way to benefit society, why only wrongdoers? In a scenario in which the authorities believe that "punishing" an innocent will deter wrongdoing and benefit society, such "punishment" would be justified. Retributive theories of punishment have their weaknesses, too, but one problem they aim to avoid is the thought that the one being punished is an object to be used. Retributivists usually argue that focusing on desert is more respectful of the dignity of the individual. The contemporary free will skeptics argue that the consequence of harm to the wrongdoer places a powerful burden of proof on the defender of free will. They often focus on extreme harm. Doesn't the retributivist approach, grounded in belief in free will, encourage us – society – to inflict more severe harm on the wrongdoer than would adopting skepticism or denial vis-à-vis free will? And in the face of extreme harm, the wrongdoer likely does not value that "respect for his dignity" that the retributivist claims to be exercising. But the free will defender can offer several responses. One is that denying that human beings have free will involves failing in respect for everybody and hence might have dire consequences overall which outweigh the benefit of less harm to the wrongdoer. A second observation draws on our lack of certainty regarding free will. When it comes to extreme harm – such as capital punishment – the *possibility* that human agents do not have responsibility-grounding free will may be enough to justify mitigating the harm. A different response based on our epistemic limitations notes that the ascription of free will is

---

18 Pinker (2008) 318. There is apparently good reason to believe that capital punishment does not actually have a significant deterrent effect. Holmes, then, may have been mistaken about the benefit he thought to achieve. Likely, the presumption that capital punishment would deter was based more on intuition than on empirical evidence. This casts an even more sinister light on his willingness to sacrifice the wrongdoer.
19 C.S. Lewis, "The Humanitarian Theory of Punishment", *Res Judicatae* 30 (1954): 224–30.

about our ability to choose. But (as explained in Chapter 2) our options may be limited by factors outside our control. That people can make libertarian free moral choices (LFMCs) is either true or false, but autonomy comes in degrees. Any particular free choice may involve very limited options, and sometimes what appears to be a free choice may not be one. Most telling, our choices are absolutely private. It is curious that retributivists like Kant focus on what the wrongdoer deserves because of what he *wills*, when the willing is not something that society can observe. The defender of free will can staunchly uphold the wrongdoer's basic ability to choose freely while granting that *how much blame* attaches to the wrongdoing can be difficult, or impossible, to ascertain. When severe harm is contemplated, this radical epistemic limitation can be invoked to justify erring on the side of less punishment rather than more. This approach entails that earthly justice is almost an oxymoron. Retributivists would do well to exercise a great deal of humility. Nonetheless, in the absence of scientific proof either way, denying free will may ground more serious risks than accepting it. Those philosophers who defend free will rarely see the justification of punishment as the main reason for valuing freedom. The main reason is that humans are a more valuable sort of being, with a special dignity, if they are free agents. To deny human freedom is to demean ourselves and our neighbors – a stance that should be avoided in the absence of conclusive evidence – and so the burden of proof lies with those who deny free will.

More Pragmatic Arguments

Bracketing the connection between free will and human dignity, there are at least several more pragmatic arguments to be made in favor of the reasonableness of belief in free will and of placing the burden of proof on those who would deny free will. The first argument has a long pedigree, going back at least to the concerns that were expressed against St. Augustine when (in his later works) he made clear his compatibilist position on human free will and divine grace. Won't it lead to moral laxity if people believe that, whatever they end up choosing, they could not help but choose it since the determining causes of their choices lie outside of their control? Interestingly, recent experiments confirm this worry about moral laxity, illustrating one way in which science can weigh in on the side of those who defend the reasonableness of believing in free will.[20]

One example of the negative effects of denying free will is offered by Kathleen D. Vohs and Jonathan S. Schooler, who conducted two

---

20 Like other experiments discussed in this work, these experiments (and the interpretations drawn from them) are open to question (see Caruso (2019): 46–9). But, unlike the conclusions drawn from many of the other experiments, the interpretation supporting the age-old thought that denial of free will inspires moral laxity has intuition on its side.

experiments to test how belief in determinism might affect people's behavior. In the first, some participants read a text arguing that people's behavior is determined while others read a text neutral on the free will issue. Then they were told to solve a mathematical puzzle where there was a "glitch" in the program which would permit cheating. Those who had read the determinist text were more likely to cheat than those who had read the neutral text. In a second experiment, some read a text defending determinism and others read a text endorsing free will and then all were told to pay themselves for performance on a cognitive task. Those who had read the determinist text tended to overpay themselves whereas those who had read the free will text did not.[21]

A list of other unwholesome consequences of denying free will is offered by Davide Rigioni and Marcel Brass. Surveying the relevant literature, they note that there is evidence that believing that one's behavior is determined increases anti-social behavior such as aggression. It also suppresses beneficial behavior, such as "the production of autonomous, independent and therefore of effort-demanding ideas". In experiments to see whether people would adjust their behavior after recognizing errors, believing that behavior is determined interfered with error-monitoring processes. Rigioni and Brass's conclusion reaffirms the traditional worry that believing that one's behavior is determined would likely lead to moral laxity:

> These findings suggest that believing in free will, that is, believing that we have some sort of deliberate and intentional control over our own behavior, is important for efficient self control. Self control requires intentional effort, or *willpower*. However if people are primed with the idea that "it would not matter anyway"—e.g. because our behavior is guided by the genetic make-up and the environment, free will is an illusion, and so forth—there might be no reason to spend that energy to implement self-control.[22]

Some suggest that belief in free will may have evolved within human societies precisely because it plays a broadly useful role.[23]

---

21 Kathleen D. Vohs and Jonathan W. Schooler, "The Value of Believing in Free Will: Encouraging a Belief in Determinism Increases Cheating". *Psychological Sciences* 19 (2008) 49–54. Moral worries about conducting this kind of deceptive experiment are discussed in Chapter 6.

22 Davide Rigioni and Marcel Brass, "From Intentions to Neurons: Social and Neural Consequences of Disbelieving in Free Will". *Topoi* 33 (2014): 5–12, at 8, 10, 11. This article supplies an extensive bibliography.

23 Roy F. Baumeister, A. William Crescioni, and Jessica L. Alquist, "Free Will as Advanced Action Control for Human Social Life and Culture", *Neuroethics* 4 (2011): 1–11; William Simkulet, "On Free Will and Evolution", AJOB *Neuroscience* 6:2 (2015): 12–13; Matthew Smithdeal, "Belief in Free Will as an Adaptive, Ungrounded Belief", *Philosophical Psychology* 29:8 (2016): 1241–52.

On the other hand, Sam Harris, in a book against free will for a popular audience, suggests that *believing* in free will may encourage bad behavior. Such belief, he holds, leads to hatred of those who do wrong and encourages cruel punishment. He reports, "I think that losing the sense of free will has only improved my ethics – by increasing my feelings of compassion and forgiveness, and diminishing my sense of entitlement to the fruits of my own good luck."[24] The free will defender – at least the free will defender of a libertarian stripe – may note that forgiveness seems out of place when behavior is determined. We forgive people when they are sorry for what they have done, but someone who holds that their behavior is determined might conclude that they could not have done otherwise and that being sorry for what one could not help but do is not appropriate. The rational wrongdoer whose wrong is determined may be sad that such things happen in the world, but he cannot repent, as if his actions were up to him. No, they were no more than his own bad luck. He is perhaps the one most "victimized" by the necessitating causes at work in the world. It is incoherent to *forgive* the wrongdoer under those circumstances. And the loss of repentance and forgiveness may be counted among the costs of denying freedom.[25]

Harris has the classic problem with punishment discussed earlier. He grants that, as a society, we have to punish wrongdoers. But they do not *deserve* the punishment; they were just unlucky. We must punish them for consequentialist reasons – to protect society.[26] But another way of stating this thesis is that we are justified in using the wrongdoer as a means to benefit the rest of us. Prevention and deterrence may well play a role in justifying punishment, but if responsibility grounded in free will is entirely abstracted from the picture, then the wrongdoer becomes a *mere* means, and anyone becomes fair game if inflicting harm upon them benefits society. The utilitarian philosopher and the free will skeptic have their responses to this last point, but here we are considering the implications of widespread, popular disbelief in free will. It is hard to imagine that these complex philosophical responses would have much impact on the vast majority of people if the belief that we do not have free will actually became widespread in society.

Still, the denier of free will can appeal to a recent study that suggests that instilling a belief in determinism encourages people to hold that wrongdoers should be punished less than they might have held without

---

24 Sam Harris, *Free Will* (New York: Free Press, 2012): 45.
25 Free will deniers and skeptics often attempt to save these reactive attitudes. Pereboom, for example, argues that we can save analogues of such attitudes while not believing that we have free will (Pereboom (2014): 178–93). Were one *sure* that free will does not exist, proposing these analogues might be better than just abandoning the reactive attitudes altogether, but while the question is open, they seem a poor substitute.
26 Harris (2012) 53–9.

that belief.[27] This could be seen as positive in that less suffering for the wrongdoer is a good thing. I mentioned above that belief in free will need not entail support for extreme and cruel punishments. When popular disbelief in free will is considered, an inclination to punish agents less severely when they are perceived to be unfree could be viewed negatively, as confirming the generally perceived connection between free will and human dignity. Our society punishes the child, the insane, and those who suffer cognitive disabilities less than the (ostensibly) responsible adult. It may be that the subjects in the study connected determinism with diminished responsibility of the sort that the law recognizes. But it seems likely that most of us would (in general) prefer to be treated as responsible adults rather than as children, or insane, or cognitively disabled. Thus, it is not clear that this study about the connection between belief in free will and in retributive punishment can be seen as evidence of a general value in denying free will.

A final pragmatic argument in favor of promoting belief in free will is that its denial would likely have dangerous political repercussions. On the plausible principle that you cannot take from someone what they do not have, it could be a quick move from widespread belief that behavior is determined (due to UCD or LCD) to the denial of political and social respect for personal autonomy. This is the theme of Anthony Burgess's 1962 novel *A Clockwork Orange*. W.R. Klemm writes that on the view that people cannot engage in deliberate, voluntary actions, "people are more likely to be victims and less able to change maladaptive behaviors. Thus society and government must help them do what they cannot do for themselves."[28] Epistocrats (those who believe that the coercive power of the state should be in the hands of those who "know best") constantly suppose that they can do a better job of running people's lives than can those people themselves. For those of us keen on liberal democracy, handing those in government yet another justification for forcing citizens to bow to the judgments of the powerful seems to be a bad move. So, again, in the absence of evidence to the contrary, it is better to maintain the view that human agents are free, responsible, and deserving of respect.

Evidence from Introspection

I have argued that there are good, practical reasons to commit to belief in human freedom, but wouldn't a more obvious defense start from our

---

27 A.F. Shariff, J.D. Greene, J.C. Karremans, J. Luguri, C.J. Clark, J.W. Schooler, R.F. Baumeister, K.D. Vohs, "Free Will and Punishment: A Mechanistic View of Human Nature Reduces Retribution", *Psychological Science* 25:8 (2014): 1563–7.
28 W.R. Klemm, "Free Will Debates: Simple Experiments Are Not so Simple", *Advances in Cognitive Psychology* 6 (2010): 47–65, at 61.

introspective experience of choosing? Surely, if you decide right now to raise your right arm and then you raise it, you experience the choice (and subsequent raising) as up to you. You recognize that you might have chosen and done otherwise. What better evidence of free will could there be? Many participants in the freedom and science debate take it that a main motive for believing in libertarian free will is this introspective evidence. John Searle writes that our conviction of our own free will arises "from some pervasive feature of conscious experience... I sense alternative courses of action open to me."[29] Mark Balaguer holds that "[t]he prima facie reason for believing [that human beings have free will] was (and is) based on introspection: We have all had the experience of freely choosing from among a number of possible options."[30] Peter W. Ross, noting that both Robert Kane and Timothy O'Conner appeal to introspective evidence, goes on to say that "all libertarians assign introspective evidence some role, for it is our feeling of metaphysically open branching paths that is the raison d'etre of libertarian freedom".[31] Shaun Nichols writes that "[t]he arguments in favor of libertarian free will typically appeal to introspection" and goes on to add that "few psychologists would countenance such arguments."[32]

Nichols argues that the libertarian intuition is based on the thought that "if our decisions *were* determined we would be aware of it".[33] He presents a significant amount of evidence that introspection is often faulty; we are frequently in the dark about the inner springs of our actions. And since defense of libertarian free will was based mainly on introspection, Nichols argues, we have good reason to reject libertarianism. However, Robert Kane questions the claim that historically the main impetus for libertarianism has been a naïve belief that our mental life is clear and open to us. He writes that "the philosophical problem of free will has arisen in history whenever persons have *questioned* the presumption that if our choices were determined, we would be aware of it".[34]

Introspective evidence will play very little role in the arguments I make in this book but it should not be discounted. Although introspection may

---

29 John Searle, *Freedom and Neurobiology* (New York: Columbia University Press, 2007): 41.
30 Mark Balaguer (2010): 2.
31 Peter W. Ross, "Empirical Constraints on the Problem of Free Will". In *Does Consciousness Cause Behavior?*. Edited by Susan Pockett, William P. Banks, and Shaun Gallagher (Cambridge, MA: MIT Press, 2006): 125–44, at 135.
32 Shaun Nichols, "How Can Psychology Contribute to the Free Will Debate?". In Baer (2008): 10–31, at 19.
33 Shaun Nichols, *Bound: Essays on Free Will and Responsibility* (Oxford: Oxford University Press, 2015): 35.
34 Robert Kane, "Free Will, Bound and Unbound: Reflections on Shaun Nichols' *Bound*", *Philosophical Studies* 174 (2017): 2479–88, at 2483.

lead us awry more often than we would like to think, it does not follow that it is always or usually mistaken. The first-person evidence provided by the experiment of deciding to raise your right arm and then (*voilà!*) up goes your arm is surely telling, at least prima facie, against those who promote the radical view that conscious choices are not among the causes of at least some of our behavior. Neuroscientists and psychologists – including those defending the radical view about the impotence of conscious choices – are not in a good position to simply disallow the evidence of introspection. The value of many experiments of many different types depends upon trusting first-person reports of feelings and beliefs.

It is plausible to hold – as neuroscientists and psychologists *do* hold in practice – that the evidence of introspection is valuable and often trustworthy. However, for the purposes of my central thesis that science has not (and probably *can*not) prove that human beings lack (or have) libertarian free choice, the introspective evidence must be invoked with caution. Unlike with the simple decision to raise my right arm and my right arm going up, there are several criteria to be met by a libertarian free choice. These criteria standardly include that the agent deliberate between genuinely open options, that he could have chosen other than he has chosen, and that his choice be up to him in some ultimate way. There is introspective evidence relevant to and supporting the claim that we have morally significant libertarian freedom. We often believe that we confront conflicting options, and our experience is that we have to engage in a sort of inward struggle (or debate) since apparently there are genuine options open to us. After the debated choice, looking back, we usually believe that (for good or ill) we could have done otherwise. This belief is especially powerful when it generates guilt and regret. What we are experiencing, on a libertarian theory, is *recognition* that we could and should have done otherwise. But even those libertarians who place more weight than I do on the evidence of introspection grant that, if one does indeed have the impression of making a choice which meets the libertarian criteria, that impression could be misleading. There could be causal forces at work that our inward gaze just misses for one reason or another. Introspection provides some evidence in some circumstances, but its evidence for libertarian freedom is far from decisive.

A second reason for not focusing much on introspective evidence for libertarian free will is that I plan to discuss morally significant freedom. I will sketch a portrait of an LFMC, and I suspect that someone engaged in making that sort of choice would not step back introspectively, while making the choice, to examine the contents and processes of their current experience. They are likely to remember the experience of struggle before choosing, and they may well feel guilt or satisfaction afterwards, but at the moment of choice the agent may be too busy making a choice to step back mentally and notice that he is making a choice. That means that for the kind of choice we are mainly concerned about we may not have clear introspective experience of the actual act of choosing. The distinction that we may sometimes be consciously engaged in mental actions without being conscious *that* we are so engaged will prove useful to bear in mind in looking at some of the free will experiments.[35] Were the evidence of introspection the only reason for believing in free will, the most rational move might be to sit on the fence in the absence of scientific evidence either way. It is the connections between belief in freedom and in human dignity, and in freedom and in virtuous and beneficial behavior, that should encourage us to commit to belief in free will and that place the burden of proof on those who would deny it.

Part II. Presuppositions against Free Will

The most common philosophical criticism of libertarianism – and it seems to be libertarianism that many scientists have in mind when they consider free will – is the "luck" problem: If there is nothing about the agent and the agent's past to cause or fully explain the agent's choosing *this* over *that*, isn't the agent's choice for *this* just a matter of luck? This point, despite being philosophical and not scientific, is often raised by scientists involved in the science and freedom debate. Steven Pinker, for example, reprises what he labels "Hume's fork": "Either our actions are determined, in which case we are not responsible for them, or they are the result of random events, in which case we are not responsible for them."[36] Libertarian philosophers have expended a great deal of time and effort trying to answer this criticism, and I have made my own contribution to that response elsewhere.[37] A review of philosophical responses to the luck problem lies outside the scope of the present work. But there are other presuppositions against free will that arise within the science and free will debate that need to be dealt with at the outset, before we can turn to the actual experimental evidence. I will look first at the problematic way in which "free will" is often described and then at the assumptions of determinism (universal or local) and physicalism.

Problematic Descriptions of Free Will

An important problem that arises in much of the experimental work – and in the literature about the experimental work – is the *Problem of Description*. Terms and concepts are not adequately defined or explained. Sometimes

---

35 I make use of this distinction in trying to address the tracing problem: How can we be responsible for forming our characters through our choices if we did not know that our choices would form our characters? See Rogers (2015): 216–35.
36 Pinker (2008): 315.
37 Rogers (2015): 174–215.

this makes it difficult to see what the claim is, and sometimes it becomes clear that the understanding at work is not relevant to free will as it has been viewed traditionally or as it has been discussed among philosophers. Some of the scientists involved in the science and free will debate do not attempt to explain what they mean by freedom or free will. The philosopher, of course, finds that a distressing lacuna. But those scientists who do make the attempt often offer a picture of free will that would be unfamiliar to most philosophers: free will involves the agent as a "homunculus", free will means that "anything goes", to be free means that one's choices appear without background or motivation. Michael Gazzaniga adopts the course of considering free will through a kind of *via negativa*.

> We can begin to understand the illusion about free will when we ask the question, What on earth do humans want to be free from? Indeed, what does free will even mean?.... When we reach for the glass of water, we don't want our hand suddenly rubbing our eye, or grasping so hard that the glass shatters, or the water to spurt upward from the faucet or turning into mist.... So we don't want to be free from the physical laws of nature.... Think about the problem of free will on a social level. While we believe we are always acting freely, we commonly want none of that in others.... We intensely desire reliability in our elected officials and indeed in our family and friends.[38]

This brief list of things we don't want to be free from doesn't go very far toward explaining what it is that Gazzaniga takes to be illusory. Furthermore, Gazzaniga (and he is not alone) portrays the believer in free will as holding that there is a homunculus "inside" doing the conscious work. He holds that we are all in the grip of this illusion:

> Do you remember the telling scene in the movie *Men in Black*, when a corpse is undergoing an autopsy? The face popped open only to reveal the underlying brain machinery, and right there was an extraterrestrial-looking homunculus pulling levers to make it all work. It was the "I," the "self,", the phenomenal center and take-charge thing we all think we have.[39]

Certainly, no one wants to admit to believing that there is a little guy inside pulling the levers. Defenders of free will are likely to insist that the morally

---

38 Michael Gazzaniga, *Who's in Charge?: Free Will and the Science of the Brain* (New York: HarperCollins, 2011): 105–6.
39 Gazzaniga (2011): 43. See also Wegner (2005): 19–20; John Banja, "Could Have Chosen Otherwise Under Identical Conditions: An Evolutionary Perspective on Free Will", AJOB *Neuroscience* 6:2 (2015): 3–11, at 9.

responsible agent is a (sufficiently) unified, conscious being, able to deliberate and to choose in consequence of those deliberations, but that is not a homunculus. The homunculus imagery seems a rhetorical device in the service of portraying belief in free will as unsophisticated. The homunculus image probably originates with Francis Crick's *The Astonishing Hypothesis: The Scientific Search for the Soul* (1994). Crick claims that most of us have this false image of ourselves.[40] I do not know whether or not that is the case, but there is nothing in the philosophically sophisticated defense of free will that would suggest a homunculus.

Some scientists who do offer a description of free will describe it in ways which make it look (at least prima facie) wildly unlikely that human agents could possess such a thing. Daniel Wegner imagines designing a person with free will:

> a person in which there is installed a small unit called the Free Willer... But what exactly do we install? If we put in a module that creates actions out of any sort of past experiences or memories, that fashions choices from habits or attitudes or inherited tendencies, we don't get freedom – we get determinism. The Free Willer must be a mechanism that is *unresponsive to any past influence* [Wegner's italics].[41]

We read in the Introduction to *Are We Free? Psychology and Free Will*, a collection of papers on free will by psychologists, that "[t]he problem may be that our intuitive concepts of free will simply don't make sense. Free will can't really mean that at any moment a person's behavior is totally unpredictable (and therefore unconstrained)."[42] John Banja, in a target article in American Journal of Bioethics (AJOB) *Neuroscience*, suggests that libertarianism entails that agents are likely to do any crazy thing: "provoking rather than fleeing from a menacing predator, consuming poison to see what happens, or randomly eating a slug may count as 'doing otherwise', but such 'freedom' will likely consign that species to extinction".[43] Daniel Wegner writes that belief in free will involves "[s]eeing one's own causal influence as supernatural"; this self-understanding, he goes on to add, "is part of being human".[44]

That having free will should entail that an agent's choices are unresponsive to past influence, that a person's behavior is totally unpredictable, and

---

40 Francis Crick, *The Astonishing Hypothesis: The Scientific Search for the Soul* (New York: Charles Scribner's Sons, 1994): 24.
41 Wegner (2002): 322. See also P. Read Montague, "Free Will", *Current Biology* 18:14 (2008): R584 under "Quick Guide".
42 John Baer, James C. Kaufman, and Roy F. Baumeister, "Introduction: Psychology and Free Will". In Baer (2008): 3–9, at 4.
43 Banja (2015): 7.
44 Daniel Wegner, "Self is Magic". In Baer (2008): 226–47, at 228.

that something supernatural must be involved does look to count against free will *ab initio*. These descriptions are very far from the paradigmatic free choice that I will be describing in the next chapter, and I take it that most libertarians would resist seeing free will in these terms. Yet sometimes philosophers – both foes and friends of libertarian free will – do suggest that libertarianism is fundamentally implausible. Among the foes, Daniel Dennett, a philosopher oft cited among neuroscientists and psychologists, holds that libertarian free will must involve an internal "coin flip".[45] Galen Strawson explains that libertarianism depends upon proposing a self that is "imagined to be in some way independent of one's CPM [character, personality, motivations]".[46] Patricia Churchland says that on libertarianism "a free choice is made when without prior cause and without prior constraints, a decision comes into being and action results".[47]

That something could come from nothing in the way these descriptions suggest does seem unlikely, and sometimes even defenders of libertarian free will express their views this way. Roderick Chisholm, proposing an agent-causal theory, is often quoted or paraphrased by the critics of libertarianism. Chisholm writes that,

> If we are responsible... then we have a prerogative which some would attribute only to God: each of us, when we act, is a prime mover unmoved. In doing what we do, we cause certain events to happen, and nothing – or no one – causes us to cause those events to happen.[48]

Even Robert Kane, defending an event-causal theory which he intends to fit well with contemporary science, sometimes explains his view in that worrisome "creation *ex nihilo*" kind of way. He writes that the connection between beliefs in free will and in human dignity is "expressed in the religious traditions by saying that humans are made in the image of God – being creators *ab initio* of at least some things in the universe, their own purposes and the actions issuing from those purposes".[49]

That we are the creators *ab initio* of our own purposes seems most unlikely. Before we ever reach the point where we might be thought to make a rational choice, we have been formed by all sorts of things over

---

45 Daniel Dennett, *Brainstorms* (Ann Arbor, MI: Bradford Books, 1978): 295.
46 Galen Strawson, "The Impossibility of Ultimate Responsibility?". In Swinburne (2011): 126–40, at 137.
47 Patricia S. Churchland, "Feeling Reasons". In *Neurobiology of Decision-Making*, edited by Antonio R. Damasio, Hanna Damasio and Yves Christen (Berlin: Springer, 1996): 181–99, at 182.
48 Roderick Chisholm, "Human Freedom and the Self", the Lindley Lecture, 1964, University of Kansas. In *Free Will*, edited by Gary Watson (Oxford: Oxford University Press, 1982): 24–45, at 32.
49 Kane (1996): 4.

which we had no control. Timothy O'Connor, a prominent defender of agent-causal libertarian free will, says that it is common knowledge that "[t]hough the buck does indeed ultimately stop with us when it comes to initiating our actions, numerous factors influence our activity, making us likely to a degree to act in this way or that."[50] And Kane, when he is actually describing his theory of "plural voluntary control" (how a libertarian free choice might work), portrays the free agent as trying to pursue conflicting motivations, which, at least early in the agent's career as a chooser, come from the agent's heredity, environment, and the other usual sources. It is the opting for this over that that is up to the agent, but that the agent should be confronting *these* particular options rather than a different set of options may well be determined by the agent's past.[51] True, the agent could have chosen other than he chose, but the agent's options are not without a respectable pedigree, and, whichever way the agent chooses, the choice is explicable through the reasons for the particular choice.[52] In the next chapter, I will be describing an LFMC, and it will be clear that a robust libertarianism does not require that free choices be produced *ex nihilo* by god-like agents.

What I have labelled the Problem of Description will come up over and over in the discussion of free will experiments. Broadly, the problem occurs when terms are used inexactly or are undefined or unexplained or when claims and theories are vaguely expressed, are misinformed or internally inconsistent, or otherwise fail to meet a reasonable standard of clarity and exactness. Whether or not "description" is a problem is context-dependent. Sometimes an analytic definition would be helpful. Often – as in the case of the LFMC I will describe in the next chapter – a general outline of the object under consideration is sufficient. But when, for example, two terms which mean different things are used as if they were synonyms, that constitutes a problem. When a theory is developed in such a way that it appears to embrace inconsistencies, that constitutes a problem. And when, as in the present case, the phenomenon in question, free will, is described in a way that does not conform to the more usual, considered understanding, that is a problem in description. And this is a problem that affects the experimental work on free will since it is crucial to know what it is that we are attempting to study ... even if we suspect that we won't find it.

Problems of Description are relatively easy to avoid. Experimenters and those discussing the experiments can carefully define or explain important terms, they can take care to express theories clearly and coherently, and, when studying a phenomenon like (purported) free will, they can offer

---

50 Timothy O'Connor, "Freedom with a Human Face", *Midwest Studies in Philosophy* 24 (2005): 207–27, at 224.
51 Kane (1996): 109–15.
52 Kane (1996): 135–7.

well-developed descriptions of what it is they hope to study. With "free will", they can try to pin down some standard understanding, either folk (which is difficult) or philosophical, or they can simply explain what they intend by the term, granting that others may use it differently. In Chapter 2, hoping to avoid a Problem of Description, I will be sketching what I take to be a paradigmatic free, morally significant, choice, an LFMC. That should promote clarity on what a proper object of study vis-à-vis human freedom would be, assuming (for the sake of argument) a libertarian approach. (Some of the criteria for an LFMC are also usually held to be requisite for a compatibilist free moral choice [CFMC]. As I said in the Introduction, if libertarian freedom survives empirical investigation, compatibilist freedom is likely to do so as well.) The description will not be fine-tuned enough to capture the differences between different libertarian theories (in that case, I would have to describe several LFMCs), but it should provide enough of a concrete example to facilitate assessing whether or not past experiments are relevant to the morally significant freedom that is the main concern in the free will debate. And having it in mind will help in considering future experiments.

Determinism

Many participating in the discussion about the experimental approach to free will make metaphysical assumptions concerning issues that are controversial within the philosophical community. One such assumption is that of causal determinism – universal or local. Science cannot proceed without allowing some philosophical presuppositions, but when metaphysical assumptions which are immediately relevant to the free will question, which have been perennially debated without consensus among philosophers, and which are not clearly labelled as metaphysical assumptions, are allowed to color interpretation of the empirical data, that constitutes the *Problem of Domain*.

Daniel Wegner writes that if a team of scientific psychologists

> somehow had access to all the information they could ever want, the assumption of psychology is that they could uncover the mechanisms that give rise to all your behavior and so could certainly explain why you picked up this book at this moment.[53]

Indeed, many scientists involved in the freedom and science debate presuppose determinism. Universal causal determinism (UCD) – in philosophy, that is roughly the theory that events at any moment of time, plus the laws of nature, entail events at any other moment of time – can no longer be

---

53 Wegner (2002): 1.

assumed due to the standard interpretation regarding the behavior of subatomic particles. But even if UCD is in question, it may be that a more local causal determinism (LCD) is operant. That is what many experimenters take their experiments to show: an agent's choices are causally necessitated by preceding factors in the near past of the choice over which the agent had no control.

Some aspects of the current debate involve questions about the possibly necessitating role of desires, motivations, and beliefs. In the next section, I will briefly address the question of physicalism and whether or not mental phenomena can, and should, be identified with brain events. For the purposes of the present work, LCD will refer to causal necessitation of an agent's choices arising from brain events, from unconscious mental events, and also from conscious desires, motivations, and beliefs. Any sort of necessitating cause that is relevant to the science and freedom debate, and that lies outside the control of the agent, is a determining cause. (I will use the locutions "determined", "determining" and so on, but when context does not make it clear whether UCD or LCD is in question, I will add the qualifiers.) Compatibilists can allow that some sorts of determining causes – some versions of LCD – are consistent with an agent's free will while some are not. And libertarians can hold that some (or even many) choices are determined. It is only the thesis that *all* choices are determined that conflicts with libertarianism.

I will understand the hypothesis that choices are probabilistically produced by the particles' nondetermined behavior – which lies outside the agent's control – as a version of LCD. A choice inevitably produced by particle behavior over which the agent has no control is still caused not by the agent but by the behavior of the particles. Positing indeterminism somewhere in the process of choosing is not enough to allow that the choice is an LFMC. Even if the particles might have "bounced" differently, nevertheless the agent chose what the behavior of the particles made him choose. But there is a caveat: If, as Robert Kane suggests, the behavior of the particles could somehow be identified (or very closely correlated) with the rational agent consciously engaged in choosing, then a choice *identified* with nondetermined brain events might be a robustly free choice.[54] I will note in the section below on physicalism and epiphenomenalism that that identification is a difficult one to make, but I leave open the thought that indeterminacy in the brain might be the grounding for libertarian free will.

That *all* of our choices are determined is not a claim for which there is currently any scientific evidence. One might appeal to common experience. Doesn't the world appear to proceed in an orderly manner? Yes, but common experience would also support the thought that we confront open options and could choose other than we choose. Why, then, do so many

---

54 Kane (1996): 128–30.

scientists assume some form of determinism? Greene and Cohen argue that neuroscience supports hard determinism (acceptance of UCD [?] and denial of free will) and note that "there is not a shred of scientific evidence to support the existence of causally effective processes in the mind or brain that violate the laws of physics".[55] In order to allow this point to count against free will, one has to embrace several debatable assumptions. One must assume that all causally effective processes in the mind or brain should be expected to conform to the laws of physics. Moreover, one must assume that our *present* understanding of the laws of physics is the last word on what sort of causally effective processes might exist. But it is sad and baseless to suppose that the discipline of physics has now said all it has to say regarding causes at work in the world such that new discoveries will never be made. One issue on which new discoveries might be forthcoming is precisely in the area of mind and brain activity, in that present physics does not deal with the stubborn fact of consciousness (about which more below). Thomas Nagel, in his *Mind and Cosmos*, argues that, in order to make sense of conscious activity as we experience it, science will need to go beyond the materialism bequeathed to us by the seventeenth century and beyond current evolutionary theory that tries to limit itself to that materialism.[56]

Finally, the question of whether there can be indeterminism at a macro level is an open one, even on the laws of physics as currently understood. E.J. Lowe cites the famous parable of Schrödinger's cat – whose fate depends on how the non-determined particle moves – as an instance of a standard story which allows the micro to be reflected in the macro.[57] On some views of how micro indeterminism functions, the indeterminacies at the level of the particles can be magnified to affect larger systems. This does not impact our predictions regarding simple systems, so we can forecast the solar eclipse or the baseball's trajectory with complete accuracy. However, it does affect very complex systems, such as the weather. This is not just an epistemic point. It may be the case that even an omniscient, but time-bound, being could not predict the weather in the distant future with perfect accuracy since the weather is genuinely not determined. And it may be that the human brain, in its complexity, is more like a weather system than it is like the solar system.[58] Thus, as noted above, it may be possible to

---

55 J.D. Greene and J.D. Cohen, "For the Law, Neuroscience Changes Nothing and Everything". *Philosophical Transactions of the Royal Society of London B*, 359 (2004): 1775–85, at 1777.
56 Thomas Nagel, *Mind and Cosmos* (Oxford: Oxford University Press, 2012).
57 E.J. Lowe, *Personal Agency: The Metaphysics of Mind and Action* (Oxford: Oxford University Press, 2008): 66.
58 Stephen Barr, Prof. Emeritus, Department of Physics, University of Delaware, in conversation.

invoke the indeterminacy that contemporary physics allows to support a libertarian theory of free will.[59]

Some scientists suggest that determinism needs to be assumed in order for the practice of the brain sciences to proceed. Patrick Haggard writes, "Neuroscience is fundamentally deterministic, in its methods, its assumptions and its outlooks. Therefore, the perspective from neuroscience requires that free will must either be compatible with determinism, or we do not have free will."[60] Daniel Wegner holds that belief in an agent-self with free will, which he persists in referring to as a "homunculus",

> undermines the possibility of a scientific theory of psychology by creating an explanatory entity that cannot itself be explained... Just as we cannot tell what God is going to do, we cannot predict what a free-willing homunculus is likely to do either. There cannot be a science of this.[61]

If the claim is that it is useful for the brain sciences to assume some sort of determinism as a working hypothesis, that does not conflict with belief in libertarian freedom. Assuming X as a working hypothesis is not the same as claiming that X, as a metaphysical thesis, is true. It is entirely consistent with libertarianism to allow that many, perhaps even most, of our choices are indeed determined. Furthermore, as I will be describing an LFMC, the situation that allows for such a choice may very well arise through a preceding causal process. Although the actual choice itself is not produced by an antecedent event that necessitates it, the brain sciences that are looking for the causes of an agent's choices need not be looking in vain. The goal of explaining the causal processes that set the stage for a free choice is surely a worthy one.

More importantly, it is demonstrably false that neuroscience and psychology must assume any sort of determinism to proceed. Some scientists may have determinism in mind as they go about their business, but the actual experiments in which they engage do not prove, and do not require, that UCD or LCD be the case. As will be evident when we look at the relevant experiments, brain science is in fact proceeding, and proceeding to

---

59 Derk Pereboom disagrees but in his discussion of physics and agent-causation his argument depends on hypothesizing probabilities for overt human actions. Just how to understand probabilities is an open question in philosophy, but it is widely granted that establishing probabilities for unrepeatable events, such as an overt human action, is a puzzling issue even in theory (see Rogers (2015): 182–93). Here I talk about trying to assign probabilities in a free choice, but many of the points are applicable to the unrepeatable case of an overt human action.
60 Patrick Haggard, "Does Brain Science Change Our View of Free Will?". In Swinburne (2011): 7–24, at 8.
61 Daniel Wegner, "Who is the Controller of Controlled Processes?" in Hassin (2005): 19–36, at 20.

uncover extremely useful and important information, without determinism under any description playing any constitutive role at all in the process. Roy F. Baumeister et al. note that "[i]n empirical fact, almost all findings from psychological research laboratories are probabilistic rather than deterministic."[62] Baumeister offers a dissenting opinion to the claim that the brain sciences must presuppose determinism:

> Personally, I resent being told that as a scientist I am forbidden to believe in free will and required to embrace total causal determinism... The reasons I offer for this refusal to be bullied... are fourfold. First, the claim that all behaviors are fully determined by external, prior causes is unproven. Second, it is also unprovable, insofar as no one can study all possible behaviors and show them to be 100% caused by prior events. Third, it is contrary to our everyday experience. We all make choices every day, and it certainly feels as if more than one outcome is possible... Fourth, it is contrary to our data, which almost invariably show probabilistic rather than deterministic causation.... determinism requires a huge leap of faith.... None of those objections proves free will to be true and determinism false. My point is simply that it is a form of unscientific fanaticism to require scientists to accept a belief that is unproven, unprovable, contrary to everyday experience, and contrary to the laboratory data.[63]

Physicalism, the Self, and Epiphenomenalism

Sometimes scientists engaged in the science and free will debate presuppose physicalism, meaning (in this context) that mental actions and events such as conscious choices can ultimately be identified with brain events. Some suggest, further, that physicalism entails that free will under a traditional description cannot exist and indeed that individual humans as unified actors do not exist. That was Francis Crick's "astonishing hypothesis": "'You'... are in fact no more than the behavior of a vast assembly of nerve cells and their associated molecules."[64] Patrick Haggard seems to espouse physicalism when he holds that "[n]euroscience treats the 'I' as being synonymous with an individual's brain."[65] He writes that

---

62 Roy F. Baumeister, Cory Clark, and Janie Luguri, "Free Will: Belief and Reality", in Mele (2015): 49–71, at 50.
63 Roy F. Baumeister, "Free Will, Consciousness, and Cultural Animals". In *Are We Free? Psychology and Free Will* edited by John Baer, James C. Kaufman, and Roy F. Baumeister (Oxford: Oxford University Press, 2008): 65–85, at 67.
64 Crick (1994): 5.
65 Haggard (2011): 9. Haggard mentions brain processes "generating" conscious experience, which suggests a distinction between the two and so perhaps he is an epiphenomenalist.

> Brain science will change our notion of free will in several ways. Most importantly, it will show that free will is not a special, transcendental faculty. Rather, it is a term given to the operations of a set of brain processes in the frontal lobes of humans, and possibly some other primates.[66]

He says that modeling brain activity must "avoid being homuncular or dualistic".[67] Steven Pinker associates belief in free will with "the traditional conception of a ghost in the machine, our bodies are inhabited by a self or a soul that chooses the behavior to be executed by the body".[68] He goes on to suggest that on a biological view of human nature, there is no "ghost in the machine".[69] He does not make his position entirely clear but this looks to be physicalism.[70]

The thesis that "you" are really a collection of brain processes involves some of the most recalcitrant issues in metaphysics. There is the problem of personal identity and the more fundamental mereological issue of what makes *anything* a discrete, unified, and individual thing. The defender of free will must grant, I believe, that human agents can be individual actors who remain the same persons over time. The moral responsibility that looms so large in the free will debate requires that the agent possess at least a minimal unity and temporal continuity. However, a segue into such complex and difficult territory would take us far afield, so I simply note that these *are* very thorny metaphysical issues on which there is no consensus. But it does seem worthwhile to say just a word on the perennial question of the relationship of the mental and the physical.

Although almost all philosophers grant that there must be a close connection between mind and brain, it is notoriously difficult to analyze mental actions and events as being reducible to brain events. Francis Crick, having offered an extensive description of the brain activity accompanying visual perception, allows that "[i]t is certainly possible that there may be aspects of consciousness, such as qualia [what is *experienced* in the course of visual perception], that science will not be able to explain."[71] But, of course, it is mental states, such as the experience of qualia, that pose a problem for physicalism. This is what David Chalmers calls the "hard problem of consciousness". He writes,

---

66 Haggard (2011): 23.
67 Patrick Haggard, "'Free Will': Components and Processes", in Mele (2015): 145–64, at 150.
68 Pinker (2008): 311.
69 Pinker (2008): 313.
70 See also Banja (2015).
71 Crick (1994): 256.

For any physical process we specify there will be an unanswered question: Why should this process give rise to experience? Given any such process, it is conceptually coherent that it could be instantiated in the absence of experience. It follows that no mere account of the physical process will tell us why experience arises. The emergence of experience goes beyond what can be derived from physical theory.[72]

E.J. Lowe says that "the thesis that mental states 'just are' (identical with) physical states is simply unintelligible".[73] Lowe rejects Cartesian dualism but adopts what he terms a "non-Cartesian substance dualism", which posits that the human agent has both physical and mental properties.[74] Colin McGinn writes, "The problem with materialism is that it tries to construct the mind out of properties that refuse to add up to mentality."[75] He goes on to theorize that "consciousness depends upon an unknowable natural property of the brain".[76] McGinn cautions against the assumption – made by many of the scientists and philosophers participating in the science and free will debate – that "*since* we understand the physical world so well it is only a matter of time until we understand consciousness" (McGinn's italics).[77] Benjamin Libet, whose influential experiments in neuroscience will be discussed at length in Chapter 3, explicitly rejects physicalism, saying, "externally observable 'physical' events and the inner observable 'mental' events are phenomenologically independent categories.... *Neither phenomenon is reducible to or describable by the other*" (Libet's italics).[78] Arguably, the most popular theory among philosophers is functionalism: a mental state is to be understood solely in terms of the role it plays in a cognitive system. Although functionalism eschews any sort of dualism, it nonetheless entails an anti-reductivist aspect due to "multiple realizability": different brain states may realize the same mental state and thus there can be no one-to-one identity between the mental state and a particular brain state. The psychological cannot be reduced to the neurological.[79] Philosophy, then, has not settled the question of mind and body in terms of physicalism.

---

72 David Chalmers, "The Hard Problem of Consciousness" in *The Blackwell Companion to Consciousness*, 2nd ed., edited by Susan Schneider and Max Velmans (Hoboken, NJ: Wiley-Blackwell Publishers, 2017): 32–44, at 40.
73 E.J. Lowe, "Self, Agency and Mental Causation", *Journal of Consciousness Studies* 6 (1999): 225–39, at 227.
74 E.J. Lowe (2008): 13.
75 Colin McGinn, *The Mysterious Flame* (New York: Basic Books, 1999): 28.
76 McGinn (1999): 28.
77 McGinn (1999): 36.
78 Libet (2004): 17.
79 This thesis is challenged by Thomas W. Polger and Lawrence Shapiro in *The Multiple Realization Book* (Oxford: Oxford University Press, 2016).

Given the evident fact of consciousness and the problems with attempting to analyze conscious activity as brain events, it is difficult to see the motivation for the assumption of physicalism. One might take it to follow from the Principle of Causal Closure: all physical effects must have purely physical causes. But then one would have to ask why we should accept that principle. Gregg D. Caruso, in the course of arguing that free will is an illusion, grants that the principle is not provable but says, "In theorizing what matters is the usefulness, fruitfulness, coherence, and success of a position."[80] But this begs the question against the one who argues that the mental has not been successfully analyzed as physical.[81] Henry Stapp, defending free will but coming to the debate from the perspective of a physicist, criticizes those who assume physicalism and the Principle of Causal Closure as failing to appreciate the scientific revolution of the past century. "Replacing the purely fictional Newtonian particles by the experience-related atoms of quantum physics converts the classically conceived world that has no rational place for causally efficacious conscious experiences into a quantum world of 'potentialities' for certain experiences to occur."[82] He goes on to note the ineradicable (and, he takes it, irreducible) role that the mental process of observation plays in the standard Relativistic Quantum Field Theory, making mind an inherent element in contemporary physics. He ultimately comes to the conclusion that "reality is more mind-like than matter-like".[83] The Principle of Causal Closure, then, is open to debate.

One might appeal to simple parsimony to defend physicalism, but the Principle of Parsimony asks us to accept the simplest theory that fits all the facts, and physicalism has trouble with the stubborn fact of consciousness. Moreover, physicalism is no more simple than Stapp's mental monism or idealism. We might start our theorizing with the ineradicable fact of our immediate acquaintance with mind stuff, note the key role of the observer in contemporary science, and then suppose that it's *all* mind stuff, one way and another. Perhaps mental events should be understood as minds operating on information that is only privately available to the subject, and physical stuff should be understood as information publicly available (in principle) to minds in general. I do not say that it would be an easy theory to work out, but nothing in the sciences refutes it and it is no less parsimonious than physicalism.

---

80 G.D. Caruso, *Free Will and Consciousness: A Determinist Account of the Illusion of Free Will* (Lanham, MD: Lexington Books, 2012): 34–5.
81 For a developed criticism of the Principle of Causal Closure, see E.J. Lowe (2008) Part I.
82 Henry Stapp, *Quantum Theory and Free Will: How Mental Intentions Translate into Bodily Actions* (Cham, Switzerland: Springer Nature, 2017): xi.
83 Stapp (2017): 6–7, 71. For a similar criticism of the "classical" physicalist approach, see Stanley Klein, "Libet's Research on the Timing of Conscious Intentions to Act: A Commentary", *Consciousness and Cognition* 11:2 (2002): 273–9.

Another possible motivation for physicalism is the thought that non-physical things or events are not empirically observable and so cannot be the subject matter of neuroscience and psychology. The brain sciences, then, must presuppose physicalism. But a point can be made against this claim that is similar to the one made above against the claim that these sciences must assume determinism. The actual experiments involving conscious experience do not require physicalism in terms of how they are constructed, and they do not provide evidence of physicalism in the data they produce.

But suppose, for the sake of argument, that we *could* analyze mental actions and events as identical to or reducible to brain actions and events. Suppose, further, that that was agreed to be the *best* way of analyzing mental phenomena. So, you, the agent, are your living body in action. That alone would not show that robust, libertarian free will does not exist. To disprove free will, one would also have to show that all those brain events that constitute your choices are determined. And that, as the concluding chapters of this book will argue, would be a difficult case to make. Throughout the course of this work, I will not assume that mental phenomena are identical to, or reducible to, brain events. However, I *will* assume that the two are very closely related, and my arguments that science has not shown that human agents lack libertarian freedom, and probably will not be able to settle the free will question in the future, are just as effective in the (I take it unlikely) event that mental states can be somehow identified with or reduced to brain states.

An alternative position among some scientists in the science and free will debate is epiphenomenalism, which (for our purposes here) will be understood to be the theory that mental events are not identical with brain events, they are caused by brain events, but they do not (in turn) cause any physical events, including brain events. This thesis may be more damaging to the case for human free will than the physicalist view. On physicalism, if mental events such as desires and choices are identified with brain events, one might argue that those brain/mental events occur in a way that is consistent with libertarian free choice. However, if, as the epiphenomenalist holds, a choice is produced by a preceding brain event over which the agent has no control, then the choice is determined. For the LFMC that I will describe, this point is more damning than the claim that our choices do not count among the causes of our overt bodily actions. This is because it is the choice itself that is the locus of freedom and responsibility, on the supposition that it has the appropriate mental history. An overt act is done freely if it follows upon a free choice. So, a disconnect between choices and subsequent actions does not, by itself, undermine the importance of free will. The proponents of occasionalism (the view that God [or something] produces the physical event on the occasion of the mental event) and parallelism (the view that God [or something] sets up the universe so that the mental and the physical run in tandem) need not deny that human agents make free choices for which they can be held morally responsible. That being said, it would certainly be concerning to discover that one's deliberations had no causal impact upon one's overt actions.

A philosophical discussion of epiphenomenalism lies beyond the scope of this work, but a couple of brief points here about causation seem in order. The nature of causation is one of those hard, perennial questions in philosophy over which there is lively disagreement today. In the free will debate, it is standard to accept a more robust analysis of causation than a bare constant conjunction, but a constant conjunction is ordinarily taken to be evidence of causation. Thus, we seem to have strong, prima facie evidence that our choices are among the causes of our actions. Furthermore, on a more robust analysis of causation, wherein the cause exercises some force or power to produce the effect, epiphenomenalism is puzzling. If the physical can exercise some force or power to produce the mental, there would seem to be some point of "contact" between the physical and the mental. But if that is the case, it is difficult to see why the causal relationship can run only one way: physical to mental but not mental to physical.

Neither determinism nor physicalism can be demonstrated empirically. They are philosophical views on which there is no consensus in the philosophical community. (Some claim that there is experimental evidence for epiphenomenalism but this claim will be shown to be mistaken.) Moreover, neither determinism (UCD or LCD) nor physicalism needs to be presupposed in order for the work of the brain sciences to proceed. In regard to physicalism, even on the thesis that mental phenomena are identical to brain events, that alone does not conflict with the claim that human agents have robust libertarian free will. But the fact that the neuroscientists and psychologists so often allow these presupposed philosophical positions to guide their conclusions raises the Problem of Domain.

It is important to get clear on what has (or can be) demonstrated empirically and what are philosophical presuppositions. Scientists doing experiments have to make certain assumptions regarding positions that are not empirically demonstrable, assumptions that philosophers might call into question – for example, assumptions about the reality of the world outside the mind, assumptions about the possibility of human knowledge, assumptions about the general validity of the inductive method, and on and on. Science could not get on without allowing some metaphysical and epistemic givens. But the brief discussion above should show that neither determinism nor physicalism is among the theses that science needs to proceed. Some scientists subscribe to determinism or physicalism (or both), perhaps being persuaded by the reasons philosophers can offer for these metaphysical positions. But it is important – especially in that scientific claims sometimes find their way into popular media – to be clear that determinism and physicalism are metaphysical theses, unprovable empirically. Many scientists may hold these views, but they are not "scientific" in the sense of being proven by some scientific practice or even playing a necessary role in the process of science.

My topic is the experimental approach to the free will question and that means that the focus needs to be on the experiments themselves. If interpretations of and conclusions drawn from the data that are derived from experiments are informed by metaphysical assumptions, that point needs to be made clearly and often it is not. For example, Patrick Haggard begins an article on free will by saying that he will "eschew metaphysical entanglements". But he goes on to assume physicalism and assess neuroscientific theories negatively if they are insufficiently physicalist. (He seems to see the only options as physicalism and substance dualism.) He writes, "neuroscientists would say that the decision should be entirely mechanistic, since the brain activity that constitutes a person's decision is simply a biophysical process". That being the case, modeling brain activity must "avoid being homuncular or dualistic". He criticizes fellow neuroscientist Benjamin Libet's claim to have found a space for free will in the ability to "veto" an action as a "form of last-gasp dualism". A model which proposes that there are no specific causes or reasons for action "has several clear advantages. The model is clearly non-homuncular and avoids problems of dualism and uncaused causes."[84] There is nothing illegitimate in Haggard guiding his assessment of certain models of decision-making based on his metaphysical commitments. The problem is that he does not make it clear that that is what he is doing. It is important to distinguish what data the empirical investigation has actually delivered, on the one hand, and what philosophy has contributed to the interpretations and conclusions on the other. Failure to make this distinction constitutes the Problem of Domain.

So, the presuppositions which some scientists bring to the study of free will need to be bracketed in assessing the actual experimental results, and the object of study – human freedom, especially morally significant freedom – needs to be described with some clarity so that the experiments will not simply miss the mark. In the next chapter, I will offer a (rather general) description of an LFMC. Focusing on libertarianism makes sense since the experimenters often assume that freedom means libertarian freedom, and, as argued in the introduction, if science cannot settle the question of whether or not human beings exercise libertarian free will, then compatibilist theories are safe from disproof.

---

84 Haggard (2015): 145, 146, 153, 158.

Chapter 2

A Paradigmatic Free Choice

Introduction

Suppose I told you that I had bought a shower curtain thinking it would match the blue in my bathroom but when I got it home I decided it had too much purple in it. I believe the use of "decided" here is quite standard. But the decision regarding the excessive purple in the shower curtain looks to be nothing like the sort of decision we are concerned with in the free will and science debate. If we are to evaluate what the contemporary experimental evidence has to say about the free will that we care about and if we are to consider what kinds of studies might be fruitful in the future, it is useful to get clear on what sort of event or action a morally significant free choice is thought to be. This effort is related to a standard problem in the scientific study of human beings: the Problem of Translation. The overarching question is: Can we "translate" what we learned in the lab to conclusions about human beings in the natural environment? (I use "in the lab" to refer to any situation deliberately set up by experimenters.) One pressing issue, call it the Problem of Translation with Regard to the Object of Study, motivates the present chapter. It has to do with the "decisions" being studied in the lab; are they sufficiently similar to the object of our concern – free morally significant choices (FMCs) – that the data from the lab can be interpreted in a way that is applicable to free will? As will be noted in subsequent chapters, the Problem of Translation also surfaces when we suspect that the situation in the lab is so removed from the natural environment that the behavior of subjects likely reflects this odd and manufactured setting. A further Problem of Translation involves the pool of subjects. If the pool is small or unrepresentative, we may fear that the data gathered using this pool do not translate meaningfully to the larger population. All of these problems in translation arise in assessing the experiments on free will, but probably the most serious one relates to the "choices" or "decisions" being studied. The question of whether they are relevantly similar to the sort of free choice that we care most about cannot be answered without *some* idea of what such a choice looks like. Hence the need for a sketch of an FMC. As I noted in the Introduction, I will make it a libertarian FMC (LFMC). Many of the scientists participating in the science and free will debate seem to assume a libertarian view, and if science has not, and cannot, provide evidence against the ability of human agents to make LFMCs, then it is very unlikely that it will be able to provide evidence against compatibilist free moral choices. I intend the sketch to be rough and general enough to apply to most versions of LFMC, such as Robert Kane's event-causal theory, Timothy O'Connor's agent-causal theory, and (in my somewhat updated version) Anselm of Canterbury's parsimonious agent-causation.[1]

I will not argue that an LFMC – or even another species of FMC – is the only sort of behavior for which we can be held morally responsible. For example, one might be morally responsible for choices and deeds determined by one's character if one is properly held responsible for the choices that helped to construct the character. Some philosophers extend the ascription of moral responsibility broadly to include, for example, instances of negligence, thoughtlessness, or forgetfulness, where the agent did not engage in a deliberate free choice and where the behaviors are not determined by a choice-constructed character. Debate over how widely to spread the net of moral responsibility can safely be bracketed for purposes of the present work. Those who believe in meaningful freedom can probably agree that, at the very least, one key locus of responsibility is the morally significant free choice. If science is unable to settle the question of whether choices can be made freely, the question of how far responsibility extends should probably be left to the philosophers.

A related question is whether or not someone making a "prudential" decision is ultimately subject to an ascription of moral responsibility. Robert Kane distinguishes the moral from the prudential but holds that moral and prudential decisions are similar in that both involve a conflict between what one believes one *ought* to do and what one has an inclination to do. In the case of the prudential choice, the conflict is between long-term goals and immediate inclinations. Moreover, both sorts of decision can be self-forming; that is, they can contribute to one's character. The examples he gives of prudential choices involve the person concerned about his weight sticking to his diet or having that beer and the recovering alcoholic taking the drink or refraining.[2] With these particular examples, my own inclination is to take the more Aristotelian tack: You have moral obligations toward yourself such that these choices are moral choices. You can be praised or blamed given which option you pursue. Perhaps there are choices between long-term goals and immediate desires that really are

1 Kane (1996); O'Connor (2000); Rogers (2015).
2 Kane (1996): 126–7.

devoid of moral content, but in general I shall take it that prudential choices of the sort that Kane discusses are a species of moral choice.

It will be helpful to propose a set of necessary elements constituting an LFMC. (This will also be useful in showing what is *not* a necessary element.) If experimental study of some relevantly LFMC-like event shows some or all of these elements to be lacking, we can conclude that the event being studied is not a free choice – at least not under the proposed description. I am using "LFMC-like" to stand for an event or act where, if it is not an LFMC, it is nevertheless similar enough to what an LFMC is thought to be that studying it can provide evidence or insight regarding the question at issue: Do human agents have morally significant free will? If, in studying LFMC-like events, we discover a reasons to believe that the elements required for a free choice are *never* present, as human agents go about their business, then we have reason to doubt the existence of free will. For example, a key element in a libertarian free choice is that the agent be able to deliberate rationally and pursue a course for which she has reasons. If, for every LFMC-like event we studied, we found that rational deliberation played no role in how the agent chose to act, we could conclude that we had evidence against free will. (This hypothesis is advanced by situationism, a theory to be discussed in Chapter 5.)

In the first part of this chapter, I will sketch what I take to be a plausible portrait of an LFMC. As the portrait gets filled in, some elements will emerge that may pose problems for the scientist who hopes to discover evidence for or against morally significant, libertarian free will. But these difficulties should not be taken as reasons to revise the portrait of freedom since it will represent a typical, though rough and general, philosophically developed LFMC. If the sciences cannot provide evidence relevant to this understanding of choice, then my point is proved. In the second part, I discuss some kinds of choices that are not FMCs in order to note the differences. There is a spectrum of events properly labelled "choices" or "decisions" – some more like, and some less like, what appear to be free moral choices. It is important to get clear on just what sort of choice is being studied, and what sort of choice *could* be studied, as we assess what science has to say, or might have to say, about meaningful freedom.

A Paradigmatic, Libertarian Free, Morally Significant Choice

In sketching an LFMC, I will adopt locutions that imply that human agents do indeed make such choices but this is just a portrait. Most of us do make choices that we *believe* to be free and to have moral content, but the thesis of this book is that science – now and in the future – leaves it an open question whether or not human agents actually make free choices for which they can be held morally responsible. A first thing to note is that, on the analysis of moral responsibility with which I am working, the locus of responsibility is the *choice*. If an overt deed follows upon the choice, the moral assessment attaching to the deed derives from the moral quality of the choice. Overtly, my stepping on your foot might appear to be the same event whether I stepped accidentally or maliciously, but I am blameworthy in the latter case and not in the former. Having chosen to step on your foot, I am blameworthy even if I miss because you suddenly move your foot. As noted in Chapter 1, this focus on the choice makes earthly justice difficult since mental events are private. We, society, must muddle through as best we can when we are called upon to judge people's behavior.[3] Making the choice itself our main concern might be misguided if all we cared about were justifying punishment, but the traditional worry about free will centers on the status of the individual and justifying punishment is a corollary.

I am assuming that there are objective moral values and so a morally significant choice is one between a genuine right and wrong. It lies beyond the scope of the present work to try to assess just what constitutes these values and how they are to be determined. (Chapters 6 and 7 will deal with ethical issues related to experimenting on human subjects.) In general, questions of value and morality belong to philosophy rather than science, although some of the experiments to be discussed do include a moral component. But – for the experimenter who is skeptical about the objectivity of moral truth – we can bracket worries about the moral content of choices to some extent and allow that a choice could be an FMC so long as the subject whose choice we hope to study *believes* that his choice is between morally better and worse options. Or even more minimally, if the subject understands that the choice he is to make is between options that involve content that is usually considered to have moral import, perhaps that would allow for an FMC. This more minimal description tries to take account of the "Huckleberry Finn" sort of situation. Huck is torn between turning runaway slave Jim in to the authorities or helping him escape to free territory. Huck's *beliefs* about the right thing to do are drawn from the claims of his slave-owning society, but he actually opts for what we, and the author, Mark Twain, clearly hold to be the morally correct decision, over the perverted belief. Thus, someone like Huck, who (we assume) holds mistaken beliefs about objective right and wrong, may still be engaged in an FMC. In any case (having the skeptic about moral truth in mind), if there is no moral truth, then it is difficult to see why anyone should care about free will. Without moral truth, there is no *moral* responsibility, and human agents do not have the elevated value, the human dignity, of being the kind of things who can choose the good on their own and who can help in the construction of their own character. We have no *moral* obligation to treat

---

3 Rogers (2015): 147–9.

people with respect. Nor need we worry about the *moral* justification for our holding anyone praiseworthy or blameworthy. In a discussion of human freedom, it seems appropriate to allow the assumption that there is moral truth.

So, what might an LFMC look like? Most libertarians agree that several criteria are required for a free choice: the agent must be capable of rational deliberation which (at least in part) produces his choice, he must confront genuinely open options, the choice for *this* over *that* must not be causally determined, and which option is chosen must be up to the agent himself. As a temporally first requirement, the agent (call him "S" for short) must be in what we can label the "torn condition", debating between morally better and worse options. For simplicity's sake, let this debate between the two options stand as a description of the torn condition. In real life, the torn condition is likely to present a much "messier" picture with a vast complexity of competing elements.[4] But in order for a choice to have moral significance, the torn condition must *at least* involve the debate between the morally better and worse options. This simple picture is adequate for the purposes of attempting to address how science has studied free will and how it might study it in the future. If science cannot decide the question of free will given this somewhat simplified paradigm of a free choice, then it is safe to say that filling in the simplified portrait with more elements would not make science's task any easier.

It is important to insist upon the point that the choice we are concerned with is a morally significant choice, meaning a choice between morally better and worse options. This will loom large when looking at choices made in experimental contexts. Choices of indifference, which I will understand to mean choices where you could legitimately flip a coin to decide what to do, cannot be FMCs. But some choices of indifference may be FMC-like. The question is, are they sufficiently similar that we can "translate" from conclusions we achieve by studying the FMC-like choice to conclusions about genuine, morally significant free choices. There are roughly three sorts of choices of indifference that will be at issue. First is the case where the options are identical or almost identical – we can call that indifference of identity. In the medieval thought experiment, aimed at undermining Aristotle's view that you pursue only what you judge most desirable, Buridan's ass was confronted by a choice of indifference of identity. The two bales of hay between which the poor creature starved were almost exactly alike, including in their distance from him. Presumably, the ass had

---

4 Eliezer Sternberg argues from the "boundless" complexity of moral choices that they cannot be the upshot of deterministic systems, since such systems can address only formally bounded problems. *My Brain Made Me Do It* (Amherst, NY: Prometheus Books, 2010).

the option to choose left or right but that was not enough of a difference to provide a reason to go either way – and the ass starves.

A second sort of choice of indifference would be one in which the options are different but still so similar that it makes no difference which you choose. Chocolate and pistachio are different in taste, and someone who liked one might dislike the other, but for those who happen to like both equally, it really doesn't matter which flavor ice cream you choose. (Ceteris paribus, if there isn't much pistachio left and that is your friend's favorite flavor, you might choose chocolate just to leave the pistachio for him.) We can call this the indifference of similarity. Neither of these sorts of choices involving indifference of identity or indifference of similarity appears to be similar to an FMC; thus, the Problem of Translation is serious when evidence from these choices of indifference is supposed to inform us concerning human freedom.

There is a third sort of choice of indifference. These would be decisions that are important and difficult and that have sweeping consequences but for which the options are equally "weighted" in terms of the strength of one's motivation and neither is morally better or worse. We can call this indifference of weight. One might be in the terrible situation of having to confront only equally bad options – a "Sophie's choice" situation.[5] One might bear moral responsibility for how one considered one's options or for how one evaluated them later, but if someone is forced to choose between equal harms, the choice itself is not a morally significant choice on my understanding. Or one might be weighing equally good options. Suppose you have decided to give money to one of two charities, but you have to choose which charity to give to, and, having done your due diligence, you decide that your money will be just as helpful given to either one. You may be praiseworthy for the initial decision to give, but opting for one charity over the other is not where the morally significant choice lies. There are many other sorts of choices which fall under choices of indifference of weight. Choices of careers and vacation spots are examples. They may be important and hard to make and have serious consequences, but (ceteris paribus) they do not have moral significance.

This choice of indifference of weight seems much closer to a morally significant choice. One intuition might be that these sorts of choices are sufficiently FMC-like that evidence regarding them translates properly to conclusions regarding FMCs. I do not agree. I take the phenomenology of an FMC to be significantly different from a choice of indifference, even where the latter choice is important. First, where one has considered one's options carefully and realized that they are equally bad or equally good, a

---

5 In the 1979 novel by William Styron, the title character, arriving at Auschwitz, has been forced to choose which of her two children will be killed immediately.

mental (or literal) coin toss is entirely appropriate. This is not the case when the agent is in the torn condition debating between the morally better and worse options. The FMC requires an exercise of "willpower", which is a different sort of action from the mental or literal coin flip. (I will continue to put "willpower" in scare quotes since I do not propose to offer a developed definition or explanation. I believe most of us recognize the experience of trying to exert a particular sort of effort to choose the better over the worse, including the long-term goal over the present gratification.) How this exercise of "willpower" goes constitutes the moral choice. One is praised or blamed for making the morally significant choice, whereas one is neither praised nor blamed for how the coin toss goes. Moreover, for many who defend human freedom, the morally significant choice is a building block of one's future character – part of the system producing settled virtues or vices. The same cannot be said for the choice of indifference of weight. So, it seems to me that evidence concerning the choice of indifference of weight likely would not translate to the morally significant choice. This is an important point in assessing the experimental approach to free will. I argued in the previous chapter that belief in free will is extremely valuable. Thus, the burden of proof lies on the one who would deny human freedom. In a situation where the experimenter uses evidence from a choice of indifference of weight to argue that human beings are not free, the burden of proof is on the experimenter to show that the evidence can translate appropriately. More on this after the main object of discussion, the LFMC, has been described.

If agent S, to make a morally significant choice, must first be in the torn condition, then he must be capable of theoretical reasoning and able to step back and consider his options. We can think of the options as being constituted by mutually exclusive desires, understanding "desires" broadly to cover reasons, motivations, inclinations, and the like. Thus, "desires" stands for whatever motivational states would lead one to pursue a particular course of action when coupled with the relevant beliefs about the situation. Were the desires not mutually exclusive, one would not have to choose. The torn condition may last only a short time or it may go on for a while. Suppose, for example, that S finds out on Tuesday that an event is being held on Thursday to which he believes he ought to go but which he does not want to go to. S may assess these options and decide – to go, let's say – almost instantaneously. His intention may be fixed days in advance, resulting in him going. Or he may dither, moving back and forth between what he takes to be the right thing to do versus what he would rather do, up until the time he starts his car to go on Thursday. Of course, if some significant new information or incident occurs between Tuesday and Thursday – he breaks his ankle or the event is cancelled because of bad weather – then even the fixed intention will have to change and will not issue in the chosen action.

The agent may or may not find himself in this torn condition very often. It is possible, if we assume that human agents make morally significant free choices, that we make them only rarely. We may make all sorts of decisions in our lives, but it may be the case that few of these decisions meet the criteria for an FMC. In fact, to my knowledge, no libertarian theory of free will entails the thesis that, if anyone has free will, then everyone must. Not only might it be the case that some (or most) free agents make morally significant choices only rarely, it is possible that some apparently normal adult human agents *never* make free choices. I do not say this is likely, just that it is possible on any given libertarian theory. Moreover, morally significant choices may be "large" or "small" in the sense that they may be about issues that are extremely important or relatively trivial. But a choice that looks to be about something trivial could turn out to have important consequences. These points are (I believe) often assumed in the philosophical free will literature, but they exacerbate the Problem of Translation for the empirical study of free will. If human agents make morally significant choices infrequently, if (possibly) some never make such choices, and if these choices are sometimes – at least apparently – trivial, then the scientist may find it difficult to isolate and focus on the sort of event that is, or that is appropriately similar to, the kind of event that the free will debate is actually about.

The requirement that the freely choosing agent must first be in the torn condition presents a further problem for scientific study: Every agent is unique. Every agent has his own life history and mental furniture. Even the same agent is different at different times. Minor factors may influence one's options. Say that S is torn between A and B but that had his back been hurting, his options might have been between B and C. Or if he had just received an acceptance on a submission to a journal, his options might have been between P and Q. Every instance of the torn condition is unlike any other, and every free choice is a unique and unrepeatable event. I do not know of any philosophers who would deny this claim. But in that science (as a rule) draws its conclusions from observing repeatable events, the uniqueness ascribed to free choices poses a formidable problem to scientific investigation.[6] One move is for the experimenter to study subjects making (apparently) FMCs in controlled circumstances such that the situation calling for the choice is (in some meaningful sense) repeatable. Chapters 5 and 6 look at experiments which take this approach. I will argue that at least some of these experiments generate severe ethical difficulties.

---

6 Some who allow the possibility of libertarian freedom, and think that science can settle the free will question, suggest that science will be able to assign probabilities to the options in a free choice. For example, see Balaguer (2010): 76–83; Robert Kane, (1996): 177. I argue that it is unlikely that probabilities can ever be assigned to options (Rogers (2015): 182–93.

Alternatively, one might study FMC-like events and explain why the data gathered are applicable to FMCs simpliciter. I suggested above that this is a problematic move. I develop this claim in Part II of this chapter where I offer a list of candidates for such FMC-like events but argue that none provides the appropriate analogy to a morally significant choice. The problem of the uniqueness of free choices will be revisited in Chapter 8.

The conflicting desires required to set up the torn condition to allow for a free choice may well be produced by something outside of the agent, S. S cannot take credit for having the desires that he has, except in the case where his desires arise from his character which has been formed (in part) by his past free choices. The torn condition that limits S's options to *these* possibilities over *those*, and that sets the stage for the free choice, may well be determined by S's past, his heredity, and so on. Thus, the sort of criticism mounted by Galen Strawson and echoed by a number of neuroscientists and psychologists, where it is supposed that libertarian freedom must entail that an agent be responsible for the options that confront him, does not connect with this approach.[7] Alfred Mele, criticizing Robert Kane's event-causal libertarian theory, argues that if the desirable options between which an agent is choosing are determined, then the agent does not have any more robust freedom than on a compatibilist account.[8] I believe this is a mistake. If the options are truly morally significant, then it makes a difference if it was up to the agent himself, and not determined by preceding causes, that he opted for this over that.[9] The thought that the options between which the agent is torn may be determined raises the issue of "moral luck". Aren't some agents just luckier than others in terms of the options that present themselves as viable? The answer is "Yes". Ideal justice would take this into account in allotting praise and blame, and earthly justice often tries to do this insofar as it is able. The defender of free will should probably just bite the bullet on the evident fact that human lives involve a lot of luck.[10] Our freedom operates within serious boundaries, yet it is sufficient to ground genuine moral responsibility and human dignity.

This point addresses one argument against believing in free will. In Chapter 1, I noted that some free will deniers and skeptics hold that, in the absence of significant evidence, one ought to reject rather than embrace

---

7 Galen Strawson, "The Bounds of Freedom", in *The Oxford Handbook of Free Will* edited by Robert Kane (Oxford: Oxford University Press, 2002): 441–60. Here Strawson talks about the kind of free will that can ground "true, unqualified responsibility-and-deservingness" (442), so perhaps he would respond that the portrait I paint of free choice falls short. The defender, in turn, suggests that Strawson has constructed a straw man, when he supposes that responsibility-grounding libertarian free will must entail that we cause ourselves and our motivations.
8 Alfred Mele, *Free Will and Luck* (Oxford: Oxford University Press, 2006): 51–2.
9 Rogers (2015): Chapter 5.
10 Rogers (2015): 109, note 14.

belief in free will; the burden of proof thus is on the free will defender. One reason is – so the argument goes – that believing in free will is likely to encourage us – society – to exercise an unwholesome self-satisfaction and to hold wrongdoers in contempt, blame them more excessively, and punish them more harshly than we would if we did not believe in free will. But recognizing this element of luck, which plausible libertarian theories are likely to include, should constitute a mitigating factor – mitigating both the self-satisfaction of those walking the straight and narrow and the blameworthiness of the wrongdoer.[11] Luck certainly plays a role in human life, and luck may limit an agent's autonomy, but a plausible libertarian theory can accommodate these facts.

In the torn condition, S struggles to pursue the two conflicting desires, call them the desire to A and the desire to B. S's "desiring" here should be understood as something that S is *doing*. "Willing" would be an equally good term so long as it is understood that one can rationally will two mutually conflicting outcomes where only one can ultimately be chosen. At some point, S chooses – A, let's say. (Whether or not there is a "moment" of choice is open to debate. There is nothing in this picture of an LFMC that requires that the choice be instantaneous as opposed to "spread" over a period of time.) This choice is described somewhat differently in different libertarian theories. Kane emphasizes the event of the agent's desiring, whereas O'Connor emphasizes the unique causal power of the agent. Anselm proposes what I have called a *parsimonious* agent-causation in that *all* that the choice for A consists in is S's desiring A to the point where the desire to A becomes an intention to A and the desire for B is no longer a live option.[12] But all of these versions require that two criteria be met if S's choice for A is truly to be considered free: First, S could have chosen B. Nothing about S, or the situation, makes it necessary that S chose A. The choice is not determined. S's choice for A can be explained (in part) by pointing to S's desire for A or reasons for choosing A. But, had S chosen B, a similar, partial explanation could have been given. No complete explanation can be given for why S ultimately opted for A over B, and that can be cognitively uncomfortable. Elsewhere, I have offered what I take to be an adequate response to this sort of "luck" problem.[13] Second, the choice was *a se*: from or "up to" S himself. It was S's doing. Kane uses the phrase "ultimate responsibility" to express the thought that the buck stops with S. That is what makes S responsible for the choice.

At this point in the process of choosing, when the agent chooses one option to the point of forming an intention – assuming the intention is fixed – the morally relevant action has taken place. Under the usual circumstances, the deed intended will follow upon the choice. I define "deed"

---

11 Rogers (2015): 147–9.
12 Rogers (2015): 81–100.
13 Rogers (2015): 174–215.

broadly to include, for example, overt bodily acts, mental acts such as focusing on some thought, and the "stillness" of *not* doing something where the options given in the torn condition were between doing or not doing the deed. (I do not intend this to be an exhaustive list of the kinds of deeds that might follow upon a choice.) But the moral status of the deed is derived from that of the choice. This is a very standard way of looking at things in the tradition that connects free will to human dignity since the primary locus of concern is not this or that individual act but the overall moral status of the human agent.

The dependence of the moral status of an act on the moral status of the preceding choice does not rule out the possibility of doing what is in some sense the right deed for the wrong reason or the wrong deed for the right reason. But this is because there is a legitimate equivocation on the terms "right" and "wrong". There is "right" and "wrong" as the terms can apply to overt deeds, where it may be better to replace them with "good" and "bad". To illustrate: Understand "good" and "bad" with regard to your preferred value theory. On most value theories, it is objectively good to help a sick child. But if you help the child only because you want to be praised for it, your act – though good in one way – is not morally praiseworthy. Your choice itself is not praiseworthy since you opted to pursue the good vainly and selfishly, although the overt deed you engaged in was objectively good. Conversely, you might, out of love, deeply desire to help the sick child but choose to do something that harms her, having made an innocent mistake about what will help or harm in this case. Your act is bad, in that it is harmful to the child, but neither your choice nor you, the agent, is blameworthy. None of this constitutes a novel way of assessing choices and acts but it is worth mentioning in order to be clear on the point that the *moral* status of an act is dependent upon the moral status of the agent's choice. The freedom that grounds responsibility and dignity is freedom with respect to choices. This will have some interesting implications for how to think about free will when it comes to considering the experiments that are purported to show that there is a disconnect between our conscious willing and our actions.

It is worthwhile to look at the aftermath of the choice and deed. The tradition that connects human freedom and human dignity often takes the development of character, through the agent's choices, to be a (or even *the*) purpose of free will. Robert Kane labels meaningful free choices "self-forming" actions or willings.[14] Individual choices and acts are (of course) very important, but more important is their cumulative impact on the agent: What kind of person are you? In both philosophy and psychology, there is a rich literature concerning character and the virtues, and many agree that it is one's choices and subsequent actions that (to some extent) construct one's character or moral orientation. This entails an important qualification to the present analysis of free choice. A human agent's choice might

---

14 Kane (1996): 124–5.

be free in the sense of being *a se* – up to the agent in a way that properly grounds moral responsibility – and yet be determined by his character if that character itself was produced by past choices that fit the description of a free choice.[15] This "tracing thesis" adds a further difficulty for the scientist who would study meaningful freedom. The discovery of preceding determining causes for some choices that are generally agreed to be properly subject to moral praise and blame would not provide evidence that *all* responsible choices may be determined. But it cannot be said that this *unfairly* disadvantages the experimenter since this "tracing thesis" is both a standard element of the traditional approach to free will and very common today among believers in meaningful freedom.[16]

A final aspect of this picture of free choice should be mentioned. It is a very typical point in Christian thinking on moral choice and I believe that many outside of that tradition would find it intuitively obvious. Yet it has had little play in the recent philosophical literature on free will. Many important choices – choices which can fit the description of an LFMC – may not issue in overt deeds at all. I am thinking especially of choices concerning one's own mental states. For example, you might be inclined to be envious of a colleague's success and choose to make a deliberate effort to adopt a different and more wholesome attitude. This choice – invisible to the outside world – may have a significant impact on your character. Chances are that if you successfully maintain the mental stance you have chosen, your behavior will reflect your changed attitude. But it may well be the case that your new practices do not follow immediately upon the choice and that they are not obvious to others.

Here is another example of an important type of choice that need not be followed – or at least not followed immediately – by any overt deed and yet may have enormous moral significance. In terms of the kind of person that you are – your orientation toward the morally good or bad – how you choose to *evaluate* your past choices and actions may be as important as those past choices and actions. I believe this is easily seen with the bad choices. Does the agent, having chosen to do something wrong and then having done it, endorse and embrace that past choice and action? Does he unenthusiastically try to make excuses for it? Or perhaps the agent regrets and utterly repudiates it. In that last case, forgiveness may be the appropriate response, and the agent may emerge from the process more securely oriented toward the good. Thus, an agent's moral orientation may be very significantly shaped by this after-the-fact choice of self-evaluation. Such an after-the-fact choice may (or may not) issue in immediate overt deeds, and that means that we, society,

---

15 Rogers (2015): 117–26.
16 Rogers (2015): 218. See note 1 for citations to contemporary defenses of the tracing thesis and note 3 for citations concerning Aristotle's explication of the thesis.

may not know of its occurrence. But that does not undermine the claim that such choices may be crucial in the life of the agent.[17]

To review: an LFMC requires that the agent be able to deliberate rationally. He must find himself in the torn condition, debating between (at least) two mutually exclusive, morally significant options. His choice for one over the other must not be determined; that is, he could, with everything about himself and the situation remaining the same, have chosen otherwise. And it must be up to agent which option he chooses. Having described an LFMC, we will find it useful to note what was *not* included among the criteria. Before the choice, open options are crucial, but that the agent confronts *these* options rather than *those* may well be determined. There is no reason to insist that the motivational structure which provides the history for the torn condition was generated by the agent himself *ex nihilo*. Furthermore, little was said about the state of mind of the agent *while* he is choosing. Must it be the case that the agent be introspecting and examining the contents of his mind as he chooses? Must he note to himself, "Now I am choosing"? Someone making an LFMC probably has enough mental work to do without taking the extra step of observing their own mental activities, and it is hard to see what the process of introspection would add to the choice. Sometimes we do deliberately introspect and perhaps we introspect a freely made choice. One piece of evidence for free will is willing some action – like raising one's arm – and attending to the willing and to the subsequent action. But if we are engaged in a serious moral choice, we may be deliberating about our options and too engrossed to introspect.

After the choice, *must* some overt deed follow? No. Although we usually think of a free choice as being aimed at doing some overt deed, that is not one of the criteria for an LFMC. Some LFMCs may be aimed at mental actions rather than doing overt deeds. Even when the choice is aimed at doing some overt deed, the doing of the deed is not where the freedom or the moral action lies. One could make an LFMC aimed at doing some overt deed but die the next moment. That would not negate the fact that one had made an LFMC. This entails the further point that a correct memory of one's deliberations and choice (or of one's subsequent deed) is not necessary for the agent to have made an LFMC. What happens after the LFMC is made does not unmake it.

With a description of an LFMC in hand, we can say a little more about the Problem of Translation Regarding the Object of Study. The most direct way to solve the problem would be to study morally significant choices, and some of the psychology experiments to be discussed have attempted to do that. These experiments raise ethical and practical issues, however, and so many of the free will experiments deal with choices or decisions that are far from the described LFMC. Thus, the Translation Problem is serious. If an experimenter concludes, based on study of a not very LFMC-like event, that human agents do not have meaningful free will, the burden of proof

17 Rogers (2015): 208–15.

principle (for which I argued in Chapter 1) entails that the burden of proof lies with that experimenter to show that the evidence translates from the event they are studying to apply properly to moral choices. This issue will come up repeatedly in the course of this work. Below I mention a few examples of decisions that have been (or might be) studied and note differences between these decisions and LFMCs. This will be useful in assessing the experiments in subsequent chapters, especially in evaluating whether or not the burden of proof can be met regarding translation from the experiments to claims about free will.

Other Kinds of Choice and Decision

A first question to consider is whether or not we can gather useful evidence from studying non-human animals. If so, that would avoid many of the practical and ethical questions involved in studying human choices. In an article entitled "Neural Basis of Decision in Perception and in the Control of Movement", A. Berthoz reports that toads exhibit the flee response in the face of targets of one shape and prey-catching behavior in the face of targets of a different shape. This occurs because "the 'decision' to trigger either type of behavior is made by a very simple neural mechanism: specialized neurons detect the main features of the targets as described above and then they mutually inhibit each other".[18] "Decision" here is rightly in scare quotes. The toad is so different from the human being that it is implausible to think that the toad "decision" is sufficiently similar to the human decision to allow us to draw meaningful parallels. But what of other primates? Adina Roskies, though she does hold that neuroscience probably cannot answer the metaphysical question of whether or not human choices are determined, suggests that we may discover evidence concerning human decision-making through recording the brain states of non-human primates. She describes an experiment in which monkeys have been trained to observe screens with dots moving to left and right. In some experiments, the greater number of dots moves randomly either to the left or to the right. In some, an equal number of dots moves in either direction. The monkey's task "is to judge the direction of overall motion of the dots and to indicate its judgement by moving its eyes". When the monkey moves its eyes, this is considered indicative of its *decision*, where the term is not in scare quotes.[19] Roskies appreciates that a responsible choice made by a human being is very different from these decisions. She locates the

---

18 A. Berthoz, "Neural Basis of Decision in Perception and in the Control of Movement". In Damasio (1996): 83–100, at 84.
19 Adina Roskies, "Can Neuroscience Resolve Issues about Free Will?". In *Moral Psychology, Volume 4: Free Will and Moral Responsibility* edited by Walter Sinnot-Armstrong (Cambridge, MA: MIT Press, 2014) 103–26, at 110.

differences as being that the responsible choice is more complex and is not stimulus-driven the way the monkey's decision is. Still, she holds that this sort of study might be usefully developed to study responsible choices.[20] If the topic is robust, morally significant freedom, though, it is not clear how the burden of proof could be met in translating from the monkeys deciding about the dots to choices resembling LFMCs. Severe Problems of Translation Regarding the Object of Study, Regarding the Situation, and Regarding the Subject Pool are likely to arise in any attempt to research free will by studying animal choices. If such studies are interpreted to suggest a lack of freedom in human beings, the defender of free will can simply point to the great difference between human beings and other animals.

There is another problem with the use of "decision" in this experiment with the monkeys and the dots. Judging the direction of the motion of the dots, even were it being done by human subjects, is much more like my deciding that my shower curtain has too much purple in it than it is like a morally responsible free choice. There are two crucial distinctions. The first is that assessing and coming to a conclusion about what is the case are not the same sorts of activity as deciding what to do. In the case of the dots or the shower curtain, the question is one of careful perception. Judging the color of the shower curtain which is before one's eyes is different from considering a future action. A second problem with holding that experiments in the family of the monkeys "deciding" about the dots is that assessing what is the case perceptually has no moral content and involves no "willpower". I am not to be blamed for my shower curtain mistake or praised for my subsequently "deciding" on the excessive purpleness. A perceptual judgment appears to be a far cry from an LFMC.

There have been experiments asking subjects to make judgments in moral situations. J. Greene et al. have studied the neural correlates of emotion and reason in moral judgments by confronting subjects with versions of the Trolley Car problems well known to philosophers. Intuitively, what should you do in the following situations: Should you save the many by switching the runaway trolley to the other track, where it will kill only the one or the few? If you are on the footbridge above the tracks, should you push the very large person next to you onto the track below, stopping the trolley before it can hit the group of people in the way? Greene et al. found that more people are willing to switch than to push and that considering pushing engages the neural centers more closely associated with emotions than does considering switching. They also suggest that a "personal/impersonal" distinction may be at work underlying subjects' intuitions.[21]

---

20 Adina Roskies, "How Does Neuroscience Affect Our Conception of Volition?" *Annual review of Neuroscience* 33 (2010): 109–30, at 118–19.
21 Joshua D. Greene, R. Brian Sommerville, Leigh E. Nystrom, John M. Darley, Jonathan D. Cohen, "An fMRI Investigation of Emotional Engagement in Moral Judgment". *Science* 293 (2001): 2105–8.

Are the choices made by subjects in these studies LFMC-like actions? I think not. Although this study is related to moral issues, it is still an instance of making a judgment about what is the case. The sorts of decisions to be made in the Trolley Car problems are much more complex than in the shower curtain example or the dots experiment, but complexity and morally relevant content do not equate to choices about what the agents actually intend to do. This point is underscored when we remember that one is likely to exercise "willpower" (perhaps unsuccessfully) and that one can be praised or blamed for making an LFMC. In discussing the Trolley Car problems with students or subjects, we are curious about their intuitions and we may be puzzled if their intuitions do not conform to ours, but we do not hold them morally blameworthy (or morally praiseworthy) for having the intuitions that they do. There is moral content in these experiments, but the moral judgments being studied are different kinds of events from LFMCs.

As I suggested above (in describing choices of indifference of weight), it could be argued that certain important – though non-moral – decisions about what to do are sufficiently LFMC-like that studying them would avoid the Problem of Translation. There are many sorts of decisions we might make which are not morally significant and yet require careful thought and make a difference to how our lives go. The choice of a career or a college or even a vacation might be such a choice. (One might imagine situations in which such choices *do* involve the morally better or worse, but here I am hypothesizing morally neutral choices.) Still these choices are unlike morally significant choices in important ways. Presumably, if one makes a deliberate and considered choice of a career, a college, or a vacation, it is because there is more than one viable option. And the different options will likely entail competing values to be weighed. In the final analysis, it is plausible to suppose that either one value will look to be the weightier or you will make a choice of indifference; that is, you will flip a mental (or even a literal) coin and just decide. If the choice follows inevitably from the appreciation of the weightier reason, it is unlike the LFMC in that there is no actual ability to choose otherwise. But if it is a coin toss situation, it is not like an LFMC either. In neither scenario must you exercise any "willpower" to choose a better over a worse option (or a long-term goal over immediate satisfaction). Moral credit is not due to you when the clear choice presented itself or you had to flip a mental (or literal) coin. Remember that we have allowed that much in your life may be locally causally determined. It may be determined that you find yourself facing these particular non-moral options. Then if the actual choice is one of indifference – the pure luck of a coin toss – there seems to be little there to ground any responsibility, even non-moral responsibility.

There is another sort of choice that might look to be similar to the morally significant choice and that is a choice made by an artist.²² It is said that the originality and creativity that we value in artistic pursuits are undermined if free will is denied. On the other hand, Paul Russell argues that a belief in libertarian free will is irrelevant in evaluating works of art and the abilities of artists. He notes that the libertarian who would insist that his metaphysics of free will must undergird our appreciation of art may find himself on a slippery slope, for if the artistic merit of works and artists requires libertarian free choice, what of other human achievements, like excellence in sports? We may admire the brilliant play and praise the player qua player. But in sports as well as in art, Russell writes, "The presence or absence of either determinism or free will, in this context, seems entirely irrelevant to these sorts of considerations and assessments. Indeed, typically these sorts of concerns are never even *contemplated*" (Russell's italics).²³

It may be that artists' choices have more in common with perceptual judgments than with morally significant choices. Perhaps there is a "logic" of artistic endeavor such that the artist is "seeing" how the work of art ought to proceed. With physicists one supposes that their theories, however new and original, are not freely chosen but are generated by attention to the evidence. I take it that we want physicists to be discovering the world, not imagining new things in the universe. Perhaps the same goes with philosophers. The philosopher meditates on the problem, and the solution, waiting in logical space, is accessed when the time is right. No choosing is involved. Maybe artists proceed along similar lines. Some, at least, subscribe to the "muse" theory, wherein the idea (or the image or whatever) is *accessed* rather than created *ex nihilo*.

With an artistic choice as with the other sorts of choice listed above, there is no advantage at all to having open options rather than just seeing what is best and including it in the work of art. With perception – like my judgment on the color of my shower curtain – and with art, it is best just to see what is in fact the case. We do not offer moral praise and blame to the artist who produces the work of art (unless moral choices were made in the course of the production). One could argue – possibly endlessly – about what goes into the process of artistic creation. My suggestion is just that artistic choices are different sorts of actions from morally significant choices. Important human choices (like the choice of career, college, and so on) and perhaps artistic choices may be more like moral choices than the

22 Robert Kane (1996): 81.
23 Paul Russell, "Free Will, Art and Morality", *Journal of Ethics* 12 (3–4) (2008): 307–25, at 313–14. Russell goes on to argue that incompatibilism is unreasonable in that (he says) it insists that free moral agents cannot be influenced by the sorts of lucky life-history events that do not trouble us in evaluating art and artists. As I noted in describing the paradigmatic free choice, an agent can be significantly influenced by lucky life-history events and still be free.

toad's "choice" to pursue or flee or the monkey's "decision" about which way the majority of the dots are headed, but they are not morally significant choices, and that is what we are mainly concerned with when we worry about whether or not human agents have free will.

A final suggestion for an FMC-like choice is a prudential choice devoid of moral content. (I noted above that Robert Kane distinguishes the prudential from the moral. However, I see the examples he gives as moral choices.) In the long tradition which produced our free will debate, prudence is a virtue. Indeed, in the Aristotelian stream in that tradition, it is a central virtue in that it assesses how the other virtues should be exercised. But if "prudential" here is taken to mean simply the realization of long-term goals, whatever those goals may be, then perhaps one can imagine a prudential choice devoid of moral content, an NMPC – a non-moral prudential choice. This choosing between the long-term and the immediate does not seem quite like a choice of indifference. Suppose, for example, one's long-term goal is to become a billionaire. (There might be something morally suspect in making that one's only, or main, long-term goal.) But one would rather buy a fancy new boat right now than invest one's money profitably. One might engage in a struggle between the options and make an effort to exercise "willpower". The subsequent choice – though by hypothesis not morally praiseworthy or blameworthy – is not really a coin flip either. This NMPC comes closer to an FMC-like event. However, I am not convinced that the hypothesis that the choice is morally neutral is realistic. In that the choice of long-term goals and the exercise of a present self-control both likely involve moral content – there are morally better and worse long-term goals, and self-control is a virtue – it might be that there really are no NMPCs. Perhaps all "prudential" choices involve some moral content and are, on some level and to some extent, morally praiseworthy or blameworthy. But for the sake of argument, I allow that there exist NMPCs and that these sorts of choice really are sufficiently FMC-like to avoid the Problem of Translation of the Object of Study were the experimenter to turn his attention to them. But a similarity close enough to avoid the Problem of Translation means that the empirical study of NMPCs will raise almost all the difficulties involved in studying FMCs.

The experimental psychologist or neurobiologist will likely argue that many of the types of choice mentioned in this section – and not just the NMPCs – are similar enough to morally significant choice that evidence can be translated from experiments concerning the former to conclusions concerning the latter. But if the evidence suggests a lack of free will, the burden of proof I argued for in Chapter 1 requires that a case be made for the relevant similarity – or at least appropriate analogy – between the non-moral choice and the moral choice. Differing intuitions on this question make it difficult to settle in the abstract. I believe that whether or not the burden of proof has been (or could be) met is a discussion that can take place only in the context of actual experiments concerning particular sorts of choice.

Regarding past experiments, some have studied what appear to be genuinely moral choices. The Problem of Translation Regarding the Object of Study does not arise in that case. But many experimenters have simply assumed sufficient similarity between morally responsible choice and other instances of choice, which often are strikingly unlike moral choice. This invites the critic to point to a serious Problem of Translation. Some experimenters, to their credit, have tried to address the Problem of Translation and make a case for sufficient similarity between whatever non-moral choice they are studying and moral choice. I will address their arguments and conclude that they are not adequate.

Suppose someone holds, contrary to my view, that many instances of non-moral choices, in addition to NMPCs, like the examples above of choices of indifference of weight, are indeed sufficiently like FMCs that the evidence from studying the former can translate appropriately to the latter. This would undermine a few of my arguments, but most remain intact. Most of the severe problems associated with attempting to study morally significant free choices will plague the study of choices which are similar to FMCs. Conversely, if one shares my intuition that the FMC is a unique sort of phenomenon, it is still the case that study of non-moral choices may provide us with very useful information regarding human agency. The goal of the present chapter was to sketch a paradigmatic LFMC. This is important in order to recognize what can be taken as the primary object of study in the experimental approach to free will. (Again, if my arguments succeed in showing that science has not, and probably cannot, settle the question concerning the existence of L [libertarian] FMCs, then the existence of C [compatibilist] FMCs is safe from disproof.) And having a clear description of an LFMC underscores the Problem of Translation which will arise often in the attempt to study free will empirically.

The next chapter looks at the discussion surrounding the Libet experiments from the early 1980s and at later Libet-type experiments. These experiments are often cited as evidence against free will, but there is much to criticize in this conclusion, including that the experiments introduce a severe Problem of Translation regarding the "choices" being studied. Libet attempts to respond to this criticism. I will evaluate his response using the LFMC sketched in the present chapter as the paradigm of a freely willed choice. I will also note a host of other problems for brain research that arise in the debate over the Libet experiments.

Chapter 3

The Libet Experiments

Introduction

Suppose a friend of yours is having car trouble. You believe you ought to help him, but you don't really want to. You debate inwardly for a little while, then make the decision to go and help. You expect a little appreciation from your friend, but he withholds that pat on the back, explaining that your decision to help him wasn't a free choice. It wasn't really up to you that you decided to help and you could not have done otherwise. Science, he goes on to say, has shown that your decision was actually produced by events in your brain which preceded your conscious choice and over which you had no control. Your friend – having heard about the Libet experiments – is glad of the help but will not give you any credit.

In the early 1980s, Benjamin Libet conducted a series of experiments which many have believed offer empirical evidence against free will. We read,

> Serious scientific study of free will and conscious volition can be said to have begun with Libet's experiments on the timing of conscious choice.... Almost all of the works involved in the recent deluge of anti-free will arguments have referenced this study ... [there has been] a steady stream of criticisms... Nevertheless, Libet's experiments have stood the test of time and become the scientific spine of the anti-free will movement.[1]

Sean Spence, in his "Prologue: Against Freedom" in *The Actor's Brain: Exploring the Cognitive Neuroscience of Free Will* (2009), reiterates this assessment of the continuing importance of the Libet experiments. He writes,

---

1 Azim F. Shariff, Jonathan Schooler, and Kathleen D. Vohs, "The Hazards of Claiming to Have Solved the Hard Problem of Free Will", in *Are We Free?: Psychology and Free Will* edited by John Baer, James C. Kaufman and Roy F. Baumeister (Oxford: Oxford University Press, 2002): 181–204, at 186.

Much of the inspiration for writing this book, and for attempting to articulate the questions that it concerns, stems from my reading of a series of experiments conducted by Benjamin Libet and his colleagues in the United States in the early 1980s.[2]

Libet himself does not take his experiments to show that human agents never have free will, but he does interpret his data as showing that the motivation producing human actions is caused by preceding brain activity of which the agent is unaware and over which he has no control. Some have taken this as evidence that human choices are locally causally determined, whereas others have disputed the experimental methods and interpretations. A review of the experiments and the debate they have generated will illustrate the Problem of Translation Regarding the Object of Study discussed in the previous chapter – Libet attempts to respond to this problem – and the Problem of Description noted in Chapter 1. And a list of new problems will be raised. (One significant worry that the Libet experiments could generate is the thought that our choices and actions are not responsive to our reasons. Most of the literature relevant to empirical research on free will and specifically concerning reasons-responsiveness deals with situationism, to be discussed in Chapter 5. I will save the extensive discussion of reasons-responsiveness until then.) Although I will be criticizing Libet's conclusions, his work has been extremely fruitful. Inspired by his ground-breaking experiments, useful and exciting study of the relationship of brain activity to human agency continues apace.

In the original experiment, a subject is asked to wait until he feels an "urge" to flex his wrist and then flex it. The subject watches a clock so that he can report the time at which he felt the urge. The flex of the wrist triggers a computer recording of an EEG (electroencephalogram) image of the subject's brain activity. Libet summarizes his conclusions: "Freely voluntary acts are preceded by a specific electrical change in the brain (the 'readiness potential', RP) that begins 550 msec. before the act. Human subjects became aware of intention to act 350–400 msec. *after RP starts*, but 200 msec. before the motor act. The volitional process is therefore *initiated* unconsciously."[3] Here is the full abstract for the original article:

> The recordable cerebral activity (readiness potential, RP) that precedes a freely voluntary, fully endogenous motor act was directly compared with the reportable time (W) for appearance of the subjective experience of 'wanting' or intending to act. The onset of cerebral activity clearly preceded by at least several hundred milliseconds the reported

---

2 Sean Spence, *The Actor's Brain: Exploring the Cognitive Neuroscience of Free Will* (Oxford: Oxford UP, 2009): 1. See also Caruso et al. (2019): 5, fn. 4.
3 Benjamin Libet, "Do We Have Free Will?" in *The Oxford Handbook of Free Will* (1st ed.) edited by Robert Kane (Oxford: Oxford University Press): 551–64, at 551.

time of conscious intention to act. This relationship held even for those series (with 'type II' RPs) in which subjects reported that all of the 40 self-initiated movements in the series appeared 'spontaneously' and capriciously.

Data were obtained in at least 6 different experimental sessions with each of 5 subjects. In series with type II RPs, onset of the main negative shift in each RP preceded the corresponding mean W value by an average of about 350 ms, and by a minimum of about 150 ms. In series with type I RPs, in which an experience of preplanning occurred in some of the 40 self-initiated acts, onset of RP preceded W by an average of about 800 ms (or by 500 ms, taking onset of RP at 90 per cent of its area).

Reports of W time depended upon the subject's recall of the spatial 'clock-position' of a revolving spot at the time of his initial awareness of wanting or intending to move. Two different modes of recall produced similar values. Subjects distinguished awareness of wanting to move (W) from awareness of actually moving (M). W times were consistently and substantially negative to, in advance of, mean times reported for M and also those for S, the sensation elicited by a task-related skin stimulus delivered at irregular times that were unknown to the subject.

It is concluded that cerebral initiation of a spontaneous, freely voluntary act can begin unconsciously, that is, before there is any (at least recallable) subjective awareness that a 'decision' to act has already been initiated cerebrally. This introduces certain constraints on the potentiality for conscious initiation and control of voluntary acts.[4]

Libet himself does not conclude that human agents have no free will. He notes that in the original volition experiments some subjects felt an urge to flick which they resisted or "vetoed" in his terminology. This led to a new experiment. Since, in the previous experiment, the uninstructed "veto" did not trigger any computer recording,

> there were no *recorded* RPs with a vetoed intention to act. [In a subsequent experiment] We were, however, able to show that subjects could veto an act planned for performance at a prearranged time. [This allowed the observer to trigger the computer recording.] They were able to exert the veto within the interval of 100 to 200 msec. before the preset time to act... A large RP preceded the veto, signifying that the subject was indeed *preparing* to act, even though the action was aborted by the subject [Libet's italics].

---

4 Benjamin Libet, C.A. Gleason, E.W. Wright, and D.K. Pearl, "Time of Conscious Intention to Act in Relation to Onset of Cerebral Activities (Readiness-Potential): The Unconscious Initiation of a Freely Voluntary Act", *Brain* 106 (1983): 623–42. Libet describes these experiments more fully, reviews how he came to perform them, and offers a philosophical assessment in his *Mind Time* (2004).

He concludes from this that "*[c]onscious will could thus affect the outcome of the volitional process even though the latter was initiated by unconscious cerebral processes. Conscious will might block or veto the process, so that no act occurs*" (Libet's italics).[5]

Problems of Description and Translation

The Problem of Description is raised immediately in that Libet sometimes says that his subjects are asked to wait until they "feel" an urge, desire, or wish to act, but they are sometimes described as making a decision or having an intention or will to act. And these are different mental phenomena. An urge or desire could be viewed as an experience of "wanting" that comes upon one passively. It is hard to imagine that, under normal conditions (a bee has not just settled on your hand and so on), anyone actually feels some urge or desire to flex their wrist. Alfred Mele describes participating in a Libet-style experiment and, since he found that he did not feel an urge to flex, he reports that he "hit on the strategy of saying 'now!' silently to myself just before beginning to flex".[6] This saying "now!" sounds much more like a decision or intention than like an urge or desire. In describing a libertarian free moral choice (LFMC), I noted that the libertarian need have no qualms about the desires or "urges" motivating the torn condition being locally causally determined, so it is important to be clear on what phenomenon is being discussed.

The Libet experiments purportedly provide evidence concerning meaningful free will. On that view, they suffer from several kinds of Problem of Translation, as has been noted by a number of researchers. First, obviously, the urge or decision to flex one's wrist, or to veto that urge having felt it, is not like any sort of meaningful choice. Libet offers two responses to this criticism. One rests on the thought that his move from the wrist flex to larger claims about human agency reflects standard scientific method. Having asked "Can we assume that voluntary acts, other than the simple one studied by us, also have the same temporal relations between unconscious brain processes and the appearance of the conscious wish or will to act?", he gives this response:

> It is common in scientific research to be limited technically to studying a process in a simple system; and then to find that the fundamental behavior discovered with the simple system does indeed represent a phenomenon that appears in other related and more complicated systems. ... We may, therefore, allow ourselves to consider what general

---

5 Libet (2002): 557, 556. See also Libet (2004): 137–40.
6 Mele (2009): 34.

implications may follow from our experimental findings, when viewed as a feature of voluntary acts in general.[7]

In order for this argument about scientific method to effectively address the Problem of Translation Regarding the Object of Study, a case would have to be made that the urge or decision to flex one's wrist is a simpler version of more complex choices (e.g., the LFMC I described in Chapter 2). But that would be a difficult case to make. If the situation is one in which the subject flexes upon feeling a spontaneous "urge", then no choice or decision at all is made. The subject does not debate about when to flex. He flexes right after feeling the urge. But if the subject actually decides or chooses when to flex, it is a choice of indifference – the indifference of identity – since there is no relevant difference between one moment and the next vis-à-vis when to flex. Many Libet-type studies carried out since Libet's original experiments repeat this methodology of asking subjects to make choices of indifference. The motivation is that roughly the same choices can be repeated in the laboratory setting, which is useful in light of the instrumentation that is needed and in that the aim is to establish a pattern of association between brain activity and choice. But choices of indifference are not simpler versions of the more complex choices we care about. They are intrinsically unlike moral choices and so the Problem of Translation arises in all of these experiments. (M. E. Schlosser argues that adopting a standard framework in psychology which distinguishes between internal and external causes – as Libet does – means that Libet-type experiments are doomed to study only choices of indifference since "free will proper" entails choosing for *reasons* and reasons involve both internal factors, like the agent's desires, and external factors, like the situation in which he finds himself.[8])

Libet offers a second response to this Problem of Translation, appealing to the point that, although what he is studying is an urge or decision to perform a simple motor act, his studies are relevant to morally significant free will since moral choices issue in actions.

> The basic initiating process for these simpler volitional acts may be the same as that for the actual motor expression of other, more complex forms of voluntary action, since the latter are manifested behaviorally only when final decisions to move have been made.[9]

He explains, "Actual motor performance of the act is both consciously controllable (in my thesis [due to the veto]) and ethically meaningful, since

---

7 Libet (2004): 148.
8 Schlosser (2014): 251–6.
9 Benjamin Libet, "Unconscious Cerebral Initiative and the Role of Conscious Will in Voluntary Action", *Behavioral and Brain Science* 8 (1985): 529–39, at 532.

it is the motor act that has a real impact on one's fellow man."[10] But, as noted in Chapter 2, some moral choices do not issue in motor acts at all; in any case, the moral action is in the choice. A subsequent action is said to be done freely, and the agent is held responsible for it, depending on the history and nature of the choice itself. Libet's responses to the Problem of Translation Regarding the Object of Study are not successful.

Another Problem of Translation arises regarding the "highly artificial if not bizarre" methodology in the lab.[11] This is the Problem of Translation Regarding the Situation. The subject is stationary, monitored, and asked to experience an urge to flex his wrist, repeatedly. But this is a far cry from the sort of situation in which people normally make meaningful choices. There is the artificial setting and the fact that the subject is following instructions. Possibly, "the instructions to produce spontaneous movements may cause the subjects to create an unusual mental state in which brain potentials trigger a previously willed decision".[12] Presumably, in order to follow the instructions, the subjects had to "manufacture" the urge since in a natural setting flexing the wrist is not something people desire to do.[13] Indeed, they had to manufacture the urge over and over. (Libet says that there was no time constraint on when the subjects could feel the urge.[14] But the subjects must have felt some pressure to get on with the experiments.) With an LFMC, the situation is one in which the mutually exclusive desires arise naturally and the agent finds himself in the torn condition debating what to do. There is no manufacturing of the desires. Again, if researchers interpret the evidence from these experiments as counting against the existence of meaningful free will, the burden of proof lies with them to show that the radical difference between the lab and the natural environment nonetheless allows translation from the former to the latter. It is important to note that these Problems of Translation are not generated by the design or the performance of the experiments. Nor do they undermine the simple data. They arise when the data are *interpreted* as applying to human free will in general, beyond (manufactured) urges to flex the wrist in the lab. Against that interpretation, these translation problems are very powerful.

Libet himself conducted further experiments involving a "veto" which he takes to provide evidence for human freedom. He instructed subjects to plan to flex and then to "veto" that plan and not flex. He found that an RP

---

10 Benjamin Libet, "Author's Response: Theory and Evidence Relating Cerebral Processes to Conscious Will", *Behavioral and Brain Science* 8 (1985): 558–66, at 564.
11 Baumeister et al. (2015): 59–60.
12 James L. Ringo, "Timing Volition: Questions of What and When about W", *Behavioral and Brain Sciences* 8 (1985): 550–1, at 551.
13 Bruno G. Breitmeyer, "Problems with the Psychophysics of Intention", *Behavioral and Brain Science* 8 (1985): 539–40.
14 Libet (2004): 126, 129–30, 141.

preceded the (supposed) expectation to act in the veto experiments and yet the subject was able to deliberately fail to act. Libet concluded that, although we might not be free to originate our urges, we are capable of freely resisting them.[15] (According to Libet, the same sort of RP found before the urge to flex the wrist in the original experiments can be observed before the veto. Mele points out that this provides evidence that it is not the case that RP *causally necessitates* the wrist flex. If it did so, it would be impossible for the subject in the veto experiments to fail to flex his wrist.[16]) Libet notes that "[v]etoing of an urge to act is a common experience for all of us. It occurs especially when the projected act is regarded as socially unacceptable, or not in accord with one's overall personality or values."[17] "Many ethical strictures, such as most of the Ten Commandments, are injunctions not to act in certain ways."[18] Libet, then, holds that his veto experiments provide scientific evidence that human agents have a robust sort of free will. Unfortunately for the defender of human freedom, these veto experiments fall prey to the same Problems of Translation as the original experiments. In fact, as Libet sets them up, the veto experiments seem to involve an even more exotic mental state on the part of subjects than did the original experiments. As Mele points out, it is difficult to make sense of the premise of the veto experiments where a (presumably rational) agent is told, before the experiment starts, that he should prepare to do something which he should then not do. How can one simultaneously prepare to do something and at the same time plan not to do it?[19] Few have found Libet's defense of free-will based on the veto experiments persuasive.

The Timing Problem

In the original Libet experiments, step 1 was for the subject to experience an urge to flex. The next step in the instructions was that the subject, who is watching a dot going around a clock, should note the time at which the urge "appeared". In that the main importance of the experiments lies in supposedly showing that the RP occurs *before* the urge is felt and in that the purported time lag is in fractions of a second, the timing is crucial and has occasioned a great deal of criticism.[20] Various timing issues raise a

---

15 Libet (2004): 138.
16 Mele (2009): 73.
17 Libet (2004): 138.
18 Libet (1985): 539.
19 Alfred Mele, "Free Will: Theories, Analysis, and Data" in *Does Consciousness Cause Behavior?* Edited by Susan Pockett, William P. Banks, and Shaun Gallagher (Cambridge, MA: MIT Press, 2006): 187–205, at 192–3.
20 William P. Banks and Eve A. Isham, "Do We Really Know What We are Doing?: Implications of Reported Time of Decision for Theories of Volition". In *Conscious Will and Responsibility* edited by Walter Sinnott-Armstrong and Lynn Nadel (Oxford: Oxford

problem that is often noted when experiments require subjects to offer a first-person report of their own mental states; first-person evidence may be open to question, and it is difficult to verify in that the subject's mental states are absolutely private to the subject. We will call this the Problem of First-Person Reporting. In the Libet experiments, this problem is intertwined with several other issues that place the introspective evidence in doubt and so I will not treat of it separately. Instead, I will canvas more specific problems related to timing, but the reason these problems arise is due to the need for first-person reporting of the time at which the subject felt the urge to flex.

A first difficulty involves an instance of what we can call the Problem of Mereology: What is it that constitutes an individual, discrete thing? Mereology is one of those vexed, perennial questions in metaphysics. It is hard enough when dealing with observable beings like ships and snails. It does not get any easier when looking at mental states and neural processes.[21] Libet takes it that there is a particular time at which the urge arises. Several critics have noted that mental events do not occur as discrete and momentary. "Considering a mental event as a discrete 'thing' with a definite beginning and end is directly imported from folk psychology and must be considered at best as prescientific."[22] Experiments undermine the generally accepted thought that "a decision to act must occur at some time and that we know that time.... The intuitively clear moment of decision then seems more like an afterthought, having no relation to the real action."[23] A decision,

> might be an ongoing developing process that continuously updates and remains amenable to changes rather than a process that converges to a final unalterable outcome at one specific point in time, and is

---

University Press, 2011): 47–60. William P. Banks and Susan Pockett, "Benjamin Libet's Work on the Neuroscience of Free Will", in *The Blackwell Companion to Consciousness* edited by Max Velmans and Susan Schneider (Oxford: Blackwell Publishing, 2007): 657–70; Thomas Bittner, "Consciousness and the Act of Will", *Philosophical Studies* 81 (1996): 331–41; Gilberto Gomes, "The Interpretation of Libet's Results on the Timing of Conscious Events: A Commentary", *Consciousness and Cognition* 11 (2002): 221–30; Patrick Haggard, "Conscious Awareness of Intention and of Action". In *Agency and Self-Awareness* edited by Johannes Roessler and Naomi Eilan (Oxford: Clarendon Press, 2003): 111–27; Uri Maoz, Liad Mudrik, Ram Rivlin, Ian Ross, Adam Mamelak, and Gideon Yaffe, "On Reporting the Onset of the Intention to Move", in Mele (2015): 184–202; Mele (2009) 30–43; Adina L. Roskies, "Why Libet's Studies Don't Pose a Threat to Free Will". In *Conscious Will and Responsibility* edited by Walter Sinnott-Armstrong and Lynn Nadel (Oxford: Oxford University Press, 2011): 11–22.

21 Colin Klein, discussing fMRI, notes that there are serious questions about just what neuroimaging is actually representing, "Philosophical Issues in Neuroimaging", *Philosophy Compass* 5:2 (2010): 186–98.
22 Banks and Pockett (2007): 663.
23 Banks and Isham (2011): 56–7.

subserved by a definite brain area or neural system. If this is the case it might not be possible to clearly map decision and intention onsets onto a single neural process or a specific moment in time... In other words, there may be no place in the neural causal chain leading to action that can be identified as the decision or the intention.[24]

So, one problem associated with subjects attempting to pinpoint the time they felt an urge lies in trying to determine the outlines of a discrete urge (or decision or intention etc.) when the mental event may not have discrete outlines to be discerned. There may not be a "moment" at which that urge arose. In that case, when pointing to a time on the clock, the subjects are just making a rough guess. But given the minute temporal measurements involved, a rough guess undermines the interpretation of the experiments.

Another problem that the timing instructions involve is that the subject must engage in some very exact introspection. This exacerbates the Problems of Translation (regarding both Object of Study and Situation) already discussed. The description of the LFMC in Chapter 2 did not include introspecting as one makes one's choice, and someone engaged in a genuinely significant choice may just be too busy to step back and pay attention to their own mental states. So, the feeling, or manufacture, of the urge (or the making of a decision) in the Libet experiments includes the extra artificiality of the subject being told to monitor his thoughts. In addition to raising the Problems of Translation produced by the requirement to introspect, introspection presents an instance of a new problem, the Problem of the Observer. The problem appears in many forms and contexts and will come up again in the course of this work. The overall issue is that, in doing research, the presence of the observer affects the process or system being monitored. This can be the case even when the observer is the one who is also being observed. John S. Stamm explains this further worry about the timing procedure in the Libet experiments:

> The constraints for temporal assessments of internal states may be designated as the analogue of the Heisenberg uncertainty principle in physics, that is that self-monitoring of an internal process interferes with the process, so that its precise measurement is impossible.[25]

---

24 Maoz et al. (2015): 194.
25 John S. Stamm, "The Uncertainty Principle in Psychology", *Behavioral and Brain Sciences* 8 (1985): 553–4, at 554. See also, J. Miller, P. Shepherdson, and J. Trevina, "Effects of Clock Monitoring on Electroencephalogiraphic Activity: Is Unconscious Movement Initiation an Artifact of the Clock?", *Psychological Science* 22: 1 (2011): 103–9.

In addition to these difficulties, Libet's interpretation of the timing sequence introduces an example of a problem that can be called the Problem of Perspective. This problem arises when the researcher fails (or apparently fails) to consider the process of the experiment from the point of view of the subject. In this case, the question is whether or not Libet (and those who conduct similar experiments) have fully appreciated all of the mental tasks that the subject must perform in order to follow the timing instructions. In order to test the accuracy of the timing process before performing the "flex" experiments, Libet conducted experiments in which subjects reported what time they felt a skin stimulus – interestingly 50 msec *before* the actual stimulus time. The assumption was that the experiences of the skin stimulus and of the urge were similar enough that – with the −50 msec accounted for – the timing reports of the subjects feeling the urge were accurate.[26] But this is a questionable assumption in that the skin stimulus experiments involved a different kind of object of awareness from the "voluntary act" experiments. One difference that could have a significant effect on the timing question is that the skin stimulus, as described by Libet, is unmistakable. One would know immediately that one was experiencing the expected stimulus. But the "urge" is a different matter. At what point does an "urge" become definite? Above I noted the Problem of Description in that Libet uses different terms for what his subjects are supposed to await – terms that mean slightly different things. Sometimes it is an "urge" and sometimes it is a "wish" or a "desire" or an "intention" or a "decision". Whereas a subject would have no trouble recognizing a skin stimulus instantaneously, a subject confronted with the instruction to wait for an urge (or wish or desire or intention or decision) might need a few hundred milliseconds to ascertain whether what he is experiencing is the very thing he has been told to experience. Thus, the relative accuracy with which subjects noted the clock time when given a skin stimulus might not carry over to the experience of feeling an urge (or wish or desire or intention or decision).

Moreover, the task of introspectively noticing that one is experiencing an urge is a different mental event from simply experiencing the urge. Paying attention to the clock requires a further effort, and noting the time on the clock at which one records that one has felt the urge is yet another task. In order to perform the series of mental tasks required to follow the instructions, the subject must hold the different elements of information in working memory.[27] A standard criticism of the Libet experiments, then, is that the brain activity which supposedly precedes the felt urge – the RP – may be simultaneous with the initial urge but appear to be earlier since the subject has to do so much between the arising of the urge and the noting

---

26 Libet (2004): 128, 132.
27 Klemm (2010): 59.

of the clock time.[28] So, even in Libet's experiments, with the simple flex, it is legitimate to be dubious that the subject's ability to note the time when he receives a skin stimulus justifies the claim that the subject can accurately report the time at which the urge arose. The objects of awareness are too dissimilar. So, the Problem of First-Person Reporting is serious. And suppose the hope was to study morally significant free will. The complexity of the mental processes involved defies imagination. There could be no experiment, analogous to the Libet experiments, where a subject is told to introspect and note the time at which he makes a morally significant choice.

Post Hoc Ergo Propter Hoc

Setting the timing worries aside, suppose that the RP did indeed precede the urge to flex in Libet's experiments. Does that show that the RP caused the urge in a way that should worry the defender of free will? Not at all. In describing the LFMC, I took one of the criteria to be that the agent be in the torn condition, debating the options, before choosing. If an RP were detectable before an LFMC, it might very well simply correlate to the torn condition, a necessary though not sufficient precursor of an LFMC. But there is a deeper concern here.[29] As Libet interprets his voluntary act experiments, RP occurs before the conscious urge arises, leading him to conclude that it is RP that causes the urge. This has been taken by many neuroscientists and psychologists to be evidence against the existence of human free will. The nature of causation is a difficult and perennial problem in metaphysics. And the question of how human beings can discover cause and effect is ancient and ongoing. Volumes and volumes have been written on these topics and it lies far beyond the scope of the present work to weigh in on these complex issues.[30] Here, in order to note possible problems for the study of human freedom, it is enough to make the simple point that in order to determine that X causes Y or is among the causes of Y, we need more than a number of instances in which X precedes Y. To hold that Y is caused by X simply because one has observed that, upon occasion, Y has followed X is to commit the post hoc fallacy: "after this, therefore because of this". If we want to figure out whether X is among the causes of Y, we should look to see whether X occurs but Y (sometimes or often) does not. Suppose we discover that X is always occurring, is constantly in the background, and often is not followed by Y. If Y occurs, of course it

---

28 Libet responds to a particular timing criticism involving switching tasks in Libet (2004): 132–4.
29 Mele (2009): 73–5.
30 For an analysis of Libet's interpretation from a philosophy of science perspective, involving a complex theory of causation, see H. Radder and G. Meynen, "Does the Brain 'Initiate' Freely Willed Processes? A Philosophy of Science Critique of Libet-Type Experiments and Their Interpretation", *Theory and Psychology* 23:1 (2013): 3–21.

will be preceded by X since X is always occurring. But I have reason to doubt that X is the *cause* of Y now that I have seen that X occurs and often is not followed by Y.[31] (Although even if X is always followed by Y, that alone is not sufficient to establish a causal connection. Think of the birds singing immediately before sunrise. We would also look for the processes involved in a connection.[32])

In the original Libet experiments, it is *only when the wrist is flexed* that the computer records the information regarding the brain states. Set aside timing problems and assume that when the urge arises and the wrist is flexed, RP preceded the urge. Add that in the veto experiments EEGs recorded a similar RP as the subjects "prepared" to flex. All of this leaves open the possibility that RP is occurring unrecorded frequently in people's brains but that it is only rarely followed by an urge to flex the wrist (or otherwise engage in simple movement). Indeed, the original and the veto experiments combined may provide evidence for RPs occurring frequently without being the causes they are taken to be. In the veto experiments, although Libet says the subjects are to "plan" to flex, what they are actually planning is to manufacture some sort of urge or feeling upon which they will subsequently *not* act. If, as Libet says, the RP preceding *this* effort was similar to the RP preceding the flex in the original experiments, that shows that similar RPs precede very different mental activities.[33] The brain activity may not be a cause of the urge at all or it may be only a partial cause or a probabilistic cause. All we know is that the urge is frequently preceded by the RP; we do not even know that RPs are followed by urges more often than not.

Studies have been conducted which suggest that this brain activity before movement in the Libet experiments (and in similar studies[34]) is something like background noise, or a sort of general preparatory activity, rather than a process that causes the urge.[35] A 2018 analysis of articles concerning Libet's, and Libet-type, experiments concludes, "While almost all papers in our review reported a general pattern of average neural activity occurring before participants' awareness of their intention to act, the relationship of

---

31 Which is not to say that X cannot be the cause of Y unless it *always* produces Y. X might be a cause if it raises the probability of Y, such that Y could not occur without X, but X might, from time to time, not produce Y. In the case of the Libet experiments, however, we do not have evidence even of probabilistic causation.
32 Radder and Meynen (2013): 10–12.
33 Alfred Mele, "Testing Free Will", *Neuroethics* 3 (2010): 161–72, at 165.
34 For example, Haggard and Eimer (1999).
35 J. Trevena and J. Miller, "Cortical Movement Preparation before and after a Conscious Decision to Move", *Consciousness and Cognition* 11:2 (2002): 162–90; J. Trevena, J., and J. Miller, "Brain Preparation Before a Voluntary Action: Evidence Against Unconscious Movement Initiation", *Consciousness and Cognition* 19.1 (2010): 447–56.

the activity to their intention still needs to be established."[36] As I noted above, were it the case that a certain sort of brain activity was shown to be a necessary precursor to an urge or a decision or even what looks to be an LFMC, that would not concern the defender of free will. Perhaps the torn condition does correlate to a specific neural process. What is worrisome in Libet's interpretation of his experiments, and in the rush of many scientists to see them as evidence against free will, is that the pretty obvious commission of the post hoc fallacy often goes unnoticed.

The Soon et al. Experiment

In 2008, a paper recording an experiment somewhat similar to the Libet experiments was published by Soon et al. under the ambitious title "Unconscious Determinants of Free Decisions in the Human Brain".[37] This paper is often quoted as evidence against free will. Although the experiment – call it the "Soon experiment" – is similar to Libet's experiments, there are two striking differences. The first is that the subjects' brain activity was being measured throughout the task using functional magnetic resonance imaging (fMRI), so the worry that in the Libet experiment the recording of the brain activity was triggered by the flexing motion does not arise. Equally important, the Soon experiment included a *choice*. One way that Libet sets out the instructions in his original experiments is that the subject is to feel an urge and flex immediately. If that is the situation, then a severe Problem of Translation arises since the subjects are not even making any kind of a choice. Moreover, in the Libet experiments, the RP that appears before the urge and the movement might just signal, at most, a vague preparatory activity. Soon et al. recognized that in the Libet experiments RP before the arising of the urge might not constitute a cause of the urge. "To rule out the idea that any leading activity merely reflects unspecific preparatory activation, it is necessary to study free decisions between more than one behavioral option."[38] They conducted the following experiment:

> The subjects were asked to relax while fixating on the center of the screen where a stream of letters was presented. At some point, when they felt the urge to do so, they were to freely decide between one of two buttons, operated by the left and right index fingers, and press it

36 Victoria Saigle, Veljko Dubljević and Eric Racine, "The Impact of a Landmark Neuroscience Study on Free Will: A Qualitative Analysis of Articles Using Libet and Colleagues' Methods", AJOB *Neuroscience* 9:1 (2018): 29–41, at 38.
37 Chun Siong Soon, Marcel Brass, Hans-Jochen Heinze, and John-Dylan Haynes, "Unconscious Determinants of Free Decisions in the Human Brain". *Nature Neuroscience* 11 (2008): 543–5.
38 Soon et al. (2008): 543.

immediately. In parallel, they should remember the letter presented when their motor decision was consciously made. After subjects pressed their freely chosen response button, a 'response mapping' screen with four choices appeared. The subjects indicated when they had made their motor decision by selecting the corresponding letter with a second button press. After a delay, the letter stream started again and a new trial began.[39]

Their abstract of their conclusions runs thus:

> There has been a long controversy as to whether subjectively 'free' decisions are determined by brain activity ahead of time. We found that the outcome of a decision can be encoded in brain activity of prefrontal and parietal cortex up to 10 s before it enters awareness. This delay presumably reflects the operation of a network of high-level control areas that begin to prepare an upcoming decision long before it enters awareness.

When the philosopher reads this abstract, the first sentence suggests that the experiment is aimed at discerning whether or not the outcome of a decision that felt "free" to the decider is actually "determined". I understand a "determined" choice to be one which is causally produced by factors outside of the agent's control which precede the choice. I take it that, when the question is human free will, this is the sort of LCD that is at issue. Soon et al. do not offer a definition of "determined" – the Problem of Description arises here – but one would prima facie suppose that they share the philosophers' understanding. (Their conclusions actually undermine this supposition. See below.) Nor do Soon et al. elaborate on the feeling of freedom, but they tell their subjects to "freely decide". Presumably, when a decision "feels" free to a subject, it feels, to the subject, as if they themselves made it, without any preceding causal determination, so they could have chosen otherwise. (If "free" and "determined" do not mean something like what I am assuming, then perhaps Soon et al. did not intend to be investigating free will as it is usually understood.) The subsequent sentences in the abstract suggest that the experiment provides evidence that a decision can be encoded and prepared in parts of the brain *10 seconds before* the conscious agent is aware of making the decision. Thus, the answer to the question about determinism is that, yes, subjectively "free" decisions can be determined 10 seconds before the conscious agent is aware of "making" them.

There is much to question in the Soon experiment, but we can start with the Problem of Description. The first thing to notice is that 10 seconds is a

---

39 Soon et al. (2008): 543.

very long time in this context. It is *such* a long time that it leads one to question what Soon et al. mean by "determined". They cannot mean that the choice of the left or the right push of the button is causally *necessitated* 10 seconds before the urge is felt to push. To see this, imagine an experiment where the subjects are given the same instructions as in the Soon experiment. But in this case the observer is able to "watch" the brain in action. When the brain activity which Soon et al. associate with the choice to push the button on the right appears, the observer can detect it. Suppose the observer detects the "right button" brain activity, waits two seconds, and then declaims (in a way that the subject will *believe* – perhaps this had to be designed into the experiment beforehand) "We'll give you $100 if you push the button on the left!" Chances are, especially given that so many of these experiments are performed using college students to whom $100 is a considerable sum, the subject will push the button on the left. If event X causally *necessitates* event Y, then if X happens, Y happens. If the "right button" brain activity *determines* the decision to push the button on the right, then the subject decides to push the button on the right. Ten seconds is such a long time that I do not see how one could frame and test a "conditional" claim about decisions being determined 10 seconds in advance. One cannot say "The 'right button' brain activity determines the decision to push the button on the right unless some new event occurs within 10 seconds after the occurrence of the 'right brain' activity." It is inevitable that lots and lots of new events will be happening within and without the subject in that long space of 10 seconds. At the most, what the preceding brain activity may be encoding represents some unconscious "preference" for this button over that, but that is not determinism and does not speak to the issue of free will.

The Problem of Translation Regarding Object of Study also looms large. The "choice" to push the button on the right or the left is yet again a choice of indifference.[40] The burden of proof is on those who suppose that this experiment is relevant to human free will to show that the choice of which button to push is sufficiently similar to an LFMC that data concerning the former can be translated into meaningful information about the latter. Libet's argument that meaningful choices are more complex versions of the same sort of thing as his urge to flex does not seem plausible, nor would a similar argument regarding the decision to push the right or the left button. Researchers may rightly point out that the current state of neuroscience severely limits the sorts of choices that can be studied in the laboratory. This is one reason why choices of indifference are the object of

---

40 Wegner (2002: 47–8) mentions an experiment in which a stimulation magnet above a participant's head apparently influenced whether he would move his right or his left finger. Perhaps right and left movements are especially susceptible to causal influences.

study but that does not address the criticism that it is illegitimate to move from that sort of choice to making claims about human freedom.

A timing issue arises for Soon et al. which again involves the Problem of Mereology (and the post hoc fallacy). The experiment had the subjects engage in the task of feeling the urge, deciding which button, and pushing, over and over in quick succession. The difficulty is to discern, in studying the brain activity, when activity related to one repetition ends and when that related to the next begins. The timing issue that Soon et al. are concerned about is whether or not enough time elapsed between trials so that brain activity associated with or reflecting the previous button push is not somehow affecting the outcome of the next right or left decision. They deliberately chose subjects who would take their time between pushes, but it is not clear that this possibly problematic timing issue can be set aside, as subsequent experiments by Martin Lagas and Katarzyna Jaworska show.

Lagas and Jaworska ran an experiment where the subjects received the same instructions as in the Soon experiment. They were able to achieve the same predictive accuracy based not on brain activity but on the previous responses of the subjects. Lagas and Jaworska note that Soon et al. selected their subjects on the basis of the subjects' previously tested disposition to evenly balance their pushes between the right and the left button and also that Soon et al. did not include data from subjects who exhibited a definite imbalance during the actual experiment. Lagas and Jaworska write,

> In conclusion, it seems possible that the multivariate pattern classification in *Soon et al.* (2008) ... was compromised by individual response bias in preceding responses and picked up neural correlates of the intention to switch or stay during a critical time window. The moderate prediction accuracies for multivariate classification analyses of fMRI BOLD [blood-oxygen-level-dependent] signals and our behavioral results call for a more cautious interpretation of findings as well as improved classification analyses.[41]

The issue in mereology gives rise to the post hoc problem when Soon et al. take it that the brain activity, which is followed by the decision and the push, must be the cause of the decision and the push. Instead, the brain activity might be the product of the decision in the previous trial.

Lagas and Jaworska also note that the predictive accuracy achieved in the Soon experiment is very modest: 0.6 (where 0.5 would be mere chance).

---

41 Martin Lagas and Katarzyna Jaworska, "How Predictable Are 'Spontaneous Decisions' and 'Hidden Intentions'? Comparing Classification Results Based on Previous Responses with Multivariate Pattern Analysis of fMRI BOLD Signals", *Frontiers in Psychology* 3 (2012): 56.

Suppose, for the sake of argument, that Soon et al. are indeed detecting brain activity that suggests that the subject is leaning toward pushing one button rather than the other. That leaves open the possibility that the subject might decide to push the other button instead and so is not evidence that the choice for right or left is determined by the preceding brain activity.[42] The neuroscientist might respond that it is the nature of the discipline to deal in probabilities. If predictive accuracy had to approach 100% in order to be evidence of determinism, then, given the way studies are conducted, such evidence could never be forthcoming, and it is unfair of the skeptic to ask for more than probabilities. The defender of free will, though, can argue that theories of free will – even libertarian theories – have usually allowed that the existence of free choices is entirely consistent with agents leaning toward or weighting or having preferences toward one option as long as the other option remains a live possibility.[43] This is not a move made recently and ad hoc to save libertarianism from the brain scientists. It just seems to accord with common experience that sometimes we may feel more drawn one way and yet end up going the other way. Or that, in a particular type of deliberative situation, most people will choose one way but a few will choose the other. (The libertarian can happily grant that sometimes one "option" really is so weighty that the choice to pursue it is inevitable, in which case we do not have an LFMC. It may be that people do not make meaningful, free choices very often.) We can call this the Problem of Probabilities. When it is said that the experimental evidence shows that, from a specific sort of preceding brain activity, a particular choice can be predicted with greater-than-chance probability – unless it is *much*-greater-than-chance probability – this evidence is not to be adduced against human free will.

The Libet experiments and the Soon experiments are often cited as showing that human agents do not have free will. But this claim far outstrips the actual data. If Soon et al. have indeed been able to observe brain activity associated with preferences for choosing right or left, that is very impressive. And even if, as Lages and Jaworska suggest, the Soon experiment instead exhibits the ability to pick up "neural correlates of the intention to switch or stay during a critical time window", that seems no mean feat. The analysis of brain activity associated with conscious behavior is an exciting field and undoubtedly will continue to render important information about how we come to think and act – information that should enable human beings to lead healthier, happier

---

42 Alfred Mele, "Another Scientific Threat to Free Will?", *The Monist* 95 (2012): 422–40, at 433.
43 Some libertarians suggest that the probabilities regarding which way an agent will choose can meaningfully be given numerical values. I find that implausible. Rogers (2015): 182–93.

lives in the future. But the Libet and the Soon experiments do not give us any reason to doubt the existence of free will. What the experiments do show is that research on free will confronts a host of problems. Attempting to approach the question of meaningful freedom through the methodology of the sciences is a much more daunting task than many have realized.

Chapter 4
Conscious Will Is an Illusion

Introduction

Suppose there is only a little coffee left in the commons room of your office building. It is the last of the coffee. You don't need it now, but you know that by lunchtime you will really want that coffee. You fear a colleague may beat you to it, so – not having time to run up to your office and grab your mug – you take the pot and hide it behind some books and papers in the commons room. When you go extract the pot for your lunchtime coffee, a colleague catches you at it. "You hid that coffee intentionally!" he exclaims. "That was pretty creepy of you." "You're wrong", you answer. "Science has shown that our intentions are caused by preceding brain events over which we have no control, and, moreover, science has shown that our intentions do not produce our actions." That being the case, you can't be blamed for your intentions, and you can't have actually done anything at all *intentionally*.

Some brain scientists have mounted a two-pronged attack on the view that human beings have free will, claiming both that our conscious choices (or intentions) are caused by preceding events over which we have no control and that those choices or intentions do not figure in the causal history of the "intended" deed. Daniel Wegner, with his *The Illusion of Conscious Will* from 2002 and subsequent related articles, is probably the most well-known representative of this approach. Michael Gazzaniga's research is cited by Wegner, and Gazzaniga offers a more recent contribution with *Who's in Charge?: Free Will and the Science of the Brain* (2011) and related articles. Other scientists participating in the science and free will debate have cited these two and added new work along similar lines.[1]

From the perspective of the tradition within which I am working, when the topic is morally significant free will, the claim that our choices are determined is more problematic than the – still very worrisome – claim that our choices do not produce our overt actions. This is because (as discussed

---

1 John A. Bargh, "Bypassing the Will: Toward Demystifying the Nonconscious Control of Social Behavior". In Hassin et al. (2005): 37–58.

in Chapter 2) traditionally the overarching concern of defenders of human free will is the moral status of the agent, which is a consequence of his free choices. On a libertarian account, if our choices are determined, then we cannot be free, morally responsible agents worthy of respect. So, if it can be scientifically demonstrated that all of our choices and intentions are causally produced by preceding events over which we have no control, the game is up for this traditional understanding of free will. Furthermore, if our choices and intentions are caused by preceding factors of which we are unaware and over which we have no control, then a crucial aspect of free choice is missing: our choices are not responsive to our reasons. The reasons-responsive criterion is often associated with Fischer and Ravizza's non-libertarian theory of freedom and responsibility.[2] Variants on reasons-responsiveness figure in many compatibilist theories of free will. And the libertarian free moral choice (LFMC) as I sketched it depends upon the agent being able to rationally assess his options such that, whichever way he chooses, he should be able to explain the reasons behind that choice. If Wegner and Gazzaniga can provide evidence that human agents neither choose for reasons nor act upon their perceived intentions, that would undermine belief in free will under many different descriptions. In the current chapter, I will argue that the evidence adduced by those adopting the "illusion" approach (sometimes called "willusionism", a term coined by Eddy Nahmias) does not show (or even suggest) that human agents do not make LFMCs. (Much of the philosophical literature dealing with the threat to reasons-responsiveness from the empirical study of free will is centered on the situationist controversy and will be discussed in the next chapter.)

The claim that our conscious choices and intentions do not causally contribute to our overt actions is less worrisome for the tradition in which I am working than is the claim that our choices are determined or that our reasons do not figure in the explanation for our choices. (In this chapter, I use the term "action" broadly. On some accounts, a deed or event which is not, at least in part, caused by a conscious intention should not be labelled an "action".) As I emphasized in Chapter 2, the moral status of an overt deed, as opposed to its goodness or badness considered from the perspective of consequences alone, is derived from the moral status of the choice. So, suppose that some agent, S, is a brain in a vat. (S may also have a mind not identical to, but associated with, his brain, but, as I mentioned in Chapter 1, for my purposes the mind/body question can safely be bracketed.) S is being "fed" a virtual reality simulation which, to S, appears to be an actual, physical universe full of objects and other people, similar (let us say) to what we take our own universe to be. S is firmly convinced that what he is experiencing is reality. And suppose

---

2 John Martin Fischer and Mark Ravizza S.J., *Responsibility and Control: A Theory of Moral Responsibility* (Cambridge, UK: Cambridge University Press, 1998).

S makes LFMCs. S believes that he can, and that he does, carry through with the overt deeds he is choosing to do. But, in reality, he can't and doesn't. He is just a brain in a vat. Nevertheless, S's moral status is the same as if he were choosing and then doing the deeds he only believes he is doing.[3] Even if agents' choices and intentions do not play any causal role in their overt deeds, their moral status as responsible agents to be respected could be the same as if their choices and intentions did play such a role. Of course, if S should come to realize his condition, the range of activities he could reasonably choose to do would be severely limited. Clearly, although he could still make LFMCs, he is far less autonomous than we who (presumably) are not brains in vats.

Of course, the claim that our choices and intentions do not contribute causally to our actions is still very worrisome. For one thing, the thesis would seem to suggest that we are constantly deceived about events very close to us, which casts doubt on our epistemic abilities in general. And if they do not play a causal role, what are choices and intentions doing in our mental landscape? It is puzzling that humanity would have evolved to engage in choosing and intending if choices and intentions don't do a job in causing actions. And we are often called upon to assess people's intentions and actions. If there is a ubiquitous disconnect between actions and intentions, then our major clues to what some agent intended – his actions including his verbal claims about his intentions – are massively unreliable. And it is difficult to see how to assess the moral status of an action if the action is not the result (at least to some extent) of the agent's intentions. So, I will address the evidence that is purported to show that our conscious intentions do not help to cause our actions. Moreover, some of this evidence comes from designing experiments in ways that are morally problematic and from interpreting experiments in ways that fail to respect participants. It will be useful, then, to review some of these experiments and their possible problems, to offer some guidance in considering possible future experiments. I begin by attempting to spell out Wegner's somewhat elusive version of the "illusion" thesis and then turn to Gazzaniga's version.

The "Illusion" Thesis

The first task is to try to get clear on Wegner's actual thesis. This – as a number of commentators have noted – is a hard job in that Wegner seems to suggest different views at different points in *The Illusion of Conscious*

---

3   I do not say that I endorse the supposition as a real possibility. Even on the assumption that you could actually sustain a conscious human brain in a vat, it might be beyond the capabilities of any science ever to convince it that it is a fully embodied agent, living and acting in a world like ours.

Will.[4] The Problem of Description comes up even in the title of the book. It is not clear what Wegner means by "conscious will". Several understandings of "conscious will" present themselves, especially because the adjective could function in at least two different ways. It could mean that the will (or act of willing) was done consciously – the agent was not sleep walking, for example. So, if we say that S "willed X consciously", we could mean that S was awake and aware, S was thinking about doing X, and S engaged in the act of deciding to X (we will assume that X stands for some action). Or it could mean that the agent was conscious *of* (or had some belief about) his own mental act of willing. Wegner's discussion of the evidence against conscious will suggests a few different meanings for "conscious will"; S "is conscious of willing X" when he is introspecting and observes his own mental state of deciding to X; S "is conscious of willing X" when he remembers himself as having been introspecting and observing his own mental state of deciding to X; S "is conscious of willing X" when he is *considering* his memory of introspecting and observing his own mental state of deciding to X; or finally S "is conscious of willing X" when, having engaged in the action X, he considers his memory of introspecting his own mental state of deciding to X and assumes that it was deciding to X that made him subsequently X.

Wegner calls his theory "the theory of apparent mental causation" and states it thus: "*People experience conscious will when they interpret their own thought as the cause of their action*" [Wegner's italics].[5] If, in order to have conscious will, agents must introspect as they are choosing or must remember introspecting or have a belief about how their choice produced their actions, then failing to have a conscious will does not conflict with the ability to make LFMCs. There is nothing in the description of an LFMC that requires that agents introspectively observe their own mental states or have certain beliefs about the causal connections between their choices and their subsequent actions. It would be useful to understand exactly what Wegner takes conscious will to be and what the connection is between belief in conscious will, or the experience of conscious will, and traditional theories of human freedom.

Beyond the term "conscious will", the Problem of Description dogs Wegner's setting out of his theory. Prima facie – given that this is a theory of *apparent* mental causation – this might seem to imply that thoughts cannot cause actions, suggesting epiphenomenalism, the view that mental

---

4 Timothy Bayne, "Phenomenology and the Feeling of Doing: Wegner on the Conscious Will". In *Does Consciousness Cause Behavior?* In Pockett et al. (2006): 169–83, at 170–3; Davies (2007): 39–60, at 50–8; Eddy Nahmias, "When Consciousness Matters: A Critical Review of Daniel Wegner's *The Illusion of Conscious Will*", *Philosophical Psychology* 15 (2002): 527–41, at 528; Sven Walter, "Willusionism, Epiphenomenalism, and the Feeling of Conscious Will", *Synthese* 191 (2014): 2215–38, at 2222 nt. 2 and 2231–2.
5 Wegner (2002): 64.

phenomena are caused by physical phenomena but cannot exercise any causal efficacy over physical phenomena and perhaps not over other mental phenomena either. Wegner offers very little argument for the thesis that our mental states are determined by preceding physical causes, but that seems to be his view. Discussing Libet's experiments, he writes,

> The Libet research, for one, suggests that when it comes down to the actual instant of a spontaneous action, the experience of consciously willing the action occurs only after the RP [readiness potential] signals that brain events have already begun creating the action (and probably the intention and the experience of conscious will as well).[6]

At the end of his book, he says that "[t]he special idea we have been exploring is to explain the experience of free will in terms of deterministic or mechanistic processes".[7] Early in the book, he associates the mechanistic with the physical.[8] In offering an explanation for why we believe in a conscious will, Wegner describes it as the "mind's compass": "Like a compass reading, the feeling of doing tells us something about the operation of the ship. But also like a compass reading, this information must be understood as a conscious experience, a candidate for the dreaded 'epiphenomenon' label. Just as compass readings do not steer the boat, conscious experiences of will do not cause human actions."[9]

However, Wegner may not be arguing that mental events in general are epiphenomenal. Early in the book, he explains that human beings adopt two sorts of explanatory systems – the mechanistic and the psychological – and criticizes the attempt to reduce the latter to the former. "The field of psychology itself has noticed that different systems of thinking seemed to be necessary for understanding mind and matter."[10] Wegner does not discuss possible ways of relating mind and matter; however, he allows that the mental has causal power over both our ideas and our actions. He writes that "it must be the case that *something* in our minds plays a causal role in making our actions occur".[11] "The automatisms and ideomotor effects become models of how thought can cause action."[12] In discussing how belief in one's own control can affect behavior, he notes, "the tendency to attribute control to self is a personality trait. Some people have more of it

---

6 Wegner (2002): 59.
7 Wegner (2002): 318.
8 Wegner (2002): 21.
9 Wegner (2002): 317–18.
10 Wegner (2002): 24.
11 Wegner (2002): 96.
12 Wegner (2002): 144.

than others, and this generalized expectancy for control influences a person's actions and choices across a wide range of circumstances."[13]

The theory of apparent mental causation, apparently, does not hold that *all* mental causation is merely apparent but only that *some* is. The overarching view seems to be that it is a mistake to suppose that our deliberations, choices, intentions, and the like figure in the causal history of our actions. But when we decide to do something, doesn't the decided-upon action usually follow? Wegner cites Hume, giving the argument that noticing a constant conjunction should not lead us to suppose an actual causal connection.[14] This can be taken as an instance of the Problem of Domain. Wegner says that the experimental evidence supports the "illusion" thesis, but he invokes a metaphysical/epistemic theory to respond to what some take to be strong and ubiquitous experiential evidence against his thesis. And citing Hume is a problematic move since Hume's skepticism toward the existence of or our ability to know about causal connections applies generally and thus would undermine all of the evidence Wegner adduces.

We may take the theory of apparent mental causation to be summed up by Wegner thus:

> The experience of conscious will arises when a person infers an apparent causal path from thought to action. The actual causal paths are not present in the person's consciousness. The thought is caused by unconscious mental events, and the action is caused by unconscious mental events, and these unconscious mental events may also be linked to each other directly or through yet other mental or brain processes. The will is experienced as a result of what is apparent, though, not what is real.[15]

Still, Wegner often gives examples in which people's *conscious* thoughts are portrayed as causally efficacious in their actions. For example,

> Unconscious action can also be understood in terms of what a person is thinking consciously and unconsciously at the time of action. It is possible that both kinds of representation of action might contribute to the causation of an action.[16]

Discussing action projection, Wegner notes that "[a]nother way action projection comes about is through the mistaken idea that one is merely stimulating, helping, or prompting the other person to act".[17] In discussing ascribing actions to a group, Wegner writes,

13 Wegner (2002): 330.
14 Wegner (2002): 13–14.
15 Wegner (2002): 68.
16 Wegner (2002): 161.
17 Wegner (2002): 219.

The husband who buys tickets for the couple to go to the Monster Truck Noise Derby may be thinking this is something his wife would actually want them to attend.... People do things in pursuit of group goals all the time, often without even checking on whether the intentions they have formulated for the group correspond with what the group would want.[18]

The example of the husband here suggests that an agent's conscious intentions, based on mistaken beliefs, can lead directly to action. Is conscious will an illusion here because the beliefs of the agent regarding the group are mistaken? But Wegner grants that "[i]n some cases, of course, the individual's intent may clearly coincide with the group's intent, and it may thus be quite reasonable for the individual to claim that the self's action was actually that of the group".[19] This seems to allow that an agent's correct beliefs may produce intentions which result in just the action that the agent intended.

In the final chapter of his book, Wegner explicitly finds a place for conscious will "because it helps us to appreciate and remember what we are doing".[20]

> Conscious will is the somatic marker of personal authorship, an emotion that authenticates the action's owner as the self.... Our experiences of will, in other words, often do correspond correctly with the empirical will – the actual causal connection between our thought and action.[21]

"And perhaps most important for the sake of the operation of society, the sense of conscious will also allows us to maintain the sense of responsibility for our actions that serves as a basis for morality."[22]

These references to "what we are doing", authorship, and moral responsibility, coupled with Wegner's occasional use of examples where conscious intentions are portrayed as causally effective regarding the intended actions, are difficult to square with the quoted statement of the theory of apparent mental causation. One possible interpretation would be to understand Wegner as making the modest case that *sometimes* there is a disconnect between our conscious intentions and our actions. The problem with this interpretation is that that case would be very modest indeed. We all knew that was the case long ere science became interested in the question of free will. We do things we do not consciously intend to do, all the time.

---

18 Wegner (2002): 217.
19 Wegner (2002): 216.
20 Wegner (2002): 325.
21 Wegner (2002): 327.
22 Wegner (2002): 328.

How often have you caught yourself humming a song you don't even like? Or, having intended to drive to the store after leaving work, have gotten distracted, turned on your mental "autopilot", and wound up at home? And we often fail to do things we intend to do: Upon receiving an email that will require a long response, you might intend to answer, so you make a mental note to get back to it, but weeks later you realize that you never responded.

Furthermore, it is common knowledge that most of our particular actions during the day are not consciously chosen. Much of what we do involves actions at which we have long been adept. When walking, we do not worry about foot placement. When speaking, we do not stop and deliberate about each word. If Wegner's thesis is simply that not all our actions are caused (or caused in part) by deliberate intentions, that would not be a startling claim and would not conflict with a very robust understanding of free will. The thesis that many of our actions do not result from deliberately made choices is consistent with the claim that sometimes human agents do in fact make LFMCs.

Another interpretation which could take account of Wegner's sometimes suggesting that conscious beliefs, ideas, and intentions do play a causal role in our actions would understand "conscious will" as requiring or involving something above and beyond these beliefs, ideas, and intentions. But what exactly is this something else? Wegner writes, "Consciously willing an action requires a feeling of doing ..., a kind of internal 'oomph' that somehow certifies authentically that one has done the action."[23] So, Wegner's thesis could be that, although conscious beliefs, thoughts, and intentions sometimes play a causal role in producing actions, conscious *will* does not since it is something more. It is this extra "force" that is illusory. But robust free will does not require this feeling of an authenticating "oomph". It is sufficient for an LFMC that the agent deliberate over open options and choose on her own. I have suggested that the LFMC may involve some exercise of "willpower" so that an LFMC is phenomenologically different from a choice of indifference, but it is not clear that this is the extra, oomphy "force" that Wegner has in mind. Some agent-causal theories introduce a special sort of causation unique to human agency, but there is no need to require that an agent be aware of a "force" which goes beyond the experiencing of an intention and then the doing of the action.

Indeed, it is not clear that the free agent even needs to be introspectively *aware* that he is engaged in *any* mental activities at the moment of choice. Several critics have pointed out that Wegner sometimes seems to assume that in order to be consciously willing something, one ought to be experiencing a feeling of consciously willing it. But, as Mele notes, in theories about free will and human action, it is not the *experience* of willing that is

---

23 Wegner (2002): 4.

held to be the cause of the consciously willed action, but the actual willing of the action.[24] I might be well aware of what I intend to do without attending to my own mental states.[25] Although looking back one might remember or reconstruct one's experience of making a choice, someone concentrating on making an important decision is unlikely to step back mentally so as to be introspectively aware of being so engaged.[26] If Wegner's thesis is that human agents often fail to observe or feel or experience an "oomph" of choice, this does not connect with the traditional discussion of human freedom.

This reinforces the point that those theorizing about free will should attempt to avoid vagueness, insufficient explanation, and inconsistencies. They should try to avoid the Problem of Description. Moreover, Wegner's sometimes focusing on the feeling or experience of willing introduces a new problem that we can call the Problem of Focus. If the question is whether or not human agents have free will, it is important that research look at (or look for) mental and physical phenomena that are among the criteria or requisites for free will. For example, awareness of an experience of willing might be *related* to human freedom. Some have argued that it is the common introspective feeling of being able to choose that provides good evidence for free will. But, as Mele points out, the presence or absence of that *feeling* is not what would make a choice actually free or unfree. That the agent be attentive to his own mental state of choosing was not among the elements in my rough sketch of what an LFMC entails. So, it may be that (at least at times) Wegner has focused on a phenomenon that simply does not figure in standard theories of free will.

Wegner's explication of his theory is not perfectly clear, but for purposes of examining his evidence, I will take it (as I believe most commentators have) that his view offers a radical contrast to any traditional understanding of free will. Wegner concludes his book with this quote from Einstein:

> If the moon, in the act of completing its eternal way around the earth, were gifted with self-consciousness, it would feel thoroughly convinced that it was traveling its way of its own accord.... So would a Being, endowed with higher insight and more perfect intelligence, watching man and his doings, smile about man's illusion that he was acting according to his own free will.[27]

---

24 Mele (2009): 148.
25 Elisabeth Pacherie, "Toward a Dynamic Theory of Intentions". Pockett et al. (2006): 145–67, at 160–4. See also Eddy Nahmias, "Agency, Authorship, and Illusions". *Consciousness and Cognition* 14 (2005): 771–85, at 775–6.
26 Rogers (2015): 229–32.
27 Wegner (2002): 342.

Wegner takes his theory of apparent mental causation to conflict with belief in free will, so I will understand his position to be this: Our actions are not caused by our conscious intentions or conscious willing. The terms "conscious intentions" or "conscious will" sometimes refer to decisions and intentions which we have while we are conscious (i.e., we are not sleep walking, etc.), but sometimes these terms refer to decisions and intentions of which we are introspectively aware or which we later remember. So, the intentions we have while conscious (and perhaps are aware of) are not among the causes of our actions. Both actions and intentions are caused by preceding, unconscious mental events. These unconscious mental events may be linked and may be caused by earlier unconscious mental events or by brain events. We form the mistaken belief that our intentions play a causal role in our actions because we notice that, very often, the intentions occur prior to the actions, the intentions are "consistent" with the actions in that the actions are what we intended, and we do not observe other, more likely, causes at work. But this is not sufficient evidence to prove that our conscious will is the cause of our actions. As Wegner argues at length, there is plenty of evidence to show a disconnect between our intentions and our actions. Thus, both may be caused by earlier, unconscious events.

Michael Gazzaniga, in his *Who's in Charge*, proposes a view somewhat similar to Wegner's. His conclusions are based on his "split-brain" experiments which Wegner includes as evidence for the theory of apparent mental causation. Gazzaniga, too, adopts the thought that conscious intentions are not the causes of our actions.

> Because consciousness is a slow process, whatever has made it to consciousness has already happened. It is a fait accompli. As we saw in my story at the beginning of the chapter [He jumps immediately at a motion in the grass], I had already jumped before I realized whether I had seen a snake or if it was the wind rustling the grass.[28]

Why does it seem to us that we form, and then carry out, conscious intentions? Activity in the left hemisphere of the brain constitutes an "interpreter", which "gives rise to the illusion of unity or purpose, which is a post hoc phenomenon".[29] Actions "are over, done, kaput, before your brain is conscious of them. Your left-hemisphere interpretive system is what pushes the advent of consciousness back in time to account for the cause of action."[30] This "illusion" theory leaves no room for *reasons* to be among the explanations for our choices and actions. What, then, is the

---

28 Gazzaniga (2011): 103.
29 Gazzaniga (2011): 109.
30 Gazzaniga (2011): 112.

evidence that, contrary to what seems obvious to experience, our reasons and intentions do not in fact guide our actions?

Evidence for the Illusion of Conscious Will

I noted in the introduction to this chapter that the more worrisome claim for the defender of our ability to make LFMCs is the point that our conscious intentions are determined. This illusion theory also conflicts with many compatibilist views in that not only are our choices determined but they are determined in a way that rules out reasons-responsiveness. Most libertarians and compatibilists agree that for a choice to be free it must, one way or another, follow upon rational deliberation. If our choices are produced the way Wegner and Gazzaniga theorize, our reasons do not play a part in the explanation. Wegner cites the original experiments carried out by Libet, writing that the "conclusion suggested by this research is that the experience of conscious will kicks in at some point *after* the brain has already started preparing for the action" [Wegner's italics].[31] Gazzaniga mentions the original Libet experiments and also the Soon experiment. He writes that the latter shows

> that the outcomes of an inclination can be encoded in brain activity up to ten seconds before it enters awareness! The brain has acted before its person is conscious of it. Not only that, from looking at the scan, they can make a prediction about what the person is going to do.[32]

In the previous chapter, I argued that there are myriad problems with these neurobiological experiments and with the conclusions which the experimenters drew from them. These problems seriously undermine the claim that a preceding brain state (not to be identified with the agent's *reasons*) of which the agent is unaware, and over which the agent has no control, causally determines the conscious intention or the action associated with it. However, the Libet-type experiments are noted only briefly in both Wegner and Gazzaniga. Wegner appeals to many other different kinds of evidence, whereas Gazzaniga focuses on his split-brain experiments. All of this evidence is applied to both of the claims Wegner and Gazzaniga defend: Our conscious intentions are determined by preceding brain/mental events of which we are unconscious, and our conscious intentions are not among the causes of the actions which seem to follow from them. Wegner and Gazzaniga do not clearly separate the two claims and the evidence for them, so the most perspicuous way to proceed will be to look at the various types of evidence they adduce and then to consider, for each

---

31 Wegner (2002): 54.
32 Gazzaniga (2011): 129.

type of evidence, whether it supports one or the other or both of the claims in question. This study will provide more examples of problems that have already arisen in this examination of the free will experiments, and it will also illustrate new problems.

People often perform apparently voluntary actions without a feeling or realization that they are doing so. ("Voluntary" here is used in a broad sense: The actions involve your body and are not simple responses to a stimulus like the knee jerking when tapped by a hammer, nor are they done against your will.) This would seem to show a disconnect between conscious intention and action. You might be unaware that you are cracking your knuckles until someone asks you to stop. You may often, in walking or driving somewhere, be so distracted by other thoughts that you are surprised to find that you have indeed walked or driven to your destination. You did it, you intended it as you set out, but you may have no feeling of doing it as you do it or memory of having done it afterwards. The individual actions required to get you to your destination are not engaged in deliberately.

A different but still common sort of example involves reacting to something before you have consciously registered what the "something" is and decided to react. Gazzaniga, arguing that conscious processes are too slow to precede our actions, gives the example of jumping immediately upon seeing a movement in the grass. Before he has consciously considered whether it might be a snake or just the wind,

> The brain takes a nonconscious shortcut through the amygdala… If a pattern associated with danger in the past is recognized by the amygdala, it sends an impulse along a direct connection to the brain stem, which then activates the flight-or-fight response and rings the alarm. I automatically jump back before I realize why.[33]

We can call these common instances of nonconscious behavior "automatic".

Wegner notes more colorful examples of people doing things that they are unaware of doing, including such phenomena as people unwittingly engaged in table turning, the moving of the pointer on the Ouija board, and automatic writing. In these cases, not only are the "actors" not aware that it is their own motion that is producing the effects, but they may attribute the movement to occult powers.[34] These he labels "automatisms" where there is no feeling of voluntariness.[35] An even more extreme example

---

33 Gazzaniga (2011): 76–7.
34 Wegner (2002): 103–11.
35 Wegner (2002): 9, nt. 3. I am not sure what the distinction is between "automatic" behavior and "automatisms". The latter term seems to be reserved for the more unusual instances of behavior over which one did not feel control. Perhaps with automatisms the behavior is such that ordinarily we suppose that one would or should feel control.

is alien hand syndrome, a neuropsychological disorder in which one hand engages in movements that are not experienced by the "owner" of the hand as his own.[36]

Related to automatisms is ideomotor action, where the entertaining of an idea results in subsequent action, but the actor does not construct a conscious intention based on the idea and is unaware that the idea has informed the action. Wegner cites a priming experiment by Bargh, Chen, and Burrows demonstrating this effect. The experimenters outline their methods and hypothesis:

> The present activation of the elderly stereotype on behavior. Participants were instructed to work on a scrambled-sentence task as part of a language proficiency experiment. The scrambled-sentence task contained words relevant to the elderly stereotype in the elderly priming condition, but all references to slowness, which is a quality stereotypically associated with elderly people, were excluded. The neutral priming condition scrambled-sentence task contained age-non-specific words in the place of elderly stereotyped words.
>
> After completing the task, each participant was partially debriefed and thanked for his or her participation. A second experimenter then surreptitiously recorded the amount of time the participant took to walk down the corridor after exiting the laboratory room. Subsequently, participants were debriefed once again with a complete explanation of the purpose of the experiment. The main hypothesis was that participants who had been primed with the elderly stereotype would walk more slowly compared to participants who had not been primed with the stereotype-relevant stimuli.[37]

The hypothesis is indeed born out, showing that ideas that do not play a role in conscious intention may nonetheless figure among the causes of subsequent action. This "priming" effect has long been taken for granted by advertisers and the general public, and recent research continues to explore various ways in which this priming phenomenon works.[38]

The examples of automatic actions, automatisms, and ideomotor actions demonstrate that people can do things where *reasons* do not figure in the history of the actions; the doing is not caused by a considered intention but rather by other factors of which the agent is unaware. Moreover,

---

36 Wegner (2002): 4–6, 106.
37 J. A. Bargh, M. Chen, and L. Burrows, "Automaticity of Social Behavior: Direct Effects of Trait Construct and Stereotype Activation on Action", *Journal of Personality and Social Psychology* (1996): 230–44, at 236.
38 See, for example, Brenda Ocampo, "Unconscious Manipulation of Free Choice by Novel Primes", *Consciousness and Cognition* 34 (2015): 4–9.

people can be brought to feel or believe that they have done things when in fact they haven't. Wegner gives the example of an experiment he conducted (he calls it the "I Spy" experiment after the name of the children's book from which pictures were taken) in which a participant and a confederate are told to move a cursor together randomly over a screen and then to stop randomly on some item on the screen. What the confederate will actually do, during the experiment, is force a stop on an item when instructed to do so. The participant, at some time near the stop, hears a word related to the item on which the confederate will stop. In a previous experiment, it was determined that hearing such "priming" words did not encourage the participant to stop on the "primed" item. The question was to see whether, when the stop had actually been forced by the confederate, the hearing of the priming word would lead the participant to feel that she had made the stop rather than that it had been forced by the confederate.[39]

> On the forced stops, a pattern of perceived intention emerged as predicted by the priority principle. Although there was a tendency overall for participants to perceive the forced stops as intended... there was a marked fluctuation in this perception depending on when the prime word occurred... perceived intentionality was lower when the prime word appeared 30 seconds before the forced stop, increased when the word occurred 5 seconds or 1 second before the stop, and then dropped again to a lower level when the word occurred 1 second following the stop.[40]

So, the participant in "I Spy" can be led to feel that she has done something intentionally when what was done (the stopping on the item) was actually done by the confederate.

Another study which Wegner mentions was carried out by Kassin and Kiechel. In this experiment, the subject is convinced, after the fact, that he has done something which he had not actually done. Here is the abstract:

> An experiment demonstrated that false incriminating evidence can lead people to accept guilt for a crime they did not commit. Subjects in a fast- or slow-paced reaction time task were accused of damaging a computer by pressing the wrong key. All were truly innocent and initially denied the charge. A confederate then said she saw the subject

---

[39] The "feeling" language is taken from the experiment. It is not clear whether the participant sometimes believes she has made the stop or whether she simply has varying degrees of a "feeling" or "perception" (undefined) of authorship.

[40] Daniel M. Wegner and Thalia Wheatley, "Apparent Mental Causation: Sources of the Experience of Will", *American Psychologist* 54 (1999): 480–91, at 489; Wegner (2002): 74–8.

hit the key or did not see the subject hit the key. Compared with subjects in the slow-pace/no-witness group, those in the fast-pace/witness group were more likely to sign a confession, internalize guilt for the event, and confabulate details in memory consistent with that belief. Both legal and conceptual implications are discussed.[41]

The purpose of the study is to help understand how police practices might encourage suspects to agree to false confessions, even to the point of confabulation (i.e., constructing false memories about the deed in question). Wegner takes the study to provide more evidence that the connection which we usually claim to observe between our reasons and intentions and our subsequent "intended" actions is only apparent and is often constructed after the fact.

More unusual examples of lack of awareness regarding what produced one's actions, followed by confabulation, arise in the "split-brain" experiments. These were experiments conducted by Michael Gazzaniga which have led him to adopt a position somewhat similar to Wegner's. In cases of intractable epilepsy, one treatment is to cut the two fiber pathways that connect the right and the left hemispheres in the brain. The two are not entirely disconnected from one another in that both remain connected to a common brain stem – an important feature allowing both sides to sleep and wake at the same time.[42] Patients undergoing this surgery apparently do not feel or behave as if their perceptual or cognitive faculties have suffered any serious diminution. But what Gazzaniga and those working with him discovered was that the right and the left hemispheres do different jobs, one striking distinction being that "one [the left] lived in a world where it could draw inferences, and the other did not".[43] This led Gazzaniga to hypothesize that different "modules" in the brain exercise different cognitive functions. Why, then, do we feel as if we are unified, conscious beings? Gazzaniga holds that a left-brain process, which he labels the "interpreter", puts disparate information together in a way that makes sense to the perceiving subject. Many experiments on split-brain patients point to this conclusion. For example, Gazzaniga describes an experiment:

> We showed a split-brain patient two pictures: A chicken claw was shown to his right visual field, so the left hemisphere only saw the claw picture, and a snow scene was shown to the left visual field, so the right hemisphere only saw that. He was then asked to choose a

---

41 Saul M. Kassin and Katherine L. Kiechel, "The Social Psychology of False Confessions: Compliance, Internalization, and Confabulation", *Psychological Science* 7 (1996): 125–8, at 125.
42 Gazzaniga (2011): 54.
43 Gazzaniga (2011): 62.

> picture from an array of pictures placed in full view in front of him, which both hemispheres could see. The left hand pointed to a shovel (which was the most appropriate answer for the snow scene) and the right hand pointed to a chicken (the most appropriate answer for the chicken claw). Then we asked why he chose those items. His left-hemisphere speech center replied, "Oh, that's simple. The chicken claw goes with the chicken," ... Then, looking down at his left hand pointing to the shovel, without missing a beat, he said, "And you need a shovel to clean out the chicken shed." ... [The left brain] interpreted the response in a context consistent with what it knew, and all it knew was: chicken claw.... What was interesting was that the left hemisphere did not say, "I don't know," which truly was the correct answer. It made up a post hoc answer that fit the situation.[44]

We know that in many cases we act before any conscious consideration occurs. Gazzaniga gives the example of jumping at a rustling sound before he is aware that it is the wind rustling the grass and not a rattlesnake. And the split-brain experiments show that people can and do confabulate the reasons for their actions after the fact. Gazzaniga concludes that our

> subjective awareness arises out of our dominant left hemisphere's unrelenting quest to explain these bits and pieces that have popped into consciousness... This is a post hoc rationalization process. ... Because consciousness is a slow process, whatever has made it to consciousness has already happened.[45]

Our actions are produced by preceding processes of which we are unaware and the interpreter then works to make sense of them. The self, including our sense of agency and the thought that we make free decisions about our actions, is an illusion.[46]

Certainly, this split-brain situation is unusual, but confabulation can occur in very humdrum cases, as the following experiment, which has nothing to do with split brains, demonstrates:

> We showed picture pairs of female faces to 120 participants (70 female) and asked them to choose which face in each pair they found most attractive. On some trials, immediately after their choice, they were asked to verbally describe the reasons for choosing the way they did. Unknown to the participants, on certain trials, a double-card ploy was used to covertly exchange one face for the other... Thus, on these trials, the outcome of the choice

---

44 Gazzaniga (2011): 82–3.
45 Gazzaniga (2011): 103.
46 Gazzaniga (2011): 105.

became the opposite of what they intended. Each subject completed a sequence of 15 face pairs, three of which were manipulated (M). The M face pairs always appeared at the same position in the sequence, and for each of these pairs, participants were asked to state the reasons behind their choice. Verbal reports were also solicited for three trials of non-manipulated (NM) pairs.[47]

The experimenters discovered that the subjects detected the changes infrequently (only about a fourth of the time). And when asked to explain why they "chose" the face which, in fact, they had not chosen, subjects confabulated, readily giving the reasons for their "choice". The experimenters draw modest conclusions about intentional choice – that our after-the-fact assessment may be in error more often than we would have assumed. But if confabulation constitutes part of the evidence for the illusory nature of conscious will, then this experiment is of special interest because of the ordinariness of the situation and choice involved.

It should be noted that Wegner and Gazzaniga seem to differ somewhat regarding the relationship of the conscious intention – in the sense of an intention of which the agent is conscious – to the intended action. For the latter, the main focus is the slowness of consciousness, so Gazzaniga explains that our awareness of our intentions is the result of the left-brain "interpreter" subsequently trying to make sense of the movements of our bodies. The "interpreter" supplies the agent with reasons, although it is not in fact those reasons which guide the agent's actions. Wegner sometimes speaks this way, he cites Gazzaniga's split-brain experiments, and his explanation for belief in "apparent mental causation" is consistent with this view. But he does say that the thought of an action is often prior to the action and so he may not share Gazzaniga's confidence that the awareness of intention is produced after the fact by a subsequent "interpreter".

Wegner offers other sorts of evidence to demonstrate the disconnect between our intentions and our actions. Sometimes we engage in "action projection": we attribute to others what are essentially actions we have performed ourselves. The famous example of Clever Hans, the counting horse, is an instance where even Hans's trainer was unaware that it was his own movements that led to Hans's apparently being able to do arithmetic.[48] Wegner also reports a much sadder example, the case of "facilitated communication", which was observed all over the world: In order to help those whose severe disorders made it difficult or impossible for them to communicate through speech or normal typing, facilitators would (it was believed)

---

47 Petter Johansson, Lars Hall, Sverker Sikstrom, and Andreas Okson, "Failure to Detect Mismatches between Intention and Outcome in a Simple Decision Task". *Science* 310 (2005): 116–19, at 116.
48 Wegner (2002): 189–92.

help clients communicate the clients' own thoughts. The facilitators would "keep the client 'on task' and help to support the pointing or typing finger and guide the retraction of the arm". Facilitators were strictly instructed not to guide the clients' responses and apparently believed in all sincerity that they were not doing so. When clients began to exhibit almost miraculous abilities to communicate through their facilitators, skeptics started to examine whether or not it might be the facilitators themselves who were unconsciously guiding the communications. Wegner notes the result (which remains the standard opinion) that it is the facilitators and not the clients who are "communicating".[49] Wegner provides many more instances of action projection: onto someone else, onto a group, onto an imaginary character, onto spirits who have "possessed" the person, onto someone as a result of hypnosis – there is no end of examples in which someone does something yet attributes the action to someone or something else. There is, then, a great deal of empirical evidence to support the claim that an action (defined broadly) may often not be the effect of reasons and a preceding conscious intention to do the action, in the sense of either an intention had by someone who is conscious or an intention of which one is introspectively aware. It is worthwhile to note that much of this evidence casts doubt on the ability of subjects (or anyone) to consistently offer accurate reports about their own mental states, underscoring that there is indeed a Problem of First-Person Reporting such as was mentioned in the previous chapter. But does this evidence provide reason to doubt that we have meaningful freedom?

Responses to the "Illusion" Claims

First, in much of the evidence provided, the Problems of Translation loom large. The first translation problem is that the behavior of the subjects often has little if anything to do with making choices and certainly not important choices. The information gained from experiments studying a feeling of having stopped a marker on a picture, for example, is unlikely to translate well to questions about whether or not human agents can make LFMCs. Further translation problems arise since the subjects often find themselves in unusual situations or constitute an unusual pool for study. This is especially true in the case of the split-brain patients. That an agent who has had a rare brain surgery might perceive things in an unusual way, behave oddly, and be led to confabulate reasons for behavior need not tell us anything about a normal agent making a "real life" choice. Even agents who are especially gullible or – as in many of the experiments – who are being lied to by someone whom it is usually appropriate for them to trust may (for these reasons) not be representative. Even just participating in an

---

49 Wegner (2002): 195–201.

experiment is a peculiar situation which might lead an agent to perceive his situation in an unusual way and behave in an atypical manner. Eddy Nahmias draws a further conclusion from the fact that Wegner's evidence for a disconnect between intention and action is frequently drawn from the unusual situation. Nahmias points out that the very reason that we find it so intriguing when purposeful behavior and conscious awareness come apart is that we recognize that as a rule the two go together and thus the very strangeness of the cases to which Wegner often appeals supports *the contrary* of Wegner's thesis.[50]

In addition to the Problems of Translation, a related Problem of Generalization arises when Wegner and Gazzaniga move from "some" to "all" frequently and without offering any justification. Science proceeds by induction, but there are methodological principles regarding how to generalize correctly from the particular instances we observe. One fundamental requirement is that the phenomena to which we are generalizing bear the appropriate resemblance to the particular instances we have observed. Libet attempted to address this issue by arguing that meaningful choices might be a more complex version of the process he studied, but Wegner and Gazzaniga do not seem to see the need for a defense of their generalizations. The move from "some" to "all" is especially problematic in that our ordinary experience would seem to demonstrate that sometimes we do indeed act in the absence of a previous intention – as when we find ourselves braking when the car in front of us stops suddenly – and at other times we have reasons to do something, we form the conscious intention to do it and then we do it. And we can tell the difference between these two sorts of cases. Think of how much decision-making, conscious effort, and attentiveness went into originally learning how to drive. The seasoned driver can brake before thinking about it precisely because of all that early conscious effort and subsequent practice.[51] Our experience, then, is against the move from "some" to "all" in this case.

Moreover, as Timothy Bayne points out, Wegner's thesis concerning how we come to believe that conscious intentions often cause our actions is rooted in our observing the frequency with which the intention is followed by the action. But ordinarily, if Y is often preceded by X and we do not discern any other causes of Y, we would count that as at least some evidence that X is a cause of Y. Thus, Wegner's explanation for why we come to believe in "apparent" mental causation provides evidence that our reasons and conscious intentions do indeed (at least sometimes) play a causal role in our actions.[52] These points raise serious doubts about the generalization moving from the point that some of our actions are not

50 Nahmias (2002): 535.
51 Klemm (2010): 61.
52 Bayne (2006): 179.

explained by our reasons and intentions to the claim that reasons and intentions *never* play a role in the causal history of our actions. But this Problem of Generalization is not addressed by defenders of the "illusion" theory.

Neither Wegner nor Gazzaniga provides much empirical or scientific evidence that our conscious intentions (and choices, if they draw a distinction) are determined and unresponsive to reasons. Both cite the Libet experiments, but nothing in Libet's findings (or in those of similar experiments) shows that choices (much less, meaningful choices) are determined. One might point to priming experiments, such as the one in which the participants walked more slowly when they had seen words associated with aging, as evidence that many unconscious factors affect our behavior, but that is consistent with our being robustly free. In this particular experiment, it is worthwhile to note that the agents apparently did what they *consciously* intended to do, in accord with their reasons for doing it – they walked down the corridor away from the room in which the words had been read – some of them just did it more slowly than they might have otherwise.[53]

In describing an LFMC, I granted that all sorts of subtle factors may go into forming the torn condition in which a meaningful free choice becomes possible. It may well be locally causally determined that the agent finds himself with *these* morally significant options as opposed to *those*. It is the actual choice that cannot be determined if the agent is to choose with libertarian freedom. Thus, it is the claim that our conscious intentions are determined, a claim which forms a consistent thread in the illusion argument, that would pose the greatest threat to meaningful libertarian freedom. But arguments or evidence for this claim form almost no part of the actual cases presented by Wegner and Gazzaniga. Gazzaniga does suggest that since we live in a physical universe governed by physical laws, we should take it that everything is determined in something like the philosophical sense.[54] Wegner holds that the practice of science conflicts with belief in free will.[55] He also reviews the standard "luck problem" critique of free will.[56] But these are philosophical points which neither author develops at length. If they are supposed to be part of the experimental practice, then the Problem of Domain arises. Making metaphysical or epistemic assumptions is entirely legitimate in doing science. The sciences could not proceed without them. But in regard to the study of free will, it should be made clear that accepting determinism or physicalism or embracing the argument that the "luck problem" shows that libertarian theories

---

53 Bertram E. Malle, "Of Windmills and Straw Men: Folk Assumptions of Mind and Action". In Pockett et al. (2006): 207–31, at 219.
54 Gazzaniga (2011): 2–4.
55 Wegner (2005): 20.
56 Wegner (2002): 322–3.

are mistaken is a philosophical assumption coming down on a particular side of much-debated philosophical issues. These assumptions are not the subject of empirical investigations. To the extent that these assumptions guide the interpretation of data and the construction of theories, the conclusions reached go beyond what the experimental results justify. The experiments that Wegner and Gazzaniga cite do not support the LCD (local causal determinism) aspect of the "illusion" case.

The "illusion" case aims much more to defend the position that it is not our conscious intentions that cause our actions. But the Problem of Focus arises when looking at the kind of evidence that Wegner adduces. Many of our non-conscious actions (i.e., we are not sleep walking but we are not immediately aware and attentive to all of the movements and behaviors we are engaged in), like driving "on autopilot", may well result from having made the earlier, reasons-responsive choice to get in the car and go to the store. Even in the more exotic cases, like the person who unconsciously moves the pointer on the Ouija board, we have no reason to suspect that the person did not deliberate and choose to "consult" the Ouija board to begin with. With the cases where someone can feel a sense of authorship for an action taken by another, as in the "I Spy" experiment, we have no evidence to undermine what we would ordinarily take for granted: that the participant *was* the actual author of her originally agreeing to participate in the experiment.[57] Indeed, in universities in the Western world, experiments on human subjects require that the subjects give their free and (at least somewhat) informed consent. The assumption at work is clearly that the participatory actions of subjects – getting to the lab and following the instructions – are the result of their rationally, freely, and consciously giving consent. If what we are interested in studying is important choices, then the evidence from automatisms (as with the Ouija board) or the mistaken sense of authorship (as in "I Spy") is taken from the wrong temporal point in the process. The interesting, reasons-based "intending" was done earlier, and the participants carried out the actions they intended. A similar point can be made concerning Wegner's example of the mistaken communication facilitators. Apparently, what they consciously intended to do was merely to help. That is what they were trying to do and believed that they were doing. That they were trying "too hard" to help in no way conflicts with the thought that they might have freely and reasonably

---

57 Mele describes the important distinctions between occurrent and standing intentions, and proximal and distal intentions (2009): 3–13, and notes that there is empirical evidence that distal intentions, such as implementing a project, do have causal efficacy regarding subsequent actions. See P.M. Gollweitzer and P. Sheeran, "Implementation Intentions and Goal Achievement: A Meta-Analysis of Effects and Processes", *Advances in Experimental Social Psychology* 38 (2006): 69–119; T.L. Webb and P. Sheeran, "Does Changing Behavioral Intentions Engender Behavior Change? A Meta-Analysis of the Experimental Evidence", *Psychological Bulletin* 132:2 (2006): 249–68.

chosen to engage in the task that they hoped would benefit the clients. So, the Problem of Focus arises because the experimental data are deliberately gathered from a point in the proceedings where actions taken without preceding intentions are possible – but only possible because intentional activity occurred earlier.

This example suggests another Problem of Focus with Wegner's (and Gazzaniga's) analysis. Both frequently isolate and study simple bodily motions, and in at least some of the experiments, it is not clear that the disconnect is actually between the agent's intention and the intended action. The physical behavior of the facilitators appears to follow directly from what it is that they are consciously intending to do: help this client right now to communicate through typing. The disconnect is not between the facilitators' *intentions* and their literal bodily motions; it is between their motions and how they *understand* those motions. Our immediate grasp of (and control over) what our bodies are doing can be faulty. One might, for example, feel a pain in the foot and yet be unable to pinpoint the exact location of that pain. Or one might intend to make a thin brush stroke but bear down too hard on the brush and make a thick one. It is easy to imagine that the facilitators, concentrating on their unusual physical task, engaged in exactly the bodily motions they consciously intended to engage in. However, through not being perfectly aware of (or perfectly in control of) what their bodies were doing, they misread the physical interaction between themselves and their clients.

A somewhat similar point can be made regarding other examples of action projection. Wegner's reading of the "Clever Hans the Counting Horse" case seems off target. The "action" that Hans's trainer was engaged in turned out to be leaning his head forward slightly and then straightening up when Hans reached the correct answer. The "action" which Hans's trainer attributed to Hans was being able to do arithmetic and record the answer by pawing the ground with his hoof. So, it is not the case that Hans's trainer was engaged in doing an action that he then attributed to Hans. Hans's trainer intended to stand still and believed himself to be standing still – at least he believed that he was not giving Hans any visual cues – when Hans performed his marvelous feats. The disconnect lies in the trainer's misreading of the position of his own body. I have allowed that the term "action" can be used broadly, but it begins to seem an abuse of the term to consider a slight, unconscious head tilt an "action". If it is an action, it is not at all the sort of action that we are concerned about when we wonder whether or not our actions are caused by our intentions. That our conscious intentions may not produce the simple bodily motions or the posture that we intend may be a consequence not of a disconnect between intention and *intended* actions but rather a consequence of our failure to read what our bodies are doing with perfect accuracy.

There are other sorts of cases, labelled "action projection" by Wegner, where agents have done things, mistakenly believing that they are doing what their group or their spouse wants to do. But, again, the focus seems off, and it is not clear that these examples are accurately labelled "action projection". In the example where the husband buys the tickets for the couple to go to the Monster Truck Noise Derby thinking this is something his wife wants them to attend, the action the husband engages in is buying the tickets. He does not attribute the buying of the tickets to his wife. His mistake is in thinking that she wants them to attend the Monster Truck Noise Derby. So, there does not seem to be any disconnect here between what the husband intends and what he does. True, there are the more exotic cases of people claiming that the actions their own bodies are engaged in are actually the actions of someone or something else. For example, someone who claims that his bodily motions are not his, but rather are authored by the spirits that are possessing him, seems to be genuinely "projecting" his actions. But these sorts of cases raise a severe Problem of Translation. They are clearly bizarre and so they do not provide evidence concerning the normal human agent going about his everyday business.

A different sort of evidence appeals to the confabulation phenomenon, but the problem remains one of focus. Certainly, the surprising readiness to confabulate should concern us in that it shows that we may make mistakes more often than we suppose as we reflect upon our past actions. This is especially of interest on the account of freedom which holds that much of the important moral business of our lives may take place after we do some deed, in our evaluation of the deed and of our responsibility for it. But even if we should confabulate after the fact in some instance of having deliberated and chosen, that does not speak to the question of the nature of the choice itself. Subsequent confabulation would not show that the choice in question did not meet all of the criteria of an LFMC. That we may sometimes be mistaken about what we have done and why we have done it does not entail that we never deliberate between options and act for reasons. Often we do remember our deliberations in a way that certainly seems to allow us to accurately report why we did what we did.

The various sorts of evidence to which Wegner and Gazzaniga appeal are not persuasive if their thesis is indeed the radical claim that our conscious intentions to act are *never* among the causes of our intended actions. Moreover, their project is subject, on several counts, to the Problem of Self-Refutation; their conclusions contradict their statements and their behavior. In this case, if their conclusions are correct, then their experiments could not be done or accurately reported. (With some argument, one might be able to direct this criticism against Libet's interpretation of his data, but the case is more obvious against the "illusion" theory.) First, if their conclusions are correct, then their conclusions cannot have been demonstrated experimentally since no one can have engaged in doing experiments. Webster's dictionary defines an "experiment" as "an operation carried out under controlled conditions in order to discover an unknown effect or law, to test or establish a hypothesis or to illustrate a known law". Whatever one thinks of appeals to the dictionary, surely it is correct that in order for an activity to qualify as an experiment it must be done "in order to" achieve a purpose. It must follow upon conscious goals. Ordinarily, we take the practice of science to represent the epitome of activity guided by reasons. But if the actions our bodies engage in are not ever guided by our conscious intentions, then the rational, purposive behavior which constitutes an experiment does not happen.

The self-refutation occurs in specific examples of experiments, as well. In the "I Spy" case, there is the participant who can be brought to feel a sense of authorship for an action she has not done. But there is also the confederate who must be able to follow the directions she receives. So, she must be able to form a rational intention and act upon it and subsequently report that she has indeed done what she was directed to do. If the confederate does not engage in the action she is told to do and is aware of doing and if she does not correctly report what she has done, then the "I Spy" experiment cannot proceed. So, the experiment can demonstrate that sometimes people experience a disconnect between what they have done and how they feel about it, but it depends upon there being an accurate "connect" between the rational intentions, actions, and awareness of actions of the confederate. Of course, this point translates to any experiment involving a confederate who is to do something.

Furthermore, in the "I Spy" experiment, the participant reports her feeling of authorship by marking down on a sheet just how much of such a feeling she had. The experiment shows a disconnect between the participant moving the marker and how she *felt* about moving the marker. But, for the data to show what Wegner takes it to show, there has to be a "connect" between how the participant felt about moving the marker and her action of *reporting* how she felt. Many of the experiments concerning conscious will involve first-person reports. But writing and speaking are physical actions. If these actions reporting the thoughts, beliefs, and intentions involved in the experiments are not causally traceable in some way to those thoughts, beliefs, and intentions, then it is puzzling that the experimenters should be so confident that the reports are accurate regarding the mental phenomena in question.[58] Furthermore, Wegner and Gazzaniga offer a lot of evidence that first-person reports are often mistaken, but if they are always (or even usually) mistaken, then much of the evidence in the experiments must be discounted.

---

58 For example, in the "I Spy" experiment the subjects were to record what they afterwards *believed* their intentions to have been, whereas Wegner reports this information as what the subjects' intentions actually were; Walter (2014): 39.

A large part of the illusion argument involves the claim that human agents – as a general matter – are not trustworthy in their understanding of what it is that they are doing and have done. But if human agents suffer from this almost ubiquitous and serious cognitive limitation, then not only are first-person reports by experimental subjects suspect, but so are the reports of the scientists conducting the experiments. Scientists are human agents, too. One way to deal with the Problem of Self-Refutation is to ignore it. One of the great divides among philosophers, going back to the Pre-Socratics, is whether or not it is acceptable to embrace a self-refuting theory. Many philosophers have been willing to defend theories involving one sort of contradiction or another. Gorgias, the Sophist, tells us that human communication is impossible. Hume explains the causes of our mistaken belief in causation. Other philosophers insist that it is irrational – or at least bad form – to knowingly hold and advance views that are internally inconsistent or that are in direct opposition to one's usual behavior and practices.

Assuming that those defending the "illusion" thesis would prefer not to be accused of self-refutation, one avenue of escape would be to claim that, as scientists, they are not (at least when they are doing science) subject to the processes which guide the mental and physical lives of the rest of humanity. But this would be a difficult claim to defend. If the behavior of scientists can be guided by rational intentions (at least sometimes), why cannot the same be said for the rest of us? Also, this setting of the scientist above the inferior mass of humankind brings up the (ethical) Problem of Elitism (to be discussed in Chapter 6) and so is an unwholesome move.

A different approach open to Wegner and Gazzaniga to escape the charge of self-refutation would be to argue that their thesis is ultimately not the radical claim that our conscious intentions are never the causes of our actions but rather that *sometimes* – perhaps in surprising ways and more often than we have supposed – our conscious intentions are not the causes of our actions. This is an important case to make but it in no way conflicts with a traditional belief in robust, libertarian free will. On the contrary, the defender of free will can hold that considering the experiments and evidence they discuss may make us better aware of how to think accurately about our own choices and actions and thus may enhance our autonomy as human agents. But if the goal is to show that human agents do not have anything like traditionally understood free will, the defenders of the "illusion" thesis do not succeed in making their case. Their defense suffers from numerous problems – of Description, of Translation, of Focus, of Domain, of Generalization, and of Self-refutation. Experimenters attempting to settle the question of free will empirically should be alert to all of these problems.

Chapter 5
Situationism

Introduction

Suppose a colleague whom you had always thought to be friendly and polite is suddenly nasty to you for no apparent reason. And suppose a grumpy and taciturn colleague is suddenly friendly and effusive, again for no apparent reason. You politely ask each of them why they are behaving in a manner atypical for them, and they say they do not know. Then the person sent to repair the air conditioning (AC) units in your building tells you that he has been able to repair the AC for the grumpy colleague, but now the friendly colleague's AC is not working. But not to worry, it's not an especially hot day and the AC will make only a barely noticeable difference. Could it be that the behavior of your colleagues is produced by a slight change of temperature? So slight that they don't even notice it? The situationist says "Yes".

Situationism, in its extreme version, holds that human behavior is explained almost wholly by the situation in which the agent finds himself. For decades in the later twentieth century, psychologists debated the situationist claim, the opposing side arguing that it is mainly character, dispositional traits, the "person" – rather than the situation – that explains behavior. The consensus now rejects the extreme situationist position and promotes some version of the view that people do possess robust traits but that these traits interact with situational elements. Daniel Lapsley writes,

> Psychologists ... seem generally nonplussed by the situationist challenge... After all, the rapprochement between social and personality psychology was sealed decades ago with more complex models of how dispositions and contexts dynamically interact.... I am aware of no generalized anxiety among personality or developmental psychologists, or among social psychologists for that matter, concerning the

alleged ephemeral nature of personality traits or the vacuity of dispositional coherence.[1]

Nonetheless, when we consider what science has to say or may have to say about free will, it is worthwhile to discuss the situationist debate, as it developed at the interface between philosophy and psychology, since it illustrates problems relevant to research on free will. After giving a quick sketch of situationism as understood by philosophers, I will outline a few of the experiments – call them "situationist experiments" – that have seen a lot of play in the philosophical literature. Unlike the Libet experiments and much of the sort of evidence adduced by Wegner and Gazzaniga, most of the oft-discussed situationist experiments do *not* suffer from the Problem of Translation regarding the behavior being studied. They actually deal with what appear to be people making morally significant choices. Thus, they are of special interest for the present work. The scientist or the philosopher who finds evidence against free will through studying an event or action which is not a morally significant choice must defend the claim that this event or action is enough like a morally significant choice that conclusions are appropriately transferred from one to the other. The defender of free will can argue that wrist-flexing, for example, is so distant from a libertarian free moral choice (LFMC) that it is just a mistake to move from evidence gained from wrist-flexing experiments to claims about human freedom. The same sort of argument is much harder to make regarding the situationist experiments.

Furthermore, it is helpful to get the situationist experiments on the table in this chapter so that they can be used to illustrate the ethical problems that can arise in studying free will. The famous and controversial Milgram experiments from the 1960s are especially useful in that there is an extensive literature concerning moral questions related to these experiments. Moreover, the Milgram experiments have been recreated recently in several different ways which supposedly avoid the moral problems with the originals. Some might look to these recreations to provide a template

---

1 Daniel Lapsley, "Situationism and the Pyrrhic Defense of Character Education", in *Moral Psychology: Volume 5: Virtue and Character* edited by Walter Sinnott-Armstrong and Christian B. Miller (Cambridge, MA: MIT Press, 2017): 171–83. See also Wiebke Bleidorn, "Moving Character beyond the Person-Situation Debate: The Stable and Dynamic Nature of Virtue in Everyday Life", in Miller et al. (2015): 129–50: at 133; Owen Flanagan, "Moral Science? Still Metaphysical After All These Years", in *Personality, Identity, and Character* edited by Darcia Narvaez and Daniel K. Lapsley (New York: Cambridge University Press, 2009): 52–78, at 56–64; Christian B. Miller, R. Michael Furr, Angela Knobel, and William Fleeson, "Introduction", in *Character: New Directions from Philosophy, Psychology, and Theology* edited by Christian B. Miller, R. Michael Furr, Angela Knobel, William Fleeson (Oxford: Oxford University Press, 2015): 1–16, at 3; Panos Paris, "Scepticism about Virtue and the Five-Factor Model of Personality", *Utilitas* 29 (2017): 423–52.

for overcoming some of the ethical hurdles involved in studying morally significant choices.

The situationist experiments, in addition to focusing on morally significant choices, are relevant to the science and freedom issue in other ways. Although the situation/person debate among psychologists did not center on the question of whether or not human beings have free will, the experimental evidence invoked in support of the situationist position could seem to count against human freedom. What the experiments were held to show was that minor situational factors exercised unexpectedly significant influence on behavioral outcomes; these were factors which the subjects apparently did not consciously consider among the reasons for their decisions and actions or which (in the view of those drawing situationist conclusions) ought to have carried little (if any) weight in the decision processes of the subjects. This evidence could tell against human freedom in two ways.

First, if recognizing certain, apparently trivial elements of a situation enhances an observer's ability to predict the behavior of an agent, it could be argued that this provides evidence that human choices and actions are locally causally determined. (And the current rejection of extreme situationism in favor of the view that it is both character and situation that explain behavior could still ground an argument for LCD.) I set this issue aside since, given my description of an LFMC, it is not a serious threat. In a human life, all sorts of causal influences are in play. That an agent is in *this* particular torn condition and faces *these* particular options may well be determined. And it may be that paradigmatic free choices occur only rarely. The situationist evidence is very, *very* far from supporting the claim that *all* choices are locally causally determined, and if the burden of proof is on the one who would deny human free will, the believer in libertarian freedom need not be too concerned about the discovery that minor factors can have a surprisingly large influence on choices and actions. Some concern *is* in order since being influenced by trivial elements in one's situation – or even elements of which one is unaware – would constitute a limitation on one's autonomy. But it would not prove LCD regarding choices.

However, there is a second way in which the situationist experiments might undermine belief in our ability to make LFMCs. What is worrisome, as Dana Nelkin has pointed out, is that agents may not be properly reasons-responsive in making decisions.[2] The illusion thesis discussed in the previous chapter also raised this problem, but mainly in discussing the situationist debate have philosophers brought it to the fore. If people make decisions which are unduly influenced by improperly weighted – or even

---

2 Dana Nelkin, "Freedom, Responsibility, and the Challenge of Situationism", *Midwest Studies in Philosophy* 29 (2005): 181–206.

unrecognized – factors, then they lack what looks to be a key element in making responsibility-grounding free decisions. As noted in the previous chapter, the reasons-responsive criterion is usually associated with Fischer and Ravizza's non-libertarian theory of freedom and responsibility.[3] Were situationism shown to be correct, many compatibilist theories would be threatened. Certainly, the question of the extent to which an agent can and does respond to reasons is relevant to the libertarian theory of free will with which I am operating. (I will be using "reasons" and "reasons-responsive" somewhat broadly. A developed analysis is not necessary for purposes of the present discussion.) In order to make an LFMC, the agent must be able to assess the morally significant options with which he is confronted. That is what the torn condition consists in. The assessment need not be perfect but it must at least recognize the morally salient features to some degree; to *what* degree lies outside the scope of the present work to decide. However, if it should turn out that agents are generally (and non-culpably) incapable of weighing their options reasonably or if they are constantly and decisively influenced by factors of which they are unaware or barely aware, then it would seem to be a mistake to ascribe to them the sort of freedom that can ground responsibility and human dignity. The literature discussing whether or not situationist experiments should undermine confidence in the ability of human agents to respond to reasons will be discussed once the most often cited experiments have been outlined.

There is a further issue related to the situationist experiments. Defenders of libertarian free will have often held that the *point* of being able to make free choices is so that the human agent can bear responsibility for his character, especially as being oriented toward the good, or not. This is what gives the human agent a special dignity. The *very* extreme situationist claim was that character plays little (if any) role in decision-making and indeed that human beings do not possess what we usually think of as character traits and dispositions. Behavior is to be explained almost solely by situational factors. Were this true, then, besides conflicting with the possibility of *rational*, free choices, it would undermine the value of free will. We cannot be responsible for our characters if there is no character to build. I noted at the outset that this extreme view has been generally rejected among psychologists, but reviewing how the philosophical debate went between the challengers and the defenders of robust character traits highlights problems in constructing and evaluating experiments involving morally significant choices.

---

3 John Martin Fischer and Mark Ravizza S.J., *Responsibility and Control: A Theory of Moral Responsibility* (Cambridge, UK: Cambridge University Press, 1998).

Evidence for Situationism

In 1999, Gilbert Harman published a paper, "Moral philosophy meets social psychology: Virtue ethics and the fundamental attribution error", which expressed the extreme situationist position and marked the entrance of philosophers into the situationist discussion.[4] Harman, citing several experiments purporting to show that it is the situation that explains behavior, writes,

> It seems that ordinary attributions of character traits to people are often deeply misguided and it may even be the case that there is no such thing as character, no ordinary character traits of the sort people think there are, none of the usual moral virtues and vices.[5]

Shortly thereafter, John M. Doris published the most significant philosophical contribution to the situationist debate, *Lack of Character*.[6] Here I offer a brief outline of Doris's explication of character traits and review his evidence for the claim that belief in such traits is misguided.

Doris proposes the following principle regarding evidence of a character trait: "If a person possesses a trait, that person will engage in trait-relevant behaviors in trait-relevant eliciting conditions with markedly above chance probability p."[7] Doris grants that there is a problem with the conditional in that it is conceivable that a person might have a trait which is often masked by another trait. He allows that "people do say things like 'he's really a nice person, he's just a little shy' by way of excusing the socially uneasy". But he does not find this a serious impediment to the case he is trying to make. "I'm doing moral psychology, not metaphysics; my interest is not in conceptual analysis but in the evidential standards governing trait attribution."[8]

Doris's target is the globalist view of character associated with Aristotle and his followers, understanding character traits to be consistent, stable, and related to similar traits.[9] In determining what sort of evidence would count in favor of there being robust character traits, Doris notes that consistent behavior in situations where almost everyone could be expected to behave that way would not provide evidence of a character trait. Rather, "it is *individuating* behavior – behavior that is outside the population norm

---

4 Gilbert Harman, "Moral Philosophy Meets Social Psychology: Virtue Ethics and the Fundamental Attribution Error", *Proceedings of the Aristotelian Society* 99 (1999): 315–32.
5 Harman (1999): 316.
6 John M. Doris, *Lack of Character: Personality and Moral Behavior* (Cambridge, UK: Cambridge University Press, 2002).
7 Doris (2002): 19.
8 Doris (2002): 16.
9 Doris (2002): 22.

for a situation – that counts as evidence for trait attribution". Doris does not dispute that, in principle, everyone in a population might have the same trait. Nonetheless,

> Individuation is evidentially significant because where trait-relevant behavior varies markedly in a situation, there is reason to think that the situation is less than optimally conducive to that behavior. Situations of this sort are *diagnostic*: unfavorable enough to trait-relevant behavior that such behavior seems better explained by reference to individual dispositions than by reference to situational facilitators.[10]

Furthermore, if we find that people in situations where we would have assumed that certain trait-relevant behavior would be elicited do not behave in the trait-relevant way, that is evidence that these people do not possess the trait in question. And if we find that their non-trait-relevant behavior seems to be significantly influenced by minor elements in the situation, that supports the situationist conclusion.

Doris chooses compassion as the trait he will examine. Although subsequent discussion in the philosophical literature highlights problems with this choice, Doris cites good reasons for his selection. Compassion is widely considered a core virtue. Noting that Aristotle does not discuss compassion per se, Doris nonetheless argues that various things Aristotle does say suggest that he would agree that it is important. Certainly, most contemporary philosophers who believe in virtues are likely to place compassion, under some description, among the virtues that lie at the center of their ethical systems. Moreover, compassion is not a "heroic" virtue that one would look for only in extreme situations and from unusually virtuous people. There seem to be many instances in ordinary life where moderately virtuous people could be expected to exercise compassion if, indeed, they possessed that virtue. Fortunately, as Doris explains, there has been a great deal of empirical work done on compassion-relevant behavior. Thus, compassion is an appropriate virtue to examine if the concern is empirical evidence related to moral character.[11]

As it turns out, many people do not exercise compassion in situations where one would have expected that they would. Doris recounts both experimental evidence and historical events, such as the case of Catherine Genovese, who was stabbed to death as her neighbors listened to her scream. Doris reports that of 38 witnesses only one called the police, at which point it was too late to save her life. He writes that

---

10 Doris (2002): 19.
11 Doris (2002): 29–30.

> failures to behave compassionately when doing so is appropriate and not unduly costly are evidence against attributing the trait... The experimental and historical records reveal that such omissions, as well as similarly incompassionate actions, commonly occur where the obstacles to compassion and the pressures to incompassion seem remarkably slight: the failures are disproportionate to the pressures.[12]

Doris holds that the experimental evidence derived from studies focused on compassionate behavior should lead us to believe that it is very trivial elements in a situation that have a profound influence on what people do.

> The disproportionate impact of these 'insubstantial' situational factors presses charges of empirical inadequacy against characterological moral psychology: If dispositional structures were typically so robust as familiar conceptions of character and personality lead one to believe, insubstantial factors would not so frequently have such impressive effects.[13]

Here I will outline a few of the experiments that Doris presents. These experiments – perhaps because Doris cites them – are often discussed in the literature. In the present chapter, it will be sufficient to review only these experiments and only as they are presented in the philosophical literature. In Chapter 6, I will go more deeply into the original reports of some of the experiments since the details can be relevant in considering how these past experiments can shed light on moral and practical issues that may be involved in the study of moral choices in the future.

Most famous are the Milgram "obedience" experiments.[14] In the middle of the twentieth century, in Germany under the National Socialists, many apparently otherwise ordinary people engaged in morally atrocious behavior which they sometimes later attempted to excuse or explain as "just following orders". This dark chapter inspired the question of whether and how ordinary U.S. citizens might be led to do immoral deeds in obedience to a recognized authority. Stanley Milgram devised a series of experiments to test for an answer.[15] The experiments were conducted between 1960 and

---

12 Doris (2002): 29.
13 Doris (2002): 28.
14 Milgram (1963); Stanley Milgram, *Obedience to Authority* (New York: Harper and Row, 1974).
15 The following is a rough and shortened paraphrase of Doris's description of the experiments (Doris (2002): 39–43). There is reason to believe that Doris's sketch, drawn mainly from Milgram (1974), reproduces some inaccuracies and lacunae in Milgram's description of his experiments. (See Gina Perry, *Behind the Shock Machine: The Untold Story of the Notorious Milgram Psychology Experiments* (New York: The New Press, 2013).

1963 with around 1,000 subjects drawn from different backgrounds. There were a number of variants on the experiment as detailed by Milgram in his *Obedience to Authority* published in 1974. Doris reports Experiment 5, and many of the iterations followed somewhat similar patterns: The subject initially becomes involved by answering an ad in a newspaper or direct mailing. When he arrives at the lab, he is met by the supposed "experimenter", who explains that the subject will be participating in a study to test the effect of punishment on learning. He is introduced to a "fellow subject", who is actually a confederate. A drawing is held to determine who will play the "teacher" and who will play the "learner", but the drawing is rigged. The subject inevitably plays the teacher who will be administering the punishment when the learner gives incorrect answers in a word-association test. The "experimenter" explains that the punishment will be an electric shock which, though painful, will not cause the learner any permanent damage. The subject is given an electric shock to demonstrate. The teacher watches the learner being strapped to a chair and then is led to the "shock generator" in a separate room from which (in Experiment 5) he can hear but not see the learner, and the experiment begins.

The teacher administers the word-association test and at each wrong answer from the unseen learner gives an electric shock – that is what the subject believes, although actually no shock is being given. The confederate learner follows a pre-established schedule of incorrect answers, and the intensity level of the (supposed) shocks increases with each wrong answer. If the subject expresses concern over the proceedings or balks at continuing, the experimenter follows a set script of verbal prods, saying firmly but politely (1) "Please continue", (2) "The experiment requires that you continue", (3) "It is absolutely essential that you continue", and (4) "You have no other choice, you *must* go on". The experimenter can also repeat the assurance that the shocks do not cause permanent damage. If the subject refuses to continue after receiving verbal prod (4), then the experiment is terminated and the subject is labelled "disobedient".

Meanwhile, as the intensity of the (supposed) shocks is increased by incremental steps from a starting point of "slight shock", the learner – actually a recording – follows a script of increasing protests and complaints. In the "Moderate Shock" level, the teacher hears the learner go "Ugh!" and then "Ugh! This really hurts." In the "Strong Shock" level, the learner complains of heart trouble, asks to be let out, and shouts that he is in pain. In the "Very Strong Shock" level, the learner demands to be let out of the experiment. At "Intense" and "Extreme Intensity Shock", the learner's demands to be let out are punctuated by "agonized screams". Finally, at the upper end of "Extreme Intensity Shock" and throughout the highest level, "Danger: Severe Shock", there is silence. The experimenter tells the teacher to treat the lack of response as an incorrect answer and to continue the punishment.

In this iteration of the experiment involving 40 subjects, one became disobedient at the second "Ugh!" and six refused to continue past the "Strong Shock" point where the learner complained about his heart and asked to end the experiment. One or two disobeyed at each level as the intensity of the supposed shock increased, but 26 (i.e., 65%) stuck with the experiment to the bitter end. And this iteration of the experiment did not represent an anomalous outcome. Doris notes that, as Milgram reported, the obedient subjects were not sadists, happily torturing a fellow human being, or blindly obedient, not concerned about the pain they were inflicting. No, the subjects were often in agony over the "requirement" to continue to shock the learner and yet so many continued to the upper limit on the "Danger" level. (The ethical implications of putting the subjects in the Milgram experiments into such an agonizing position will be discussed in Chapter 6.)

Doris raises the possibility that many of the subjects did not really believe that they were administering actual shocks, but points out that all the evidence is in favor of most subjects believing they were shocking the learner. He concludes that the Milgram experiments support situationism.

> What the experiments do highlight, once more, is the power of the situation; the majority of subjects were willing to torture another individual to what seemed the door of death without any more direct pressure than the polite insistence of the experimenter.[16]

The Milgram experiments are striking in that, as the situationist would have it, a relatively minor element in the situation – the firm but polite instruction from the experimenter – produces not just a failure of compassion but also outright cruelty. The Milgram experiments involve subjects who do seem to be making moral choices and so the Problem of Translation regarding the Object of Study seems to be avoided. (That is how it looks prima facie, but a closer look may undermine this impression.) And the subjects are ordinary people who answered an ad, so the Problem of Translation does not arise concerning the pool of subjects. It is the case that Milgram's subjects are in an unusual situation in that they are in a lab, and so the Problem of Translation Regarding the Situation is a concern, but Doris reviews other experiments where the designed situations come much closer to mimicking everyday life. These experiments do not elicit cruelty, but Doris argues that they do demonstrate that subjects' exhibiting compassionate or non-compassionate behavior is due to minor elements of the situation.

In the "Good Samaritan" experiments, subjects were Princeton Theological Seminary students invited to participate in a study of religious

---

16 Doris (2002): 42.

education and vocations.[17] Students/subjects filled out a questionnaire in one building and then were told to go to a second building where they were to give an oral presentation. They were told, as they prepared to depart for the second building, that the condition was one of "high hurry", "medium hurry", or "low hurry". Between the first and second buildings was a confederate slumped in a doorway portraying someone possibly in distress. The point of the experiment was to see how the instruction concerning the "hurry" condition might affect whether or not the subject would stop to help the person apparently in need. Nothing of great importance was hanging on the student's delivering the oral presentation, nor did the student have any special relationship with the experimenter – they had just met. Yet the hurry level exercised significant influence on whether or not the subject stopped to help the person apparently in distress. When the hurry level was "low", 63% stopped; 45% stopped when the hurry level was "medium". But when the hurry level was "high", only 10% of the seminarians stopped to help. Doris assesses the experiments:

> It is difficult to resist situationist conclusions. Subjects were hurried but certainly not coerced. ... Once again, there is the appearance of disproportion; in this case the demands of punctuality seem rather slight compared with the ethical demand to at least check on the condition of the confederate.[18]

Another sort of experiment examines the impact of being in a group on helping behavior. There have been numerous studies on this issue; experiments have been configured in different ways, and explanations for failing to help have differed with the nature of the experiments. In one experiment cited by Doris, college students believe they are participating in a marketing research survey.[19] A young woman gives them the survey, then, disappearing behind a curtain, apparently falls and screams – the falling and screaming are actually a recording. When subjects were alone, 70% offered help, but only 7% did so if in the presence of a confederate who was unresponsive to the apparently injured woman. In explaining their failure to help, subjects reported being unsure about what to do or having decided that the situation was not serious.

---

17 J.M. Darley and C.D. Batson, "From Jerusalem to Jericho: A Study of Situational and Dispositional Variables in Helping Behavior", *Journal of Personality and Social Psychology* 27(1973): 100–8. The following is a rough paraphrase of Doris's description of the experiments (Doris (2002): 33–4).
18 Doris (2002): 34.
19 B. Latane and J. Rodin, "A Lady in Distress: Inhibiting Effects of Friends and Strangers on Bystander Intervention", *Journal of Experimental social Psychology* 5 (1969): 189–202; Doris (2002): 32–3.

A somewhat different helping experiment asked for participants to discuss the difficulties for college students in urban environments. [20] Either subjects are alone in a cubicle (ostensibly for the sake of privacy) speaking to a single other student (actually a confederate) or the subject is isolated in a cubicle but believes himself in communication with six others as part of a group of equally isolated participants (actually a confederate and five recorded "participants"). In both scenarios, the subject hears the confederate supposedly having a seizure. In the case where the subject believed that the situation involved just him and the one having the seizure, 100% intervened. In the case where the subject believed that there was a group, only 62% did so. Here Doris notes that the researchers suggest that the explanation has to do with "diffusion of responsibility". Doris writes, "The operative processes are doubtless complicated, but one general implication of the group effect studies seems fairly clear: Mild social pressures can result in neglect of apparently serious ethical demands."[21]

Finally, we can look at an experiment that presents an even less dramatic situation than those involving apparent falls and seizures. There is a great deal of evidence that one's mood affects one's decisions, and a minor element in the situation can (it is argued) elevate one's mood and significantly influence one's choices and behavior. The experiment Doris cites involves the experimenters sometimes placing a dime in the coin return of a phone booth in a shopping mall.[22] (The experiment was done when lots of people used phone booths and a dime was worth something.) As the caller leaves the phone booth, a confederate in the experiment drops a stack of papers. The question is: Will finding the dime increase the probability that the caller will help pick up the papers? The answer seems to be a resounding "Yes!" Of 16 callers who found the dime, 14 helped pick up the papers. Of 25 callers who did not find a dime, only one helped pick up the papers. Again, the compassionate behavior seems to be significantly influenced by the minor situational element, suggesting that it was the dime, rather than the character of the callers, that explains their behavior.

The mundaneness of the situation is noteworthy in this experiment for several reasons. Doris notes that compassionate behavior in the case of helping to pick up the papers could hardly be considered heroic – one is not, for example, called upon to help someone who may be seriously hurt or suffering – and this suggests that most people do not have even a very modest disposition toward compassion. Moreover, the situational element, the finding of the dime, is the sort of thing one might barely notice or

---

20 B. Latane and J.M. Darley, *The Unresponsive Bystander: Why Doesn't He Help?* (New York: Appleton-Century-Crofts (1970): 95–101; Doris (2002): 33.
21 Doris (2002): 33.
22 A.M. Isen and P.F. Levin, "Effect of Feeling Good on Helping: Cookies and Kindness", *Journal of Personality and Social Psychology* 21 (1972): 384–8; Doris (2002): 30–2.

remember as one goes about one's daily activities. Doris writes that "[t]he crucial observation is not that mood influences behavior – no surprise there – but just how unobtrusive the stimuli that induce the determinative moods can be".[23] In this experiment perhaps more than in the others cited, one can easily suppose that the agents made no conscious connection at all between the operant situational element (in this case, finding the dime) and the action upon which they decided (in this case, helping to pick up the papers). I would add that the ordinariness of the dropping of the papers may be relevant to how we assess the conclusions of the experiment. In unusual situations, such as an unseen woman suddenly (apparently) falling and screaming, our thought and decision-making processes may be clouded by the unusual situation into which we are thrust. But someone dropping papers is pretty ordinary and shouldn't cause any cognitive confusion.

None of these experiments provides evidence for local causal determinism (or for indeterminism) as human agents choose and act. But they do raise concerns about the extent to which we are able to assess our options and act for reasons, and they could cast doubt upon whether or not human beings can form their characters by their choices and actions if, as Doris has argued, we do not have characters to form. Thus, it will be worthwhile to survey the philosophical responses in connection with the issue of acting for reasons and with the issue of character. Examining the situationist experiments, and debate over how they should be interpreted, can help us think about moral and practical problems related to the construction and interpretation of future experiments relevant to free will.

The Challenge to Reasons-Responsiveness

If it is shown that many or most of our decisions are based on reasons that are woefully inadequate to justify or explain those decisions or on reasons that are irrelevant to our decisions or that our decisions are often very significantly influenced by elements in our surroundings that we barely notice, such that we cannot even label them "reasons", this proves a challenge to responsibility-grounding free will. In order to make an LFMC, the agent has to be able to deliberate about the options with which he is confronted. This introduces the Problem of Description; what does it mean to have the capacity to act for a reason? And what constitutes a reason, in any case? One response that appears in the philosophical literature argues that an agent can be properly held responsible for an action even if the mental buildup to the action does not rise to the level of a careful weighing of the proper reasons. What counts regarding responsibility for a particular choice and action, so this response goes, is that the agent have the *capacities* to recognize and respond appropriately to reasons, even if the situation

---

23 Doris (2002): 30.

in question is such that the agent does not exercise these capacities. Possibly, this response continues, the capacities admit of degrees, and likely the evidence of the situationist experiments shows that agents are less reasons-responsive than we would like to think. Nonetheless, the subjects in the situationist experiments were probably *capable* of responding properly to reasons and so can bear the moral responsibility for their actions.[24]

Markus Schlosser notes that if the issue is subjects having the *ability* to recognize and respond to reasons, the very fact that they are able to decide to participate and show up for the experiments would seem to prove a certain degree of reasons-responsiveness.[25] Marcela Herdova and Stephen Kearns point out that in the Good Samaritan experiment a majority of the students who had received the instructions with the "low hurry" condition did stop to help the confederate. These students had the capacity – exercised in a situation which did not put the "high hurry" pressure on them – to recognize and respond appropriately to reasons. That being the case, it is plausible to think, they argue, that the "high hurry" students *had the ability* to recognize and respond appropriately to reasons. Both the "high hurry" students and the "low hurry" students might have been only moderately reasons-responsive as agents, and the "high hurry" situation was enough to mute the exercise of the capacities in the students who failed to help, but since the capacities to recognize and respond to reasons were there, those unhelpful students can properly be blamed.[26] Even though the agent's choices and actions are not the result of assessing and responding to reasons appropriately, the agent can be responsible.

The discussion of this possible defense of the reasons-responsiveness, and hence responsibility, of subjects in the situationist experiments takes place largely within a compatibilist context (or at least a context that allows compatibilism). That context permits the possibility that, owing to the situation, the subjects inevitably chose what they chose. In the particular situation, their choices may have been locally causally determined. Nevertheless, they are responsible in that they possessed the appropriate capacity, although they could not exercise it.[27] The account of free will I am working with does allow that there are choices and actions for which

---

24 Michael McKenna and Brandon Warmke, "Does Situationism Threaten Free Will and Moral Responsibility?", *Journal of Moral Philosophy* 14 (2017): 698–733.
25 Markus E. Schlosser, "Conscious Will, Reason-Responsiveness, and Moral Responsibility", *Journal of Ethics* 17 (2013): 205–32, at 230.
26 Marcela Herdova and Stephen Kearns, "This is a Tricky Situation: Situationism and Reasons-Responsiveness", *Journal of Ethics* 21 (2017): 151–83, at 161.
27 Herdova and Kearns discuss the debate between Fischer and Ravizza and Manuel Vargas, where the latter relativizes the capacity to the situation. They hold that Vargas might conclude that the subjects in the situationist experiments are not responsible, while Fischer and Ravizza would conclude that they are. Herdova and Kearns defend Fischer and Ravizza's side of the question (Herdova and Kearns (2017): 173–8).

the agent can be held morally responsible but which are not immediately preceded by a rational and informed analysis of the options. If an agent's decision is determined by the agent's character, which was formed by LFMCs, then the agent is responsible for the character-determined choices.[28] But this responsibility must be traceable to the earlier choices. Thus, the agent must, at some point in his career, have made some LFMCs. And that requires having been in the torn condition, able to assess his morally significant options, at least to some extent, and choose one or the other *a se*. Thus, the agent must, sometimes, be in a position where he does consciously recognize and evaluate his motivating reasons. His reasons must be occurrent and "visible" to the agent. If this is how human free will is understood, then pointing to unexercised and possibly unexercis*able* capacities does not constitute an adequate response to the threat posed by situationism to reasons-responsiveness.

Another issue of clarification arises regarding what constitute reasons. Much of the literature regarding situationism and reasons-responsiveness suggests that only *good* reasons are reasons; the morally preferable reason is the appropriate reason, and the subject apparently failing to act upon it has failed to be reasons-responsive. So, the students in the Good Samaritan experiment who are in the "low hurry" situation (and stopped to help) can be described as exercising their moderately reasons-responsive capacity whereas the students in the "high hurry" situation who failed to help were not reasons-responsive. This is not the picture that emerges from my description of an LFMC where the assumption is that the agent is consciously considering competing live options, such that both the morally better and morally worse options have their attractions. Suppose, for the sake of argument – I will question this supposition below and offer some defense for the unhelpful seminarians – that at least some of the students in the "high hurry" condition who saw the person apparently in need of help, but who went on by, debated within themselves along these lines:

> That person might need my help, and I ought to help those in need. I feel drawn to help that person. On the other hand, as an important student at Princeton Theological Seminary it is critical to my self-esteem that I always present a superior face to the world and that includes never being late.

Suppose, further, that these students recognized (on some level) that helping was the morally better course and that hurrying on (as self-centered)

---

28 Some philosophers include thoughtless acts and omissions in the scope of what an agent can be responsible for. I leave that an open question and focus on the choices and acts for which one is clearly responsible, if one is responsible for any choices and acts at all.

was the morally worse course. If this was how the students assessed their options, then each option had a certain appeal. Although they chose the worse course of action, their choice was not irrational.[29] They acted upon their considered reasons. It was just that they chose to follow their reasons for doing something morally wrong. This would not undermine Doris's thesis that few (if any) people possess a robust virtue of compassion. But if the question is whether or not the Good Samaritan experiment shows that people often fail to choose and act for considered reasons (unless we assume that there are not reasons for wicked choices), it is possible to interpret the experiment as leaving the reasoning of the students intact.

I do not believe we can offer the same sort of analysis for the dime in the phone booth. Here we might allow that most people's default position is to be mildly thoughtless unless prompted to be otherwise by a mood enhancer. The way the experiment is set up suggests that the subjects had almost no time to make a choice to help or not and so perhaps they didn't find themselves in the torn condition at all. In this case, they did not "act for reasons". Are they blameworthy when they failed to help and praiseworthy for helping? On my account, that is a hard question to answer. If they didn't actually make a decision, then they cannot be praised for *choosing* well or blamed for *choosing* badly. But intuition suggests that, in general, when people help that is praiseworthy and when they don't that is blameworthy. The intuition can be explained – on the theory of free will I am working with – by noting that split-second decisions may flow from one's character (*pace* situationism) constructed over the years. And, prima facie, we may judge that adults ought to have worked on developing a helpful character and so are praiseworthy when they help and blameworthy when they fail to do so, even if they do not explicitly deliberate and choose.

The evidence of the dime experiment suggests that most people occupy an intermediate state of character, but we just don't know how responsible a stranger in a shopping mall is for their character. The subjects in the dime experiment were never debriefed, so we don't know what their thinking about the situation was. The business of life is hard and perhaps for many people the "mildly thoughtless" setting represents a trajectory toward the good. Perhaps some of those who did not find a dime would have cursed or laughed at the woman dropping the papers a year ago but have practiced enough patience since then to just walk on by. If we understood their history, we might not consider them blameworthy. Perhaps the fact that merely finding a dime caused many people to help shows that the "mildly thoughtless" setting is actually pushing the needle toward the good side of

---

29 If salvation is the ultimate goal for these seminarians, then (in the final analysis) it is irrational, as against one's ultimate best interests, to make the immoral choice. But on the proximate level, where the students are not considering final destinies, their choice to knowingly do the wrong thing seems to be rational.

the virtue scale, and a lot of people are better than situationism suggests. (These are simply suggestions to point out that the conclusions from this experiment can be viewed from different angles.) The bottom line here is that subjects may not have acted for good reasons at the time and yet may be responsible for split-second decisions in certain circumstances. One point to emphasize is that the decisions made in the Good Samaritan situation seem less "immediate" than in the dime experiment. One supposes that it took a little while to approach and then pass the person apparently in need of help. So, possibly the Good Samaritan decisions were of a different nature than the decisions – if indeed there were decisions – made in the dime experiment, and questions about reasons-responsiveness and responsibility need to be approached differently in the two cases.

Another concern related to reasons-responsiveness is that a good case can be made that the defenders of situationism frequently downplay the power of the reasons at work. The situationist thesis requires the claim that it is insubstantial factors in the situation that produce behavior. But often what the situationist takes to be an insubstantial factor may appear to be very significant to the subject. This point offers another version of the Problem of Perspective. In discussing the Libet experiments, I noted that the experimenters may have failed to appreciate the various elements involved in the task that the subjects were to perform as these tasks appeared to the subject. In the case of the situationist experiments, the problem is that the experimenters and those (like Doris) interpreting the data may have failed to understand how the options looked to the subjects. At least in some cases, even if the subjects are not operating with *good* reasons (i.e. reasons embracing generally accepted values), they are operating with *understandable* reasons. We can see how the subjects could nonculpably hold the views they may have held that prompted their behavior.

This is a point that has been made in the literature, but I believe it can be developed more fully and made even more forceful.[30] This critique is especially relevant to the Milgram experiments. Doris holds that these experiments support situationism since so many of the subjects were "willing to torture another individual to what seemed the door of death without any more direct pressure than the polite insistence of the experimenter".[31] But it is very clear, as Doris himself notes, that many of the subjects found this "pressure" to be agonizingly powerful. Milgram reports that subjects were often observed to "sweat, tremble, stutter, bite their lips, groan, and dig their fingernails into their flesh".[32] He quotes an onlooker,

---

30 John Sabini and Maury Silver, "Lack of Character? Situationism Critiqued", *Ethics* 115 (2005): 535–62; E.J. Wielenberg, "Saving Character", *Ethical Theory and Moral Practice* 9 (2006): 461–91.
31 Doris (2002): 42.
32 Milgram (1963): 375.

I observed a mature and initially poised businessman enter the laboratory smiling and confident. Within 20 minutes he was reduced to a twitching, stuttering wreck, who was rapidly approaching a point of nervous collapse. He constantly pulled on his earlobe and twisted his hands. At one point he pushed his fist into his forehead and muttered: "Oh God, let's stop it." And yet he continued to respond to every word of the experimenter and obeyed to the end.[33]

Subjects sometimes suffered uncontrollable seizures. "On one occasion we observed a seizure so violently convulsive that it was necessary to call a halt to the experiment."[34]

The subjects in the Milgram experiments obviously did not find the pressure "insubstantial". Those who moved to the higher levels of shocks were deeply distressed. Is it possible, if we make a point of trying to see the situation from the subject's perspective, to offer an explanation of their behavior which ascribes to them understandable reasons for doing what they did? Doris grants that, at least for some of Milgram's experiments, the fact that they were conducted under the auspices of Yale might have produced obedience "through institutional intimidation". Beyond being intimidated, subjects might have reasonably trusted that an institution of the stature of Yale would not endorse scientific experiments that could seriously harm someone needlessly. But apparently the results of the experiments were roughly the same when conducted outside of the Yale setting.[35] More important is the fact that the authority in question in the Milgram experiments claims the backing of science. In modern American culture, many people exhibit an almost religious faith in the goals and methods of science and in the integrity, wisdom, and beneficence of scientists. To disagree with a scientist or to assert that scientists may be doing something wrong is to declare yourself a benighted ignoramus. The obedients in the Milgram experiments were, as far as they knew, obeying not just any authority but a scientific authority – and a scientific authority who had likely already conducted numerous such experiments – thus someone whom they had the strongest reasons to trust.

In recent American history, there have been debates over allowing scientists to engage in activities that some have found morally objectionable – cloning human beings, for example. And two sorts of arguments have been adduced to defend the activities. There is the consequentialist argument that the worrisome activities are morally justifiable by the greater good that will be produced. But sometimes one hears this sort of claim: "Yes, there are moral concerns, but if we don't allow it, scientific progress will be

33 Milgram (1963): 377.
34 Milgram (1963): 375.
35 Doris (2002): 49.

impeded". This is the sort of position that the student of history – including and especially the history of the regime that inspired the Milgram experiments – finds chilling.[36] On the face of it, the claim seems to be that scientific progress is such a great good that it should trump moral concerns. But perhaps it isn't meant this way. Perhaps the underlying assumption is that scientific progress will be so beneficial that, in the long run, the future benefits would outweigh the present harms. So, perhaps the apparent "primacy of science" claim was really a version of the consequentialist argument. In any case, this position, that the advancement of science should override (some people's) moral concerns, is a position that one hears, mutatis mutandis, regarding many public issues. Thus, it is not far-fetched to suppose that the obedients in the Milgram experiments might have imbibed a faith in science and scientists from the surrounding culture. Then they would understand it as perhaps even a *moral* duty to continue with the experiments in the interest of ultimately serving the greater good.

Moreover, in introducing subjects to the ostensible "learning" experiment, the experimenter makes a point that punishment is often seen as a teaching tool (e.g. with parents spanking children). But, says the experimenter, "we know very little about the effect of punishment on learning, because almost no truly scientific studies have been made of it in human beings".[37] So, the good to be achieved by the experiments is not just some unknown future benefits but possibly the sparing of generations of children from pointless pain. Thus, in addition to valuing science in a general way, the subjects may be hoping that this particular scientific exercise will yield a significant and specific benefit. This thesis provides a more plausible explanation for their behavior than just that, at great cost to themselves, they were brutely subservient to authority because of the situation but for no good reason at all.

The power of the subject's commitment to science is a theme which Milgram himself emphasizes.[38] Indeed, it is noteworthy that neither Doris nor Harman discusses Milgram's own theoretical analysis of the behavior of his subjects. The philosophers extract very different conclusions than does the scientist, demonstrating the (obvious) point that experiments are open to multiple interpretations. Milgram proposes that human beings are, in the right circumstances, prone to undergo an "agentic shift" – that is, to come to understand themselves as the agents of an appropriate authority

---

36 Ridiculous as Nazi ideology may look in hindsight, in the first half of the twentieth century National Socialism claimed for itself the titles of "progressive" and "scientific". And many educated people, including many educated people in the United States and the United Kingdom, bought the advertising. *The Prime of Miss Jean Brodie*, a novel by Muriel Spark, published in 1961, offers a fascinating insight into the appeal of fascism.
37 Milgram (1974): 18.
38 Milgram (1974): 9, 59, 63–4, 70, 142–3, 176.

rather than as independently acting and hence responsible actors.[39] Prima facie, this might look to be yet another attack on free will, but Milgram does not see it that way. For one thing, the agentic shift admits of degrees. It is true that some people in some circumstances may be unable to resist the demands of the authority to which they have committed, but others may be capable of rejecting the authority, even as they feel some pull to obey.[40]

More importantly for the question of reasons-responsiveness and the Problem of Perspective, Milgram holds that one does not undergo the agentic shift unless one shares (or comes to share) the ideological stance of the authority to which one is willingly obedient.[41] In the case of his own experiments, he believes that what allows for the agentic shift (among other criteria) is that the subjects and the experimenters share a commitment to the value of science. The subjects will have imbibed this position from the culture, but the experimenters also make a point of explaining the value of the (faux) memory experiment. If there is indeed an agentic shift, it does not destroy or negate the subject's reasons for obeying. The reasons for engaging in the experiment to begin with help to prompt the shift, and the subject shares these reasons with the authority. It is possible that, once confronted with the authority, some subjects could not "detach" and disobey. In this case, their deliberations and decision-making (if not instances of morally significant choices) may have occurred before they ever entered the lab, at the point when they decided to answer the newspaper ad and show up to be interviewed for the experiment.

This suggests one pattern that the Problem of Focus can follow: most of the meaningful choices relevant to experiments involving free will may have taken place before the participant enters the lab, so if the experimenters hope to study phenomena relevant to free will, they are looking at the wrong point in the process. With the Libet experiments, it is often noted that the deliberation and decision-making occur before the experiments begin, when the subject is deciding to participate. The same holds true of many of the experiments which Wegner takes to show the lack of conscious will: Surely, part of the history of the subject's showing up at the lab for the experiment involves having decided to do so. If Milgram is right about the agentic shift, it may well be that some subjects, once in the lab, were literally unable to disobey the authority to whom they had committed. But this would be a special situation regarding a special relationship to

---

39 Milgram (1974): 123–34. David Kaposi writes that "Milgram's *retroactive* explanation and reference to a supposed 'agentic state' have always been considered the weakest points of his project". He notes that this assessment is shared by "both those sympathetic and critical to Milgram's account in general" (David Kaposi, "The Resistance Experiments: Morality, Authority and Obedience in Stanley Milgram's Account", *Journal for the Theory of Social Behaviour* 47 (2017): 382–401, at 385).
40 Milgram (1974): 197.
41 Milgram (1974): 142–3.

authority. It is not evidence of any overall lack of free will for human agents. Milgram himself insists on this: The relevant choices may come well before one finds oneself obeying an authority, at an earlier point where one has the option to accept or to reject that authority.[42]

David Kaposi suggests that rather than suffering an "agentic shift", some subjects might simply have felt coerced.[43] Suppose, as Milgram argues, that most of the subjects did indeed believe that a scientist – sometimes backed by the authority and prestige of Yale University – was actually insisting that they go on delivering truly dangerous shocks to a person who might die from them. From that perspective, the subject might cease to view the authority as "legitimate" and come to worry that the experimenter is a criminal – a criminal with whom he, the subject, is effectively alone in the lab. In the presence of an apparently bona fide mad scientist, one might honestly feel threatened and hence not free to stop. (When the experiment is over, the subjects do not say they felt threatened, but that might be a function of their great relief at discovering that they had not shocked someone almost to the point of death.) All of this highlights the importance of trying to understand how the subjects might be viewing their situation.

The case that the subjects in the Milgram experiments were responding to reasons – reasons that they shared with the experimenters – can be underscored when we consider the thought that a good case can be made that those running the Milgram experiments – the confederates and Milgram himself (I have been calling them "the experimenters") – were inflicting serious suffering on the subjects. That is, there is a telling similarity between the behavior of the subjects and that of the experimenters, except that the experimenters delivered actual pain.[44] There is some evidence that Milgram himself recognizes this. Gina Perry reports Milgram arguing with a subject who was being interviewed well after the experiments had taken place. The subject claims not to have believed that he was really shocking someone, his argument being that Yale would not have allowed an experiment which might kill someone to go forward. Milgram's response to this is to note how another subject had said that "this [the experiment itself] is one of the most distressing experiences of his life." And yet Yale allowed the experiment to be carried out.[45]

---

42 Milgram (1974): 199.
43 Kaposi (2017): 395–6.
44 The similarity between the behavior of the subjects and the behavior of the experimenters has been noted in the literature; Diana Baumrind, "Some Thoughts on Ethics of Research: After Reading Milgram's 'Behavioral Study of Obedience'", *American Psychologist* 19 (1964): 421–3, at 422; Diana Baumrind, "Is Milgram's Deceptive Research Ethically Acceptable?", *Theoretical and Applied Ethics* 2 (2013): 1–18, at 7; Steven Patten, "The Case that Milgram Makes", *Philosophical Review* 86 (1977): 350–64; Perry (2013): 215–16, 270, 273, 287.
45 Perry (2013): 224.

True, the actual experiments delivered more psychological suffering than physical pain, but psychological suffering can be enormously painful. And, as Milgram reports, the psychological anguish did often lead the subjects to suffer convulsions and to inflict physical suffering on themselves, such as digging their fingernails into their flesh. Moreover, while each subject was involved in (apparently) inflicting suffering on only one learner, the experimenters inflicted suffering on hundreds of subjects. Presumably, after a number of iterations of the experiment, the experimenters recognized that they would likely be inflicting suffering on the next subject. The subjects did not know at the start of the experiment that they would be inflicting suffering.

If we asked the experimenters "How could you bring yourselves to cause such psychological pain to strangers?", the initial answer would probably be "The subjects agreed to participate in the experiment, they suffered no permanent harm, and it was very important to conduct the experiment in order to gain scientific knowledge." Of course, the subjects did not agree to be subjected to the particular harms which were inflicted on them. And whether or not the subjects suffered permanent harm is debatable. These issues will be taken up in Chapter 6.[46] Here the point is that the experimenters would likely give exactly the reasons for participating in the experiment, and pursuing it to such extreme levels, that the subjects could give. So, a case can be made that the subjects could offer reasons for their behavior and these are the sorts of reasons that are widely accepted. True, those subjects who pursued the experiment to the highest levels were (apparently) inflicting greater harm on the learners than the experimenters were on the subjects. But I will argue in Chapter 6 that the experimenters could well be inflicting significant harm on the subjects, so the difference here is merely one of degree.

The experimenters might try to exonerate themselves by pointing out that the subjects could have stopped the psychological suffering by refusing to go on with the experiment. But, first, that fails to appreciate what should have been obvious to them after a few dozen experiments and that is that the subjects apparently felt *enormous* pressure. Perhaps, as I have suggested, the subjects understood it as a duty to continue with the experiments, or perhaps they were in the grip of Milgram's "agentic shift" or simple fear. In that case, they might have literally been unable to disobey, which makes the inflicting psychological suffering on them rather worse, it seems to me.

---

46 Milgram offers several responses to ethical criticisms. For example, he notes that the majority of the subjects, when questioned after having the hoax explained, said that they were glad to have participated in the experiments (1974: 193–202). However, some of Milgram's responses open him to the charge of misrepresenting the situation (Perry (2013): 216–24).

Moreover, that same point is available to the subject – at least up until the point of the final silence from the learner. In some of the experiments, the learner is apparently not strapped down. The subject hears him (apparently) pounding on the wall.[47] In some, the subject has seen the learner strapped to a chair, but – judging by the scene in Milgram's film *Obedience* and by the photograph in Milgram's 1974 book (page 25) – it's just an office chair. A determined adult could easily overturn it and disconnect those electrodes. (In the film, the learner does in fact free himself from the straps since we see him setting up the recording and we have not seen anyone duck back to undo the straps.)[48] The learner says he wants to stop and he wants to get out, but as far as the subject can judge, there is very little to prevent the learner from removing the electrodes and halting the experiment. (Remember Milgram's quoting the *subject* who continues with the experiment even after saying "Oh God, let's stop it.") And the learner (apparently) keeps on answering the questions in the word-association test even after he has (apparently) been shocked really painfully, says he has a heart condition, and says he wants to get out.

Moreover, David Kaposi notes that careful attention to one of the standardly reproduced transcripts suggests that, from the subject's perspective, it could look like the learner is siding *with* the experimenter who says to continue and *against* the subject who wants to stop. This happens when the subject says they ought to stop and the learner is (apparently) silent, not backing up the subject's requests.[49] The learner is, of course, just a recording which cannot take account of what the subject has to say. But from the subject's perspective, the learner's (apparent) behavior could suggest that he intends to continue in spite of the pain. The subject may assume that the learner, though in pain and (sometimes) asking to get out, plans to stick with the experiment until someone in authority tells him that he can stop. The subject may assume that both he and the learner are doing their duty by suffering in the interests of advancing scientific knowledge. The point, again, is that the *reason* which the experimenter could give to excuse his inflicting greater and greater suffering on the subject can also be given by the subject vis-à-vis the learner.

But here is a possibility to distinguish the experimenter's reasoning concerning harming the subject from the subject's reasoning concerning (apparently) harming the learner. I do not say the experimenter actually

---

47 Milgram (1974): 32.
48 In ABC's *Primetime* segment about Jerry Burger's 2007 recreation of the Milgram experiments (available on YouTube), the subject who is shown makes the point that if the learner had wanted to, he could easily have gotten out of the straps.
49 Kaposi (2017): 391.

had this in mind, but it is possible.[50] Perhaps, as the subject moves upwards on the scale of shocks, the experimenter begins to consider him guilty of immoral behavior. Milgram frequently describes the situation with which he confronts his subjects as one where they must opt between making the morally right choice or obeying the authority which demands they do the wrong thing.[51] So, while the subject is (apparently) inflicting suffering on an *innocent* person, the experimenter's reasons may include the judgment that (in some sense) the suffering of the subject is *deserved*. That would explain why the subject is anguished over administering the shocks while the confederate playing the experimenter maintains his cool and polite demeanor (and Milgram watches silently through a one-way mirror) as the subject begins to convulse.

This suggestion, that the experimenter may hold the subject morally culpable, highlights not only the importance of trying to consider the situation from the subject's perspective but also the importance of being careful in assessing what constitutes a morally responsible choice. It is worthwhile to consider the extent to which the subject ought to be considered guilty of a wicked choice and even whether the subject should be considered guilty at all. If Milgram is right about the agentic shift (or Kaposi is right about the coercive fear), at least some of the subjects may have had no option but to obey. In that case, they were not making morally significant choices. But there is another scenario that would rule out morally significant options, a scenario grounded in an important distinction that was made in Chapter 2. I noted that some important decisions with sweeping consequences may nevertheless be choices of indifference and should not be considered morally significant choices at all. The "Sophie's choice" situation in which one is forced to choose between options that one judges to be equally bad (or equally good) does not constitute the sort of morally significant choice for which free will is crucial. Whichever way one chooses, one is not actually morally blameworthy (or praiseworthy) since one was forced to choose and, as far as the options went, there was no distinction in moral status. Flipping a coin would be an entirely appropriate way to decide the question.

Suppose for the sake of argument that some (or even many) of the subjects in the Milgram experiments assumed a consequentialist argument: the good to be achieved in the long run will outweigh the immediate pain caused to the learner. They could have considered it their duty to continue

---

50 Milgram himself, throughout his 1974 book detailing and analyzing the experiments, is confident that what the obedient subjects are doing is wrong, but his attitude toward them as human beings seems ambivalent. Sometimes they are ordinary people caught up in a terrible situation and sometimes they are little Eichmanns. This would not be inconsistent if Milgram were truly of the opinion that Eichmann wasn't a bad person, but he does not come across as willing to go that far.
51 Milgram (1974): xi, 6–7, 41–3.

with the experiment although it was causing such pain to themselves and (as they believed) to the learners. If that was the case, then the subjects might have judged themselves forced to confront morally equivalent options – options which each involved causing some harm but also doing something morally right. They could continue to do their duty, causing pain to both themselves and (as they believed) the other participant in the experiment, or they could stop the pain of the experiment and fail in their duty to help in the advancement of scientific knowledge – knowledge which might produce outweighing benefits in the future. It is just possible that at least some of the subjects were thinking along these lines. In that case, their choice was a choice of indifference and not a morally significant choice, if by that we mean a choice with moral right on one side and wrong on the other, and they are not blameworthy for opting for obedience over disobedience.[52] So, although the decision in the Milgram experiments to continue to shock or to stop appears, at least from Milgram's point of view, to be a moral decision between morally better and worse behavior, from the subject's perspective it might not be a moral choice at all. In that case – if one hoped to apply Milgram's data to the free will issue – the Problem of Translation Regarding the Object of Study has not been avoided after all.

Here is a different scenario. As they begin to grow uncomfortable administering the higher levels of shock, some subjects want to stop the experiment, recognizing to some extent that it is wrong to cause pain to the learner. But then these subjects think something along these lines: "If I insist that we stop, what will the experimenter think of me? He will probably consider me a benighted ignoramus! I certainly don't want anyone to think that about me!" But this concern about how the experimenter will think of him seems to be self-centered and hardly a good reason to continue to inflict pain. If the subject views his options as continuing to shock or to stop the experiment and be considered stupid, then these clearly seem morally worse and better options, and the subject who continues to shock has made a morally significant choice for the worse.

There are a number of morals to be drawn from these scenarios. One involves the Problem of Description; caution is required to distinguish a morally significant choice from some other type of decision. As I emphasized in Chapter 2, the focus in the free will debate over the centuries has almost always been on morally significant decisions. A judgment between two options of morally equal status is a version of a choice of indifference. Someone could argue that even if it is different from an LFMC, it may be sufficiently LFMC-like that what science can discover about the making of

---

52 Mario F. Morelli makes the point that Milgram's subjects might have viewed their options as two, opposing moral claims; "Milgram's Dilemma of Obedience", *Metaphilosophy* 14 (1983): 183–9, at 187–8.

the judgment can be translated to the morally significant choice. But, given my argument in Chapter 1 that the burden of proof lies with the one who would deny free will, if the situationist wants to use these possible choices of indifference as evidence for his position, he will have to make the case that translation is appropriate.

A second point is that in both scenarios the subjects choose for reasons, although only in the first – on the assumption that the consequentialist argument is plausible – could they be considered good reasons. Finally, both scenarios illustrate the point that, contrary to what the situationist holds, the elements that produce the behavior may be very substantial indeed, at least when seen from the subject's perspective. Even the desire not to be considered a fool – although surely no *philosopher* would let that override a perceived moral duty – can be extremely powerful.

The situationist does have a final move to make in defending the thought that the Milgram experiments support situationism. I have offered the argument that if the experimenters in the Milgram experiments can appeal to understandable and perhaps even powerful reasons for their behavior – if they are not just responding to their situation – then the same can be said for the subjects, and Milgram's data do not provide evidence for situationism. But in response the situationist is free to stick to his guns and negate the consequent: The behavior of Milgram's subjects shows that people simply respond to the situations in which they find themselves and the same goes for the experimenters. But this would be a difficult move to defend. First, the experimenters – especially Milgram – devoted a great deal of thought, time, and effort to *constructing* the situation. It seems bizarre to hold that they are the pawns of their own creation. Second, if the experimenters are not engaged in methodical and well-thought-out behavior – behavior driven by understandable (if not good) reasons – then the experiments which are constituted by that behavior are not trustworthy. If the conducting and analysis of the experiments by the experimenters are ultimately just people responding non-rationally to their situation, then we cannot suppose that they provide the evidence that the situationist holds that they provide.

The Problem of Self-Refutation arises vis-à-vis the situationist's interpretation of the data. The problem is similar to that discussed in the previous chapter regarding Wegner's claim that people's behavior is not caused by their consciously willing it: If, as Wegner's argument entails, conscious intentions are not guiding the behavior of those who believe themselves to be conducting experiments, then they have not actually engaged in conducting experiments since (by definition) an experiment requires goal-directed actions. The situationist claim that scientific evidence shows that people's behavior is not based on reasons but rather is the result of minor elements in their situations would certainly conflict with any standard theory of human freedom. But it also conflicts with the claim that people are capable of conducting experiments and gathering evidence. Thus, the position is self-refuting. If it is granted that the behavior of the experimenters in the Milgram experiments is similar to the behavior of the subjects, the more plausible conclusion is that the subjects may have good reasons for their behavior, and the situationist's claim that they are manipulated by *insignificant* elements in their situation is not supported.

I do not believe this point about the power of the situational element when seen from the perspective of the subject can be made regarding the dime experiment (though more on the dime experiment below), but with the Good Samaritan and with the Lady in Distress (and other experiments dealing with the group effect), it may be that situationists systematically downplay what constitutes a very powerful pressure from the point of view of the subject. Perhaps it shouldn't be, but it is. Take the seminarians in the "high hurry" condition. They are attending Princeton Theological Seminary, sure evidence that from childhood they have absorbed and practiced the academic virtues of being punctual and following instructions superlatively. To fail to be punctual and follow instructions might well be extremely difficult for such a person. (Here the Problem of Translation could arise regarding the pool of subjects.) Perhaps they concentrated so hard on their need to arrive on time that they failed to notice the person apparently in need of help, or if in some sense they "saw" him, the awareness of the situation did not rise to the level of deliberation and so no choice was made.[53] It would be difficult to construct an interpretation of the Good Samaritan case in which the student does recognize that there is a person apparently in need of help where failing to help could be anything but wrong. (The confederate did not, apparently, present a threatening appearance, which might justify not helping.) But those who failed to help may have had reasons (from their perspective, *powerful* reasons) not to help.

A similar point can be made about the group studies. The evidence seems clear that people are likely to help someone apparently in need when by themselves, but if they are with others who fail to respond to the apparent need, they are much less likely to help. Again, the situationist understands being in the non-helping group as an insubstantial element of the situation. But there are a number of reasons why most people might find that the inaction of the group exerts powerful pressure on their decision-making.[54] In a group, the members may hold that their own responsibility is diminished – they have no more duty to help than anyone else, and these others are not helping. Moreover, at least in Western culture and at least in some contexts, it is considered rude to tell other people

---

53 Dylan Murray suggests this in noting that the seminarians could be suffering a kind of akratic failure; "Situationism, Going Mental, and Modal Akrasia", *Philosophical Studies* 172 (2015): 711–36, at 723.
54 Sabini and Silver (2005).

that they are behaving in a morally wrong way. It is not hard, apparently, to protest the behavior of others when you are in a large, supportive group. But to be the lone voice speaking out against the unanimously agreed-upon behavior of numerous (or even one or a few) others can require a great deal of courage. And to be the lone helper surrounded by those who ignore the situation states, by your actions, that you believe the others are not doing what they ought to. And that exposes you to the serious fear of censure. You can easily imagine the others thinking that you ought to mind your own business and not behave in that holier-than-thou fashion.

Most importantly, in my opinion, is the thought that the solitary subject, seeing the inaction of others, may well be thinking simply that they must know something that he doesn't.[55] Epistemic humility seems a virtue in the vast majority of cases and presumably it has been bred into us as serving a vital evolutionary function. That we automatically trust the authority of the others is just necessary for our survival. As small children, we learn language from those around us. We imbibe the rules and mores of our society from family, friends, neighbors, and the others with whom we come in contact. As children grow and become educated, they had better take it for granted that their math teachers, their language teachers, their history teachers, and the rest know a lot more than they do. Learning requires trust.

Academia, it should be noted, operates through consensus. The different disciplines, and sub-areas within the disciplines, move forward because there is – as a general practice and on a fundamental level – agreement on methodology and agreement on how to evaluate colleagues, institutions, and publication venues. The sciences could not make progress if there were not a tendency to come to a consensus on the primacy of certain theories, require your students to embrace those theories, and treat outliers as kooks. (Philosophy as a discipline is perhaps less concerned with achieving consensus but that attitude is itself a majority stance which goes largely unquestioned.) It is entirely reasonable to entertain the possibility, when we find our views and inclinations at odds with those of the rest of the people around us, that it is we who have missed something that the others have seen. Indeed, that seems like the correct default position, prima facie. Surely, the ingrained tendency to want to conform to the group – a tendency that in most situations will guide us aright (Who wants to see non-conformist drivers on our roadways?) – can exert a very powerful pressure. So, perhaps many of the subjects in the group studies were thinking: "Everybody else must know something that I don't. I'd better act the way they act." If so, their behavior was based on pretty strong reasons.

---

55 Sabini and Silver cite the very telling study in which people could be led to deny the obvious evidence of their senses if others unanimously disagreed with their perception (2005): 554–5.

The downside of this way of thinking, of course, is that sometimes your teachers are mistaken, the consensus is wrong, and the kooks have it right. A great value of these group studies is precisely to show how powerful the effect of the group can be, underscoring the point that it is well to recognize the conformist tendency and then try to step back and consider the situation carefully and ascertain whether or not the group really does see something that one has missed. The decisions of the subjects in the group experiments are understandable, but it is hard to argue that they were correct to fail to help. They may have been operating on barely conscious (or even non-conscious) assumptions or attitudes regarding the others, assumptions or attitudes which are understandable. But the evidence they had was that someone needed help. Epistemic humility is a good thing, but under the circumstances, one supposes that compassion should have trumped it. Still, they acted for reasons, the sorts of reasons that are appropriate under many (and possibly most) occasions. When the situationist experiments are approached with the possible perspectives of the subjects in mind, they do not provide evidence that people ordinarily fail to act for reasons. But perhaps they do show that people often fail to assess their situation properly. And that is useful information to have.

The Challenge to Character Building and Virtue Ethics

The situationist debate actually focused on the question of whether character traits or elements in a given situation better explain the behavior of human agents, and the current consensus among psychologists is that both are important. People do have robust traits, but the traits are expressed within particular situations, so the elements in the situation influence how (or whether) a trait is manifested. But even though extreme situationism is no longer a popular position among psychologists, philosophers got interested around the turn of the twenty-first century and have continued to discuss the question. Harman and Doris explicitly criticize virtue ethics and the concept of character building from a situationist perspective, and many philosophers have responded to this criticism in various ways, arguing that the experiments simply do not provide the evidence that situationists supposed they did.[56] In the tradition within which I am working, one of the core values of being able to make free choices lies in one's being the sort of agent who can be responsible for his character. So, looking at the philosophical defense of character is relevant to the question of human free will. The discussion is also useful in thinking about the difficulties with

---

56 Doris should probably not be labelled an "extreme" situationist. He allows that similar contexts may elicit similar behaviors and so people may have local, rather than global, character traits ((2002): 65–6).

constructing, conducting, and interpreting experiments having to do with human choices and actions.

First, it is well to make a few (rough) distinctions. I will use the terms "trait" or "character trait" similarly to the way Doris uses them. Traits exhibit

(1) *Consistency*. Character and personality traits are reliably manifested in trait-relevant behavior across a diversity of trait-relevant eliciting conditions that may vary widely in their conduciveness to the manifestation of the trait in question.
(2) *Stability*. Character and personality traits are reliably manifested in trait-relevant behaviors over iterated trials of similar trait-relevant eliciting conditions.[57]

But "reliably manifested" needs qualification. First, given the current consensus about the interaction of traits and situations, we should understand "reliably manifested" to be context-sensitive. Second, the manifestation of a particular trait will be limited by Doris's third criterion for a trait: "*Evaluative integration*. In a given character or personality the occurrence of a trait with a particular evaluative valence is probabilistically related to the occurrence of other traits with similar evaluative valences."[58] Prima facie, this looks to be implausible. Why should someone who is, for example, compassionate be likely to be courageous or honest or loyal? But here we need to appreciate the standard distinction between one's overall character and this or that particular character trait. This brings up both the Problem of Description and the Problem of Focus in the situationist literature.

Harman's seminal article defending situationism is essentially an attack on Aristotelian (or Aristotelian-inspired) virtue ethics: "If there is no such thing as character, then there is no such thing as character building."[59] The "character" one wants to build (presumably) is not a "bundle" of separate, isolated traits. It is acceptable to understand "character" to refer to the integrated mix (or web) of traits a person has. But how to relate this mix of traits to the question of whether one should be thought to have an overall good character, bad character, or something in between is more complex than it might appear at first. At first glance, it might look like one could just tot up the traits, note whether they are virtues (like compassion) or vices (like gluttony), and then do the math. Does the agent have more virtues than vices? If so, then the agent has a good character. But that is too simple. For example, someone with numerous good qualities may possess

---

57 Doris (2002): 22.
58 Doris (2002): 22.
59 Harman (1999): 328.

a vice of such strength and seriousness that we feel inclined to ascribe a bad character to them in spite of these positive traits.

A more important complication is directly relevant to the "reliable manifestation" of a trait. On the Aristotelian view (which I set out in a rather simplistic way, sufficient for current purposes), virtues consist in habits of properly moderating natural inclinations whereas vices consist in habits of failing to do so. But what constitutes "proper moderation" is relative to the individual and to the situation. This is not because there is no objectivity to what is proper. What is proper is objective, and the test is whether someone is behaving in a way conducive to their flourishing. But the differences between individuals and situations mean that "proper moderation" varies from person to person and situation to situation. Someone who is a glutton, and someone who is not, might eat the same amount of food, for example. Whether you are eating too much, too little, or the right amount depends on a host of factors – factors about you as an individual and about the particular situation.[60] That's why it's so easy to miss the mark and so hard to hit it. And that is why *practical wisdom* is required if the goal is to become the virtuous person and lead the good and happy life. One needs to be good at *understanding* the moral and non-moral facts about the situations in which one finds oneself.

In discussions of traits and virtues, it is important to remember what Aristotle and common sense teach: that a trait we might assume to be simply a virtue could, without the guidance of practical wisdom, directly issue in evil choices and actions. For example, the willingness to face danger and death to defend a cause one believes in might usually be labelled the virtue of courage. But if the cause is foolish or wicked, then it is wrong to face danger and death to defend it.[61] If the agent's mistaken belief that the cause is important and good was arrived at nonculpably, then perhaps we cannot hold the agent morally blameworthy. The "courageous" Nazi might have absorbed National Socialist values from his culture, and the option to consider it critically might never have arisen. But his "courage" is not the courage of the virtuous person who understands when it is appropriate to face danger and death for one's cause.

Doris includes "evaluative integrity" as one of the criteria of a "globalist" conception of character traits, which is the sort of Aristotelian approach he intends to attack. But he focuses on one particular trait: compassion. He explicitly declines to define "compassion", saying "My arguments are not contingent on any particular understanding of compassion; I could as easily couch discussion in terms of what psychologists rather colorlessly call 'prosocial behavior'.., inasmuch as ethical reflection is preoccupied with

---

60 Aristotle, *Nicomachean Ethics* 2.6.
61 Doris (2002): 21.

such conduct."[62] But compassion, understood as a disposition to empathize with other people and to want to help them, is a perfect example of a trait that requires the guidance of practical wisdom if it is to issue in virtuous choices and actions and contribute to the construction of the overall virtuous character and life. For example, suppose a student comes to you begging for a higher grade than they have earned because if their grade point average falls they will lose their scholarship. You might feel great compassion for the student, but it is (at least arguably) wrong to give students higher grades than they have earned. You must squelch your compassion and act upon your commitment to larger goods: fairness in grading, adherence to the rules, the value of scholarship money ultimately going to the better students, and so on. Someone who simply let their empathy and desire to help run rampant without the guidance of practical reason might end up doing a great deal more harm than good. Traits that lead you aright (in general) may lead you astray as well, and the virtuous person – at least Aristotle's virtuous person – is able to discern when to exercise and when to try to curb a particular trait. Good character, then, is not just possession of a set of traits that are usually considered to be prosocial or virtuous.

Doris appreciates this point. He defends his characterization of global character traits as requiring "evaluative integration" by noting that Aristotle and his followers hold versions of this thesis; perhaps having one virtue requires having them all or perhaps all of the virtues are actually manifestations of a single overarching disposition.[63] But the *empirical evidence* that Doris and Harman discuss does not address the notion (or the possibility) of the overall virtuous person. It deals with this or that trait, like compassion or honesty. It may be that the nature of the experiments necessitates studying traits as discrete, but on the Aristotelian account it is difficult to make sense of traits, at least of virtues – how they are possessed and how they manifest themselves in behavior – without understanding them through the lens of the overall unified virtuous character. The experiments may necessitate the narrow focus but that vitiates the evidence which is supposed to undermine the Aristotelian approach. Of course, Doris will argue that there is no such thing as a unified character, but isolating individual traits to study seems to shoulder aside the possibility of a unified character from the beginning and may entail that the study of the discrete traits is skewed because the possibility of the unified character is bracketed.

Thus, there is at least something of a disconnect between the situationist's study of "character traits" and the concern – especially in its Aristotelian mode – for building character. This will prove important in

62 Doris (2002): 29.
63 Doris (2002): 20–1.

evaluating the evidence and underscores again the value of being exact concerning what philosophical concept we are considering and what empirical evidence we are observing and interpreting. But, certainly, if it should turn out that (by and large) people behave as they do only because of the situations they find themselves in, then not only must we deny robust character traits but we must deny overall character as well, and character building is a lost cause.

Happily for the project of building a good character, there is apparently plenty of empirical evidence in favor of human agents possessing robust traits, including traits that can be considered virtues. Jayawickreme et al. write, "in light of the totality of the evidence presented, psychologists across the field have accepted the evidence and concluded that both situations and persons are powerful."[64] They explain,

> Although each individual varies considerably in his or her behavior, each individual also has a central point or tendency around which he or she varies… While people may act very differently in different situations, their typical behavior remains highly consistent from week to week.[65]

Evidence for the reality of traits includes "observer-target" and "observer-observer" agreement; that is, when people describe their traits, there is considerable agreement between the person themselves and their acquaintances. Furthermore, people describe themselves in similar ways across time – in their 30s and in their 60s. The study of twins who have grown up apart suggests some genetic basis for some personality traits. And trait attribution is a good predictor of outcomes for the agent in a host of areas such as academic achievement, job performance, marital quality, mental health, and length of life.[66]

What to make, then, of the evidence from the situationist experiments? In fact, these experiments may provide evidence in favor of at least some people having robust traits.[67] One way to discern the existence of a trait is to observe the differences between people in similar situations.[68] Some – albeit

---

64 Eranda Jayawickreme, Peter Meindl, Erik G. Helzer, R. Michael Furr, and William Fleeson, "Virtuous States and Virtuous Traits: How the Empirical Evidence Regarding the Existence of Broad Traits Saves Virtue Ethics from the Situationist Critique", *Theory and Research in Education* 12 (2014): 283–308, at 298.
65 Jayawickreme, et al. (2014): 302.
66 Jayawickreme, et al. (2014): 290–1.
67 Doris allows the possibility of "pure types", people who are pathologically consistent in their behavior. But he holds this sort of person to be abnormal. He takes account of the general reliability of most people's behavior by positing "local" traits – people will behave in a roughly similar way across roughly similar situations; Doris (2002): 65–6.
68 Jayawickreme, et al. (2014): 288–9. Doris (2002): 19.

a disturbingly small minority – of the subjects in the Milgram experiment which Doris reviews refused to continue the experiment from an early point after the learner first says that he refuses to go on.[69] These subjects, at least, exhibited compassion. And it appears that they exhibited it in a situation in which only a very compassionate person would do so. I argued above that understandable reasons may have occurred to some of the subjects who continued with the experiment. For those who stopped, we can hypothesize that such reasons might have occurred to them, but compassion might have trumped these reasons. (Alternatively, the few who stopped might have been more skeptical than the others about the consequentialist argument justifying present harm in the interests of scientific advancement or more skeptical about the trustworthiness of scientists. But being skeptical can be seen as a character trait.)

One thing the Milgram experiments show is that the initial assumption of the experimenters, that most people would behave with compassion and defy authority, was just mistaken. This initial assumption may simply fail to appreciate the power of the desire to obey a trusted, legitimate, and scientific authority. But rather than demonstrating the lack of such a trait as compassion, perhaps what the experiment shows is that, in the face of the powerful desire to be obedient to authority, only the *extremely* compassionate person can summon the willpower and the courage to be defiant. Similarly, mutatis mutandis, with the Good Samaritan experiment and the group effect experiments. Those few who chose to help did so despite (at least possibly) experiencing the powerful inclinations which led to the other subjects failing to help. What the experiments may show is that *very* compassionate people are rare, not that most people do not possess at least a modest degree of compassion. (Remember that one of Doris's reasons for choosing to examine the virtue of compassion is that it need not be heroic. But, at least possibly, the compassionate people in the experiments, if not "heroic", at least rose above the level of the modest, all things considered.)

This demonstrates an important (if hardly new) methodological point about interpreting experimental evidence: the same evidence admits of different interpretations. And how one interprets the evidence may depend upon one's initial, pre-experiment, assumptions. Doris's situationist argument depends upon subjects' behavior falling short of experimenters' expectations. In discussing the criterion of consistency, Doris notes that he is not insisting on some "absolute and general standard". Rather, the problem for those who would defend robust traits

> is that for important examples of personality and character traits, there is a marked disparity between the extent of behavioral consistency

---

[69] Milgram (1974) describes other versions of the experiment in which all or most of the subjects do refuse to continue to the upper reaches of the shock machine.

that familiar conceptions of the trait lead one to expect and the extent of behavioral consistency that systematic observation suggests one is justified in expecting.[70]

Suppose that "familiar conceptions" of compassion led the experimenters in the Milgram, Good Samaritan, and group effect experiments to expect that many people would show compassion by stopping the experiment early or helping the person apparently in need. Indeed, Milgram took a survey of a number of psychology students, asking whether or not they expected many of the subjects to continue to the higher levels of electric shock, and these students predicted that very few would continue.[71] As we know, in these experiments, many people failed to do the compassionate thing. The situationist conclusion is that expectations failed because few people are even moderately compassionate. An alternative interpretation, illustrating again the Problem of Perspective, is that the expectations failed because the subject's experience of the strength of the *very substantial* elements operating against doing the compassionate act was not appreciated by the experimenters beforehand.

Suppose, for the sake of argument, that the situationist experiments do indeed show that very few people possess even moderate compassion as a global trait. Perhaps the few who behaved compassionately do, but they do not represent the generality of humankind. Does this provide good evidence for situationism? Only if Doris's (and Harman's) move from the lack of compassion to the lack of global traits generally is justified. The Problem of Focus arises in that the focus on compassion may just be misplaced. It is true that Doris has good reasons for choosing compassion as the trait to examine: it is central to our moral thinking and there is a significant body of empirical evidence concerning helping situations. But even on the (dubious) supposition that the situationist experiments show that few people are even moderately compassionate, this allows for different interpretations. The situationist suggests that the lack of compassion is good evidence for the lack of global traits in general. An alternative interpretation is that although people possess all sorts of robust global traits, compassion is often not among them.

Doris grants this possibility but holds that the compassion looked for in the relevant experiments is extremely minimal.[72] It is not clear how this answers the suggestion of the alternative interpretation: Perhaps people possess all sorts of robust global traits, and *even minimal* compassion is often not among them. Or perhaps a better analysis would be that although many people do have minimal compassion, it is easily overridden by other

70 Doris (2002): 20.
71 Milgram (1963): 375.
72 Doris (2002): 31–2.

traits such as a tendency to obey authority or (among excellent students) a felt need to be punctual or a tendency to defer to other members in a group.[73] Doris mentions the possibility that one trait may be overridden by another, but he does not find this a worrisome point, saying "I'm doing moral psychology, not metaphysics; my interest is not in conceptual analysis but in the evidential standards governing trait attribution."[74] But when we examine the evidence from the situationist experiments – especially when the observed behavior of the subjects is surprising – it seems appropriate to consider all of the live options. (It is not clear why Doris labels that move "metaphysics".)

Positing that many people possess compassion weakly seems a good way to read the dime experiment. Even a minimally compassionate person may fail to help when they're busy and trying to make arrangements for getting something done – the subjects were just coming from making a phone call in a phone booth in a shopping mall, after all. (Some of us will remember how annoying pay phones could be.) But those who did help might be judged to be minimally compassionate since all it took to nudge them toward behaving compassionately was finding the dime. It may be that compassion is somewhat rare and often a bit thin where it is found; in that case, it is unusually sensitive to situational factors. Although Doris's reasons for focusing on compassion were well taken, it may turn out that compassion is an especially problematic trait to study if the question is whether or not people have robust traits in general.

Strongly compassionate people may be rare, and Aristotle's attitude – with which common sense would likely agree – is that virtue in general is rare and requires a great deal of time and effort to achieve.[75] At least in some circles, the thought that virtue – including a robust and properly directed compassion – is uncommon does not come as a surprise.[76] But this need not mean that there is no character and the project of character building should be abandoned. Micah Lott draws the analogy with developing

---

73 Christian Miller suggests that one explanation for the results in the standard situationist experiments could be competing virtues; Miller (2014): 221–2.
74 Doris (2002): 16.
75 Nafsika Athanassoulis, "A Response to Harman: Virtue Ethics and Character Traits", *Proceedings of the Aristotelian Society* 100 (2000): 215–21; Christian Miller, *Character and Moral Psychology* (Oxford: Oxford University Press, 2014): 202–3.
76 The point that virtue is rare might appear to conflict with my methodological claim that human beings ought to be thought to have great dignity and value, unless proven otherwise; a claim entailing that a serious burden of proof lies with the one who would deny free will, since part of our presumptive value derives from our being free agents. But the traditional view is that humans have *metaphysical* value because of the kind of thing we are. The worst human being among us has this sort of value. The moral value of the virtuous person is a different phenomenon. The two sorts of value are related in that (at least according to the traditional defender of free will) one cannot really have the moral value if one is not the sort of thing that has the metaphysical value.

expertise in some skill. The minimally proficient in the skill might be rather rare and the genuine expert might be exceedingly rare, but it does not follow that the skill is not a reality, nor that one should abandon the aim to master it.[77]

The importance of character building brings up one more criticism of the situationist interpretation of the situationist experiments. This one points to a different Problem of Focus: If human agents develop their characters over time through the choices they make and if attempting to build a virtuous character is a long process, then the momentary snapshot of a choice taken during an experiment may not tell us much at all about whether or not the subject has certain character traits. And we would need to observe the agent over a long period of time to ascertain whether or not they have a stable character or perhaps a character in progress for good or ill.[78] There have been studies conducted over long periods of time which do indeed indicate that human agents have robust traits.

As mentioned at the beginning of the chapter, the consensus among psychologists now is that character is real and powerful but that part of what it means to have a certain character involves how one responds to different situations. But, although extreme situationism is no longer a going concern, the discussion above illustrated a number of problems – especially Problems of Description, Focus, and Perspective – that need to be taken into account in attempting to study human free will. The experiments which are often cited in the situationist literature are especially interesting because many of them study what at least appear to be moral choices. In so doing, they raise ethical questions about experiments using human subjects. To this point, the problems generated by the review of the empirical study of freedom have been practical problems, but in the next chapter I discuss these situationist experiments to make the case that experimenting on free will raises special ethical concerns.

---

[77] Micah Lott, "Situationism, Skill, and the Rarity of Virtue", *Journal of Value Inquiry* 48 (2014): 387–401.

[78] Athanassoulis (2000): 219; Christian Miller, "Social Psychology, Mood, and Helping: Mixed Results for Virtue Ethics", *Journal of Ethics* 13 (2009): 145–73, at 165.

Chapter 6
Ethical Issues in Experiments with Human Subjects

Introduction

The previous chapters have introduced a list of practical problems facing the study of human free will. But there are moral problems as well. In order to study human freedom – unless one is prepared to face huge Problems of Translation – it is necessary to do research on human subjects and on human subjects engaged in something akin to morally significant choices. In discussing the situationist challenge to free will, I noted that many of the experiments cited do indeed deal with moral choices or something very similar. But these experiments also raise ethical questions. In this chapter, I survey a number of ethical issues that have arisen over the past several decades, focusing especially on the Milgram experiments since they have generated an extensive literature among psychologists and philosophers, and they involve subjects apparently making moral choices. In that moral choices are especially constitutive of who a person is – what kind of person they are – such choices are deeply personal and bear a special kind of value. This means that experiments on such choices introduce an extra level of ethical concern. A thorough discussion would be too extensive for the purposes of the present work, but enough can be said to add a number of ethical problems to the list of hurdles facing experimentation on free will. In Chapters 7 and 8, I will consider how a future scientist, not suffering from the limitations that present-day neuroscientists and psychologists must deal with, might go about attempting to settle the question of free will in light of the list of problems, practical and ethical, that the research to date has illustrated.

A first ethical question to consider when studying human beings is: When, if ever, is it morally acceptable to deceive the subject of an experiment? The answer to this question is tied to the further question concerning whether participation in the experiment itself is likely to cause harm to the subject or to wrong him in some way. This issue is clouded by the difficulty of sorting out what truly constitutes harming or wronging the subject.

Possible justifications for deceiving, and even harming or wronging, the subject appeal to the value the experiment may ultimately produce, but this generates questions about what sort of values are in play, how to assess them, and when the benefits should be held to justify the costs. And the cost/benefit calculus needs to include consideration of whether or not the benefits derived from the "costly" experiments could have been achieved through some alternative, non-deceptive, non-harmful, non-wronging method. A final issue that falls under the heading of "respecting the subject" involves how to understand and represent the behavior of subjects. Many who discuss the various experiments I have mentioned earlier in this work interpret the behavior of the subjects in a negative light when there are less demeaning interpretations which are consistent with what the subjects have said and done (at least as this behavior is recorded). Any of these questions would be worthy of a book, and I do not propose to offer an exhaustive discussion of any of them. My hope is to set out the issues sufficiently to make the case that, at the very least, the future study of human agency is likely to pose many, serious ethical questions. To that end, I will present the moral problems as forcefully as I can but without attempting to propose and rebut all the possible responses that could be made to the ethical difficulties I raise.

Deception and Informed Consent

Stanley Milgram conducted his obedience experiments in the early 1960s, and in the succeeding half a century, they have generated a continuing debate over the ethical issues they raise. As described in Chapter 5, the Milgram experiments depended upon deceiving the subjects into believing that they were participating in a learning and memory experiment. As Milgram describes in his 1974 book, *Obedience to Authority*, great pains were taken to convince the volunteers for the "learning" experiment, first of all, that they were participating in an experiment on the role of punishment in memory and learning and, second, that they were indeed administering shocks of higher and higher voltage to a fellow volunteer.[1] Clearly, the subjects in Milgram's experiments had not given their *informed* consent. They had not agreed to participate in the experiment in which they were participating, generating a serious Problem of Deception.

But why is it important that experimenters inform subjects? Most of us are comfortable with falling short of the truth in some instances. Many trivial cases of social etiquette require saying things that are not strictly true. And the catastrophe cases where telling the truth does enormous harm

1 Milgram (1974): 13–23.

seem intuitively – at least to many – to justify deception.[2] Classic examples include confronting the Gestapo at your door as you are sheltering the family of Jews in your attic and lying to your seriously ill loved one because the doctor has told you that the truth might kill them. Few will accept the principle that one should always tell the truth. But still, deliberately deceiving another person, in most cases, seems to require serious justification. The importance of informed consent is discussed in *Ethics in Research with Human Participants*, a collection of essays written by a task force convened by the American Psychological Association (APA) in 1994.[3] The collection was published by the APA in 2000 and is included (as of this writing in 2020) on the APA's list of books for sale. I do not find anything in the collection to conflict with the "Ethical Principles for Psychologists and Code of Conduct" on the current (2020) APA website.[4] The collection of essays offers a more extended discussion of the issues and standards set out briefly on the website. This collection can be taken to express the considered opinion of those representing the APA (with the obvious qualification that some members of the APA may disagree with some of the positions stated in the collection and in the standards presented on the website). Chapter 1, by M. Brewster Smith, presents the "Moral Foundations of Research with Human Participants", and the first of the five foundational principles is "Respect for Persons and Their Autonomy". Smith writes, "Researchers respect the human participants in their investigations as persons of worth whose participation is a matter of their autonomous choice."[5] Under "Respect for People's Rights and Dignity" on the list of general ethical principles on the APA's current website, we read that "Psychologists respect the dignity and worth of all people, and the rights of individuals to privacy, confidentiality, and self-determination."[6]

Smith's spelling out of the principle of respect echoes the 1979 Belmont Report (included as Appendix C in *Ethics in Research with Human Participants*), "Ethical Principles and Guidelines for the Protection of Human Subjects of Research" from the National Commission for the Protection of Human Subjects of Biomedical and Behavioral Research. This commission was established by the U.S. Congress in 1974 through the

---

[2] Sissela Bok presents a ringing endorsement of truth-telling and a thoughtful canvas of the myriad dangers of lying, including deception in social science research, but even she grants that it is morally permissible to lie sometimes (*Lying: Moral Choice in Public and Private Life* (New York: Pantheon Books, 1978): 32–46).

[3] Bruce D. Sales and Susan Folkman, editors, *Ethics in Research with Human Participants* (Washington, DC: American Psychological Association, 2000).

[4] https://www.apa.org/ethics/code/.

[5] M. Brewster Smith, "Moral Foundations in Research with Human Participants" in *Ethics in Research With Human Participants* edited by Bruce D. Sales and Susan Folkman (2000): 3–10, at 5–6.

[6] https://www.apa.org/ethics/code/. Under "General Principles: Principle E".

National Research Act.[7] (The 1970s saw a great deal of debate and review concerning ethical issues related to experiments with human participants and produced new guidelines for health sciences in general and psychology in particular. The extent to which the notoriety of the Milgram experiments was among the catalysts for this increased concern is an open question.[8]) The report elaborates on three "Basic Ethical Principles", which the commission holds to be "generally accepted in our cultural tradition". The first in the list is "Respect for Persons", of which the first prescription is that "individuals should be treated as autonomous agents" where

> An autonomous person is an individual capable of deliberation about personal goals and of acting under the direction of such deliberation.... To show lack of respect for an autonomous agent is to repudiate that person's considered judgments, to deny an individual the freedom to act on those considered judgments, or to withhold information necessary to make a considered judgment, when there are no compelling reasons to do so.[9]

The APA statements emphasize the connection between respect for other human beings and recognition of their autonomy and freedom. Deception fails to respect the other as a free agent. In general, lying is wrong because, as Sissela Bok writes, the deceived

> see that they were manipulated, that the deceit made them unable to make choices for themselves according to the most adequate information available... most of us would resist loss of control over which choices we want to delegate to others and which ones we want to make ourselves, aided by the best information we can obtain.[10]

I argue that the burden of proof is on the one who would deny free will since to deny someone's freedom is to demean them. The ethical principles of the APA reflect this perspective. Insisting that experimenters must obtain a participant's informed consent before engaging in an experiment is one way to exercise this respect and that entails not deceiving prospective subjects.

---

7 Appendix C in Sales and Folkman (2000): 197–205.
8 Thomas Blass, *The Man Who Shocked the World: The Life and Legacy of Stanley Milgram* (New York: Basic Books, 2004): 280–3; James H. Korn, *Illusions of Reality: A History of Deception in Social Psychology* (Albany, NY: State University of New York Press, 1997): 148–50; Arthur G. Miller, *The Obedience Experiments: A Case Study of Controversy in Social Science* (New York: Praeger, 1986): 134–7.
9 Belmont Report in Sales and Folkman (2000): 198–9.
10 Bok (1978): 20–1.

But we have already granted that it is legitimate in some cases to deceive others. Given the connection between respect and truth-telling, deceit means either a lack or an overriding of respect for the one deceived, but there are times when the morally appropriate move entails not respecting someone or entails allowing our respect to be overridden by more pressing concerns. Saying that respect is "overridden" here means that our respect for the person in question is in no way lessened by the situation but that even more morally pressing concerns require us to view our respect as secondary to these concerns. In the Nazi example, given that the policeman at the door is the minion of the vicious regime, it is probably morally appropriate to fail in respect for him or at least for him qua his official position. With the example of the seriously ill loved one, our respect may be legitimately overridden by our immediate concern to give him the best chance at surviving his illness. The subject in an experiment probably does not have much in common with the Nazi policeman. There is not likely to be anything about his character or about his role as subject that would justify failing to accord him the respect that we ordinarily owe to our fellows. But could the importance of doing research on human beings sometimes override the principle of respect such that it is legitimate to deceive potential subjects?

It would be difficult to argue that deceiving the subject in the experiment in social psychology is analogous to lying to the patient about his life-threatening condition. The deception in the experiment is not done for the benefit of the subject, nor is it likely to be a matter of saving a life, at least in the immediate future. Some point to the use of placebos in testing drugs as an analogy for deceiving subjects in behavioral experiments.[11] The use of placebos in testing is common practice to which no one has ethical objections. But this analogy is not apt. The subjects in these drug tests are not being deceived. Current ethics codes would not allow such deception. Subjects are told that they will be receiving either the drug being tested or a placebo and that is the plain truth. One might apply this analogy to the Milgram situation if Milgram had explained to his subjects before the experiment began that either the experiment would be about the effect of punishment on learning and memory or it would be about whether or not they, the subjects, could be brought to act like (in Milgram's view) guards at Auschwitz. That would have been the truth, but chances are few would have volunteered to participate, and those who did would not have behaved "naturally" since, guessing which side of the disjunct they found themselves participating in, they might have preferred not to appear to have much in common with a guard in a Nazi extermination camp. For Milgram's experiment to proceed, he had to deceive would-be participants.

---

11 Marian W. Fischman, "Informed Consent", in Sales and Folkman (2000): 35–48, at 45.

One suggestion has been that the experimenter inform would-be participants that some information may be withheld from them, which might include even the purpose of the experiment.[12] Participants *agree* to have information withheld from them, so this could seem to be approaching informed consent producing a situation similar to the use of placebos in drug tests. However, the analogy is still distant in that, with the drug test, the participant knows that he will be in one of only a small, fixed number of possible situations, and what the possible situations involve has been explained to him. Thus, the participant in the drug tests can evaluate the different scenarios and make the informed decision that he could (or could not) accept finding himself in any one of them. In the social science setting, if the would-be participant is told only that he will not be told some of the important facts about what the experiment involves or what it is about, then he is more or less agreeing to he knows not what. Perhaps trust in the integrity and beneficence of experimenters would lead many people to agree to participate on these terms, but it seems wrong to label this agreement *informed* consent.

Adopting this move would probably not have served Milgram well. A significant number of subjects in his experiments said that they suspected that the experiment was some sort of hoax and the shocks were not real.[13] If they had been warned beforehand that they might be misinformed, the numbers of the suspicious would likely have risen considerably and that would undermine the point of the experiment. The current APA code of ethics does not suggest that researchers who plan to deceive subjects should inform would-be subjects that they may be misled, so it is not clear that the suggested move has gained much traction.

Although the Milgram experiments are now considered morally controversial, deceptive experiments are currently used widely in social psychology, and the APA holds that it is ethically acceptable to deceive subjects as long as certain criteria are met. "Psychologists do not conduct a study involving deception unless they have determined that the use of deceptive techniques is justified by the study's significant prospective scientific,

---

12 Fischman (2000): 42; Christopher D. Herrera, "Ethics, Deception, and 'Those Milgram Experiments'", *Journal of Applied Philosophy* 18 (2001): 245–56, at 250. Milgram suggests establishing a group of prospective subjects, where members will participate in a number of experiments and to explain to the whole group that some of these experiments might involve deception and stress. Alternatively, the experimenter might describe his experiment to a group of people to ascertain the view of the "reasonable person" regarding whether or not they believe they would be willing to consent to participate. Milgram grants that the next person might disagree with the consensus of the group, but "'presumed consent of a reasonable person' seems better than no consent at all". (Stanley Milgram, "Subject Reaction: The Neglected Factor in the Ethics of Experimentation", *The Hastings Center Report* 7 (1977): 19–23, at 23.)
13 Milgram (1974): 172 (Table 7).

educational, or applied value and that effective nondeceptive alternative procedures are not feasible." They do not "deceive prospective participants about research that is reasonably expected to cause physical pain or severe emotional distress". And they explain the deception to the participants as early as they can.[14]

These criteria point to deep and complex issues. What constitutes, and how do we determine, the prospective value of an experiment? What constitutes, and how do we determine, harm to the subjects where harm is considered to be physical pain or severe emotional distress? Can one *wrong* someone even though one has not caused them physical pain or severe emotional distress? And what is meant by "feasible", in asking whether or not effective nondeceptive alternative procedures are feasible? "Feasible" can mean "possible" or it can mean "convenient".

Psychologist Diana Baumrind, beginning when Milgram first published the results of his experiments, has written a series of articles criticizing deceptive research. In a 2015 review of Gina Perry's *Behind the Shock Machine: The Untold Story of the Notorious Milgram Psychology Experiments*, Baumrind discusses the APA code of ethics and notes that where the code asks the researcher to judge that there are no effective alternatives, "effective alternative may be interpreted by the researcher as one that is as convenient and thrifty as the deceptive procedure". She argues that the widespread use of deceptive research is "motivated more by convenience than necessity". And she notes that "harm" is not defined to include lying to the participant.[15] Baumrind is referring to the APA code from 2002, but the most recent version raises these same issues. I will discuss each of the APA criteria for allowing deception briefly, underlining ethical problems that confront experimentation on free will. Perhaps these problems can be overcome, but they need to be recognized and addressed.

Harms to Subjects

That many of Milgram's subjects suffered severe emotional distress, and even physical pain, in the course of his experiments is not a matter for dispute. Milgram describes this stress and pain in the original report of his experiments.[16] And he notes it briefly in responding to the suggestion that many, or most, of the subjects did not believe that they were really shocking another human being.[17] But when he comes to defend the moral acceptability of his experiments, he writes that the subject experienced

---

14 https://www.apa.org/ethics/code/. Under Section 8: Research and Publication, at 8.07.
15 Diana Baumrind, "When Subjects Become Objects: The Lies Behind the Milgram Legend", *Theory and Psychology* 25 (2015): 690–6, at 691, 695.
16 Milgram (1963): 375–7.
17 Milgram (1974): 171.

"momentary excitement", and momentary excitement "is not the same as harm".[18] His assessment does not find many supporters.[19] It is generally agreed that Milgram's subjects experienced significant harm during the experiments and this was harm that they had by no means consented to suffer. The codes of ethics established by the APA in (and since) the 1970s look to rule out deceptive experiments involving the sort of harm that Milgram's subjects experienced during their participation. Experiments which involve deception, but which are foreseen to cause only minimal emotional distress, are permitted. But this judgment raises two questions concerning harms.

First, might it not be the case that the subjects experience ongoing distress after the completion of the experiment? This is an important question since the APA guidelines suggest that at least part of the process of making the decision about the ethical acceptability of an experiment involves a cost/benefit analysis.[20] But counting the overall costs to the participants may be difficult. Take the case of a subject who experiences only a little stress while engaged in the experiment but after the completion of the experiment suffers moderate anxiety due to having participated in the experiment and who suffers this anxiety periodically for the rest of her life – decades and decades, let's say. The consequentialist philosopher would almost certainly hold that the cumulative weight of this ongoing (if episodic) anxiety should be factored in when assessing how much harm the subject suffered. Arguably, the subject experiencing this moderate anxiety suffers more harm than someone who, during an experiment, briefly suffers *severe* distress but is not anxious afterwards. The point is that the experimenter projecting that his experiment will not cause physical pain or severe distress to his subjects *during the experiment* may be engaged in an inadequate cost/benefit analysis.

There is a second question related to the first: Given the extreme variability in human beings, might it not be the case that what looks to the experimenter as likely to produce only trivial distress might actually cause severe distress – or ongoing moderate distress? And might not different

---

18 Milgram (1974): 194. Regarding the allowable level of harm, Milgram argues that an acceptable, though harm-causing, experiment would be one that is likely to produce negative effects that do not do permanent damage and "do not exceed in intensity experiences which the subject might encounter in ordinary life" (Milgram (1977): 21). But many terrible experiences might fit these two criteria, including broken bones and automobile accidents. These do not seem to be helpful criteria.
19 Milgram attempts to deflect criticism concerning the harm caused by noting that, before the experiments began, he could not have known that so many of his subjects would go as far as they did (Milgram (1974): 194–5). This is a weak response in that, after the first 10 or 20 iterations, the pattern involving harm should have emerged.
20 Arthur G. Miller entitles his chapter covering the moral debate over Milgram's experiments, "What Price Knowledge? The Ethics of the Obedience Experiments" and concludes in favor of the value of the experiments, writing that real harm "could result from *not doing* research on destructive obedience". Miller (1986): 88, 138.

subjects respond differently? Assuming a connection between the deception and the stress-causing element in the experiment, the *deceived* subject could not have given informed consent to the suffering or even to the risk of suffering. Here the Problem of Perspective arises in an ethical context. And it is exacerbated because not only does the assessment of harm require trying to see things from the subject's point of view, but the experimenter must take into account that different subjects might experience different levels of harm.

Although the clear consensus is that Milgram's experiments caused an unacceptable level of distress to his subjects during the time they were participating, there is debate about the extent to which they may have suffered ongoing emotional distress. Milgram says that he debriefed his subjects after each iteration of the experiment, but during the months in which the experiments were being conducted, the debriefing did not tell the subjects the truth. They were told that the shocks had not really been very severe and the (confederate) learner would then emerge and tell the subject that he, the learner, had been overreacting. The shocks had been painful, but no real harm was done – essentially that the (confederate) experimenter had been telling the truth all along.[21] The subjects received a more accurate description of the experiments, including some information about the conclusions, roughly a year after they had been finished.

Milgram explains that the aims of the "debriefing" immediately after participation in the experiment were, especially in the case of the obedient subjects, to decrease their stress and to make them feel better about their behavior.

> After the interview procedures were undertaken to assure that the subject would leave the laboratory in a state of well being [sic]. A friendly reconciliation was arranged between the subject and the victim, and an effort was made to reduce any tensions that arose as a result of the experiment.[22]

"Obedient subjects were assured that their behavior was entirely normal and that their feelings of conflict or tension were shared by other participants."[23] This explanation of the debriefing is puzzling. As Milgram describes the experiments and the behavior of many of the subjects, he

---

21 Perry (2012): 65–94. Perry points out that in his early papers about the experiments, although Milgram uses the term "dehoax", which might lead one to think that the subjects were told the truth about the experiments immediately after their participation, he does not say that this is the case. In that his experiments ran over the course of two years, if he had told the early subjects the truth, it might have gotten out and made it impossible to conduct the later experiments.
22 Milgram (1963): 374.
23 Milgram (1974): 24.

takes it that, as the maximum voltage was approached, many subjects sincerely believed that they were actually causing very extreme pain, perhaps even death, to the learner.[24] Certainly, one assumes that subjects were delighted to discover that the learner had not really undergone the terrible harm. But, unless they were amazingly un-self-reflective, they would have recognized the fact that they had been willing to shock, and indeed had engaged in the action which they believed to be shocking, an innocent stranger to the point where he is unresponsive. In the previous chapter, I suggested the possibility that at least some of the subjects believed that they were doing their duty to science and that they understood their choice to continue shocking as the lesser of two bad options. In that case, the hope that they would "leave the laboratory in a state of well being" is well founded. The subjects could believe that they had done their duty, and, fortunately, they had been mistaken about the harm that that involved.

But if this was indeed the perspective of a significant number of the subjects, then Milgram's conclusions are undermined. He saw himself as studying *destructive* obedience, so if some or many subjects believed – with some reason – that they were acting dutifully, this does not seem to be "destructive" obedience. On the other hand, it is very standard in the literature to accept Milgram's starting assumptions and hold that the behavior of the obedient subjects was just evil. Suppose the subjects saw their behavior in the same light. Were that the case, although they should rightly be happy to discover that their beliefs about the harm done to the learner were mistaken, this should not change their assessment of their own behavior. What they chose to do and what actions they actually engaged in are not altered by the trickery of the experiment. The subjects should not feel a bit better about themselves and their behavior when they discover that the harm they intended failed to transpire.[25] So, continuing dismay about their performance is among the possible harms that the subjects may (and possibly should) have suffered consequent upon the experiments.[26]

It is possible that, by some strange coincidence, those who volunteered for Milgram's experiments *were* amazingly un-self-reflective. They shouldn't feel more satisfied with their own behavior when they discover that it was ineffective, but perhaps they actually do. In that case, Milgram can suppose

---

24 Milgram (1974): 171–4.
25 It is true that, with the criminal deed, we often punish successes more than failed attempts. There are various ways to account for this, but it would be odd to hold that the inadvertent failure is morally very different from the success relative to the choices, behavior, and character of the agent. See my "Retribution, Forgiveness, and the Character Creation Theory of Punishment", *Social Theory and Practice* 33 (2007): 75–103, at 92–4.
26 Damage to the self-image of the subject is one of the many harms that Diana Baumrind discusses in her article critical of deceptive research published shortly after Milgram's original report of his experiments came out (Baumrind (1964): 421).

that his debriefing did the job. The subjects were able to leave the lab feeling fine. This hypothesis is unlikely given what Milgram has to say about his set of volunteers. And if the unlikely scenario were true, that would cast doubt on Milgram's findings; he would have been studying a set of subjects a significant number of whom exhibited an extreme lack of self-reflectiveness, and (at least possibly) people who are that unreflective about their choices and behavior may be unusually easy to lead, in which case the Problem of Translation Regarding the Pool of Subjects arises.

The debriefing should not provide much comfort for minimally self-reflective people. And the more they learned about the experiments – for example, when they received the more complete debriefing well after the series of experiments was finished – the more dismay they might feel. The current APA code of ethics says that participants in deceptive research should be told the truth as early as possible. The question of how to proceed when debriefing causes more harm than good is a difficult one.[27] Milgram is very explicit, in his 1974 book, that the inspiration for the experiments was questioning how Nazi war criminals could have done what they did. Intuitively, it seems that one might suffer emotional stress at thinking that one has acted like a Nazi war criminal. It might not be severe stress, but periodically, as one remembered one's participation, one might suffer the stress of the painful memory.

Although, as I will discuss below, Milgram believes he has the evidence to show that subjects did not suffer lasting harm, he himself inadvertently supports the thesis of the possibility of ongoing harm. When, roughly a year after the series of experiments had ended, he sent out the more complete report concerning the experiment and conclusions to the subjects, he also sent out a questionnaire. Among the questions was one concerning the degree of belief that the learner was really getting painful shocks: 56% fully believed, 24% had doubts but thought it was probable, 6.1% weren't sure either way, 11.4% thought probably not, and 2.4% were sure that the learner was not getting shocks. One way to read this is that many of the participants seriously entertained the thought that the experiment was a setup. Since this could undermine Milgram's conclusions, he offers a response.

> It is simple, indeed, for a subject to explain his behavior by stating he did not believe the victim received shocks, and some subjects may have come to this position as a post facto explanation. It cost them nothing and would go a long way toward preserving their positive self-conception.[28]

---

27 Lorraine D. Eyde, "Other Responsibilities to Participants" in Sales and Folkman (2000): 61–73, at 65–71.
28 Milgram (1974): 173–4.

Milgram's thesis seems to be that a subject, a year or more after the fact, is likely to present a false report of his beliefs at the time of the experiments; the subjects may be deliberately fabricating or may be honestly misremembering an unpleasant episode, but either way Milgram is granting that, owing to the experiments, their "self-conception" is in need of maintenance a year after their participation.

Furthermore, however the subjects might have felt about their own behavior, the subjects may have continued to suffer stress due to others knowing that they had participated in the experiments. Milgram notes that, on the questionnaires, some of the subjects reported that they had learned something important about themselves from the experiments. One such subject includes "As my wife said, 'You can call yourself Eichmann'".[29] One assumes that the wife was merely making a light-hearted reference to the enabler of genocide. Nevertheless, knowing that your loved ones, your friends and neighbors, or just generations of readers of psychology textbooks may think of you as morally on a par with a Nazi war criminal might cause you ongoing stress. Subjects are listed by numbers in the files and Milgram used pseudonyms in his book, so perhaps only those whom subjects told (and those whom these in the know told) would know by name who had actually participated and how far along the shock machine they went. But the thought that even a limited group of others is aware of your unseemly behavior might be a continuing source of emotional stress. And even if you appear only as a statistic for the general public familiar with the Milgram experiments, the thought that a vast crowd considers your behavior infamous and evil might cause you discomfort down the decades. This could be the case even if your memory of the event and your considered estimation of your behavior are that you felt torn between duties and did the best you could.[30] The suggestion here is that the amount of emotional stress experienced after participating in the experiment could add up over time so that it is even more significant than the intense (but short-lived) suffering during the experiment. Again, this was a harm of which not even the possibility had been suggested to the subjects before

---

29 Milgram (1974): 55.
30 Gina Perry (in personal correspondence) writes, "What I found most unsettling was the way Milgram presented his subjects as willing torturers capable of working in 'death camps' in newspaper articles, TV talk shows and the like and yet he had not intimated to his subjects that this was the interpretation he put on their behaviour. Anyway, I could go on but I feel very strongly about this as I spoke to some subjects as you know and it was a terrible experience not just during the experiment but living with the shame afterwards (even for those who were technically 'defiant')." She makes the point that often the "shame" had to do more with being duped and participating in the experiments, since, as she notes, significantly more of the "obedients" than of the "disobedients" said they had doubts, or serious doubts, that anyone was being shocked (Perry (2012): 139, citing Milgram (1974): 172).

they agreed to participate in the experiments. This needs to be factored into the cost/benefit analysis.

The question of ongoing harm from damage to the subject's self-image and from shame due to the attitudes of those who know you, and those who don't, is especially important to emphasize because it does not seem to figure in the ethical thinking of the APA. There is evidence for this in the fact that version 5 of the Milgram experiments was recreated in 2007 by Jerry Burger, having passed the scrutiny of his institutional review board (IRB).[31] (Version 5 is described in the previous chapter.) Burger's replication involves some important differences from the original experiments. Probably most important is the fact that, although the shock machine was a close copy of Milgram's and included switches up to the "Danger, Severe Shock" level, when subjects showed that they were willing to continue past the 150-volt point, the experiment was stopped. The 150-volt point was important because at this point the learner is yelling, complaining that his heart is bothering him, and demanding to get out. Burger noticed, in studying Milgram's data, that 79% of subjects who were willing to continue past this point went all the way to 450, the point at which the learner fell silent. Burger writes that "[t]his observation suggests a solution to the ethical concerns about replicating Milgram's research". Experimenters would be able to make a reasonable estimate concerning what the participants would have gone on to do had the experiment not stopped at 150 volts, but they could "avoid exposing [participants] to the intense stress Milgram's participants often experienced in the subsequent parts of the procedure".[32]

Burger's replication departed from the original in several other ways. Would-be participants were screened twice for signs that being involved in the experiment might cause them significant distress. (For obvious reasons, they were also screened to find out whether they had heard about the Milgram experiments.)[33] And the possibility of deception was presented up front. The consent form which participants signed included the following:

> I may not be told the entire purpose of the study prior to participation. The experimenter may withhold information about the nature of the study or provide misleading information. However, the full purpose and nature of the investigation...will be revealed to me at the end of my participation.[34]

---

31 Jerry M. Burger, "Replicating Milgram: Would People Still Obey Today?" *American Psychologist* 64 (2009): 1–11.
32 Burger (2009): 2.
33 Burger (2009): 5.
34 Burger does not explain this in his 2009 article, but he writes it in a personal communication to Thomas Blass, "From New Haven to Santa Clara: A Historical Perspective on the Milgram Obedience Experiments", *American Psychologist* 64 (2009): 37–45, at 43.

Participants were told repeatedly, and in writing, that they could quit the experiment at any time and still keep the $50 they had been paid to participate. It is not clear, though, how subjects processed this information since, during the experiments, Milgram's original prods were used. Thus, when subjects hesitated, they were told that the experiment required their continuing, that it was absolutely essential that they continue, and that they had no other choice but to continue. That is, when it counted, they were told they couldn't quit.[35] Two more departures from the original were that (1) the sample shocks given to the subject and learner at the beginning were smaller than in Milgram's experiment and (2) the subjects, we are told, were fully debriefed immediately after their participation.[36]

Burger holds that, given the number of subjects who expressed willingness to continue past the 150-volt point, his data reflect Milgram's. "Consistency needs and self-perception processes make it unlikely that many participants would have suddenly changed their behavior when progressing through each small step."[37] Burger notes that, since participants had been told clearly beforehand that they could leave the study at any time, it ought to have been easier for them to quit than in the original experiments.[38] Burger's replication of version 5 was less stressful for participants during the experiment than Milgram's original. And Burger's subjects were perhaps somewhat more aware of the possibility of deception given the statement on the consent form about being possibly misled. Burger does not include any information concerning how many of the participants might have believed that they had indeed been misled. That seems important information since one could suppose that some (or many) of those who were willing to go beyond the 150-volt point might have just been playing along.

Burger's recreation is less harmful to subjects than Milgram's original experiment, but contrary to Burger's supposition, not all the ethical problems have been solved. Volunteers were originally solicited through ads asking for people to participate in a memory study, and the entire setup continued this deception, even though the consent form did raise the possibility that the experimenter could mislead. Subjects were led to believe, and apparently many *did* believe, that they were shocking a learner in a memory experiment. (If this was not the situation, then the experiment seems pointless.) At the end of the experiment, they are told that it was really they who were the subjects, although Burger does not go into detail

---

35 Burger (2009): 6.
36 Burger (2009): 2.
37 Burger (2009): 9.
38 Burger (2009): 9.

on the debriefing.[39] The concern that subjects could suffer ongoing stress is raised by appreciating that the entire experiment was suggested by the producers of a television show, ABC's *Primetime*. At the beginning of the segment, the connection is made between the Milgram experiments and Burger's recreation. The segment is labelled "A Touch of Evil". Burger's conclusion is that the great majority of participants in his experiment would have gone on to the bitter end, as did their predecessors in the earlier experiments. True, the subjects in Burger's experiments may comfort themselves with the fact that they did not actually go to the dangerous shock level. And they can tell this to others. But – to put it in the worst light from the perspective of the subject – the scientist in charge believes, and has advertised to a wide television audience, that they *probably* would have behaved like Nazi extermination camp guards. Might this not cause ongoing, cumulative harm in the form of damage to their self-image and shame? Less harm than the original experiments but harm nonetheless? And harm which, again, participants could not have anticipated and so it is harm to which they could not have given their *informed* consent.

Appreciating the possibility of this ongoing harm does not entail the conclusion that the costs of the Milgram experiments, and Burger's recreation, outweigh the benefits. What is worrisome is that the possibility of this cumulative harm does not seem to play any role at all in the way Burger (and presumably his IRB) thought about the replication. Perhaps this is because there is evidence that participants – including Milgram's subjects – say that they were happy to be involved in these experiments and opine that such experiments should continue. A brief look at this evidence will help in assessing the costs and benefits.

With the final report sent to subjects about a year after the experiments were finished, Milgram sent a questionnaire which included a question about whether or not they were glad to have participated in the experiment. Milgram reports that 92% of subjects returned the questionnaire and that 84% said that they were glad (or very glad) to have been in the experiment.[40] Furthermore, Milgram says that he initiated a study in which a psychiatrist examined 40 subjects, focusing on those he felt most likely to have suffered adverse effects from their participation and found (quoting the psychiatrist's report) that none showed "signs of having been harmed by his experience.... No evidence was found of any traumatic reactions."[41] Milgram argues that "the participant, rather than the external critic, must

---

39 Burger, in personal correspondence, says, "I routinely told participants that the study was based on previous research using similar methods. I provided more details, including Milgram's name, when they wanted to know more about those experiments."
40 Milgram (1974): 195.
41 Milgram (1974): 197.

be the ultimate source of judgment".[42] And there have been other studies which look to provide empirical evidence that people do not mind being deceived when participating in experiments.[43]

On the other hand, there is a significant literature casting doubt on Milgram's claims. As I noted above, Milgram himself seems to undermine his evidence in responding to the point that just under half of the subjects, on the questionnaire accompanying the final report, said that they had doubts about whether or not the learner was actually being shocked. He says that this response would "cost them nothing and would go a long way toward preserving their positive self-conception".[44] But a similar explanation could be given for subjects saying they were glad to participate (i.e., they had excuses to make).[45] Diana Baumrind writes that saying they were glad to participate could be a way for subjects to "affirm their agency by denying that they have allowed themselves to be treated as objects, and when queried by an experimenter, most will say that they were glad to have been subjects".[46]

Milgram adduces more evidence from the interviews conducted by the psychiatrist who found no harm done to the subjects. Milgram says that he instigated these interviews and that the subjects interviewed were those judged most likely to suffer some ongoing distress. Gina Perry, in her painstaking search through the records in the archives at Yale, discovered a different story. Perry writes that "It was in February 1963 that Yale, concerned over the treatment of Milgram's subjects, initiated the series of follow-up interviews."[47] Equally important, "In total, Milgram invited more than 140 people, 20 percent of his original group of 780 subjects. Only thirty-two showed up."[48] The sample of people interviewed by the psychologist was very small and it was a self-selection of those willing to come "back to the lab" for another encounter. Thus, the evidence of these interviews counts for little to justify the claim that participants did not feel that they had been harmed. Simply deceiving someone involves failing to respect them or overriding respect for them. Different people may weight the value of truthfulness differently. Those who were not worried about being deceived may have felt comfortable returning for an interview, whereas those who held truthfulness in higher

---

42 Milgram (1974): 199.
43 L. Christensen, "Deception in Psychological Research: When is its Use Justified?" *Personality and Social Psychology Bulletin* 14 (1988): 664–75; Herrera (2001): 248; Miller (1986): 93–6, 106–9.
44 Milgram (1974): 174.
45 Gina Perry (2013): 140–1.
46 Diana Baumrind, "Research Using Intentional Deception: Ethical Issues Revisited", *American Psychologist* 40 (1985), 165–74, at 169.
47 Perry (2013): 216.
48 Perry (2013): 217.

esteem might have felt more wronged and hence have chosen not to respond to the request for an interview.

But suppose, for the sake of argument, that subjects really were just happy, after the fact, to have participated in Milgram's deceptive experiments. One way to explain this phenomenon is to see it as of a piece with their behavior during the experiment. Some (or many) may have felt a powerful commitment to science and an exaggerated faith in the integrity and beneficence of scientists. Perhaps their commitment and their faith were so strong that even participation in the deceptive experiments couldn't shake these attitudes. They may have been glad to participate for the same reasons they were willing to administer the shocks. This possibility raises an interesting dilemma for Milgram.

Milgram asks us to trust the ethical stance of the subjects when it comes to whether or not such experiments are morally acceptable and should be continued. And this is not unreasonable on my suggestion that subjects, though perhaps a bit naïve regarding science and scientists, are *not* choosing to act in violation of clear moral norms. This hypothesis considers the subjects to be at least adequate moral reasoners. But then Milgram's own assessment of the point of his studies is undermined. On the other hand, Milgram's view was that being willing to continue shocking the learner was morally wrong. He implies that the subjects themselves would have recognized the wrongness.[49] Milgram suggests that subjects were willing to allow the influence of the scientist to override their own moral sense to the point where they were willing to do something evil. But perhaps, later, as they are asked how they feel about being in the experiment, subjects try to recall their state of mind during the experiments. On Milgram's account, they were experiencing an "agentic shift" which produced a perspective rendering other duties, duties which Milgram portrays as of little or no moral weight, more important than the moral duty not to harm an innocent. But, with that memory in mind, their answer to the question about whether or not they were glad to have participated might reflect a morally skewed perspective. And in that case, Milgram is mistaken in his claim that the feelings of the participants are the best way to judge the experiments. If (as Milgram supposes) the moral compasses of his subjects were easily diverted from true north, then their contentment with having been in the experiments may not represent a trustworthy moral evaluation.[50]

Here is a different thesis to explain subjects' (purportedly) not feeling that they were in some way harmed by the deceptive experiments: Deception is so ubiquitous in our society that people are not surprised or dismayed when they find out that they have been lied to. Bryan Benham argues from the ubiquity of deception to its acceptability in research. He writes,

---

49 Milgram (1974): 6–7.
50 A somewhat similar argument is made by Steven Patten ((1977): 358).

"insofar as deceptive research practices are analogous/parallel to those accepted forms of deception, then such research is ethically permissible". One of his examples of accepted deception is the doctor who is dealing with an anxious patient and gives him a placebo.[51] But this is not a good analogy. First, in the placebo example, the doctor is (one hopes!) deceiving the patient for the patient's own immediate benefit. The deceptive research in question is not done for the benefit of the subjects. More importantly, many of us would hold that it is wrong for the doctor, however well intentioned, to deceive the patient that way. The suggestion here is that many of Milgram's subjects are complacent about having been deceived because they have often been misled, and expect to be misled, by many of the people and institutions that they deal with all the time. And perhaps they feel comfortable and justified in frequently deceiving those with whom they deal.[52] But rather than taking this as evidence that deceptive experiments are morally acceptable, we might see it as a disheartening indictment of our culture and perhaps a call to those with some influence to attempt to encourage truthfulness. So, even if we allow that subjects in deceptive experiments like Milgram's were glad to participate and do not feel harmed, it has not been shown that these feelings accurately reflect a plausible and considered moral stance.

Wrongs to Subjects

The APA code of ethics establishes criteria which discourage deceptive research when it is likely to cause harm to subjects, where harm is understood as physical pain or severe emotional distress. But there are other serious wrongs that can be done to people, which do not fit this understanding of harm. The possibility of such wrongs should be taken into account when considering asking subjects to participate in research where they will be uninformed or misled and so cannot make an informed decision to agree to being wronged. Two sorts of wrongs are especially relevant to the attempt to study human subjects making morally significant choices. One has to do with putting subjects at moral risk (the Problem of Moral Risk) and the other involves violating a right to privacy (the Problem of Privacy).

Many defenders of free will hold that by making morally significant free choices we help construct our own characters and so can be (to an extent) responsible for the sort of people we become. This means that there is a

---

51 Bryan Benham, "The Ubiquity of Deception and the Ethics of Deceptive Research", *Bioethics* 22 (2008): 147–56, at 150, 152.
52 I had a student, a double major in philosophy and psychology, who argued for the acceptability of deceptive experiments by pointing out that when he was waiting tables, if someone asked him to recommend an appetizer, he always picked the most expensive one, whether he liked it or not, since that way he would get a bigger tip. Since deceiving customers this way is acceptable, so is deceptive research.

great deal at stake in making moral choices. Confronted with a choice, someone is in a position of moral risk. They might choose well, but they might choose badly. And even what looks to be a relatively trivial choice can have significant consequences for the subsequent character of the agent.[53] Arguably, it is wrong to put people at moral risk without their consent. The Milgram experiments (purportedly) put the subject in a situation where he was forced to make a moral choice. He was put at moral risk without having agreed to it. This seems to be a wrong done to the subject, although it is not harm in the sense of physical pain or severe mental distress.

But aren't we often confronted with temptations which set the stage for morally significant choices in everyday life? Certainly. But it does not follow that it is legitimate for someone to construct such situations and place unknowing subjects in it. Minor traffic accidents happen all the time and may call for morally considered responses, but social psychologists do not travel the highways causing minor traffic accidents to study how people behave during and immediately after a minor traffic accident. (The APA's prescription against experiments producing severe emotional stress and physical harm would rule out causing more serious traffic accidents.)

Ironically, if this issue of moral risk is taken seriously, the debriefing in the Milgram experiments, which was supposed to mitigate the moral concern about having caused the subjects significant emotional stress, exacerbates the problem of putting subjects in a situation where they may do damage to their characters. In the debriefing, according to Milgram, he encouraged the subjects – including the obedient subjects – to feel good about themselves. The aim of the debriefing was to counter whatever stress the subjects may have suffered during the course of the experiment. Apparently, the psychology code of ethics at the time suggested that this was the proper aim of a debriefing and in general it seems an admirable goal.[54] But it can be argued that in the case of the Milgram experiments something is badly amiss. Milgram repeatedly says that the experiments forced the subjects to choose between obedience and doing the right thing.[55] And the surprising conclusion, he holds, is how often people are willing to do the wrong thing. And this is how the experiments are usually portrayed.

I have suggested that some (or many) of the obedient subjects may have judged that they were doing their duty toward science. And roughly half had doubts (or serious doubts) about whether or not the learner was actually being shocked.[56] But suppose Milgram is correct that many of his subjects made *evil* choices. Or simply grant that Milgram sincerely believed

---

53 Rogers (2015): 123.
54 Perry (2013): 78.
55 Milgram (1974): xi–xii, 4, 6–7.
56 Milgram (1974): 172.

that many of them had made evil choices. In that case, should Milgram have told the subjects that their behavior was "normal"? Milgram says that his job is not to make a moral judgment on the subjects but rather just to observe their behavior.[57] On the one hand, he, and many who discuss the experiments, do imply a very negative judgment on the subjects. But in the debriefing, the obvious implication which the subject could draw is that Milgram, the scientist in charge, judges that the subject's behavior was morally acceptable. I argued above that the self-reflective subject might well have ongoing qualms about what he has done. The aim of Milgram's debriefing, as described in his original 1963 article and in his 1974 book, was to silence those qualms and make the subjects feel comfortable with their behavior. But, arguably, this goes beyond simply putting the subject at moral risk. It actively encourages the subject to embrace his own wrongdoing.

If the choice Milgram's subjects faced was really between right and wrong then, when subjects made the wicked choice, it just seems morally mistaken to try to convince them that what they have done is acceptable, even where the goal is to make them feel better. Granted, if the subject's decision regarding how to assess his behavior during the experiment is itself a free choice, then it is ultimately the subject's doing if he should embrace the view that he has done nothing wrong. Milgram's debriefing would only provide a tempting excuse. But, in conducting experiments, scientists do not have the right to deliberately strew a subject's path with temptations that would not have been there otherwise. And this is especially the case if the subject has not had the opportunity to give his informed consent to participation in the morally risky experiment. It is worrisome that the APA code does not recognize moral risk to the subject. This raises the problem that the pattern in the Milgram experiments (and in the Burger recreations) of placing unwitting subjects in situations where they have to make moral choices and then encouraging those who choose badly to be comfortable with their own wrongdoing may often be repeated in psychological experiments. Furthermore, it is worth noting that developing a bad character could lead (by various paths) to the sorts of harms that the APA *does* recognize as problematic in regard to deceptive research.[58]

There is another sort of wrong that does not play a role in the APA criteria for when deceptive research is acceptable: violation of an experimental subject's right to privacy in a situation in which the violation does not cause physical harm or severe emotional stress. The case can be made by looking at James Rachels's oft-quoted argument against consequentialist thinking in his classic textbook on ethics, *The Elements of Moral Philosophy*.

---

57 Milgram (1974): xi.
58 Rogers (2015): 123–6.

Consequentialism dominates the perspective of the APA documents, as the arguments for overriding respect for people's autonomy show. Rachels proposes that people have rights which ought not to be violated even if no harm or damage is done to them. He gives the following example, which is a variation on a real-life case.

> Here is an (imaginary) related case. Suppose a Peeping Tom spied on [a woman] by peering through her bedroom window, and secretly took pictures of her undressed. Further suppose that he did this without ever being detected and that he used the photographs entirely for his own amusement, without showing them to anyone. Now under these circumstances, it seems clear that the only consequence of his action is an increase in his own happiness. No one else, including [the woman], is caused any unhappiness at all. How, then, could Utilitarianism deny that the Peeping Tom's actions are right? But it is evident to moral common sense that they are not right. Thus, Utilitarianism appears to be unacceptable.[59]

In Rachels's example, the woman's right to privacy is violated. What is meant by a "right" and when and where people have rights, if they do, are all enormous issues. But at the very least, many will agree with Rachels's "moral common sense" that the Peeping Tom should not have been peeping and that he wrongs the woman by doing so.[60] The experiments purported to reflect on free will which I have been discussing in this work, including the Milgram experiments, do not raise the question of privacy directly, but it is an important one.[61] I will say more about neuro-ethics and brain privacy in the next chapter, where I will be allowing that in the future it will be possible to "peep" into people's brains and read their minds, so it is useful here to discuss the Problem of Privacy.

Respect for privacy, though not associated with deceptive research, does figure in the current APA code of ethics, in connection with appreciating the dignity of the individual. Under "General Principles", we read, "**Principle E: Respect for People's Rights and Dignity:** Psychologists respect the dignity and worth of all people, and the rights of individuals to

---

59 James Rachels, *Elements of Moral Philosophy* (4th ed.) (New York: McGraw-Hill, 2003): 105.
60 A test of the claim that the woman is wronged is to change the example a little: Peeping Tom owns the house next door to his, and, in the empty room across from his bedroom window, he sets up a painting of a naked woman at which he then peeps from his bedroom. Creepy, certainly, and Tom is still an unappetizing character, but there is no woman being wronged (unless we add a lot more to the story about the painting).
61 Currently, Milgram's documents and tapes are "sanitized" so they do not give names. When the records are declassified in 2039, names will be released as well. Gina Perry (2013): vii, and in personal correspondence.

privacy, confidentiality, and self-determination."[62] The privacy concern in this document, and in *Ethics in Research with Human Participants*, is mainly that the psychologist not share someone's name or identifying information inappropriately.

> Privacy within the context of sociobehavioral research can best be protected through informed consent...The right to refuse to participate in research or to answer questions is central to protecting privacy and is an essential component of informed consent...Anonymity provides excellent protection of privacy.[63]

One motivation for protection of privacy is that a subject might be deeply embarrassed by information revealed after the research, thus violating the APA prescription not to cause severe emotional stress.

But what about a deceptive experiment that appears to be an invasion of privacy, but that could apparently be allowed, given current APA guidelines?[64] Here is an imaginary example: Members of the Psychology Department and members of the Fashion Department want to study athletic women's self-body-image, especially as it relates to choice of clothing and interactions with other women. They advertise all over campus for volunteers stating this as the purpose of the study. And it *is* the purpose of the study. As explained to the volunteers, over the course of a semester, they will get together once a week for some group sport. Each week they will be assigned a different type of outfit, and they will be observed in order to address the question of whether the difference in dress seems to affect how they interact during the sport. But the team of researchers believes that a deeper and more interesting question is whether or not being clothed *at all* has a significant effect on the body image of athletic women. So, the weekly sport will be played in a somewhat overheated gym with a communal women's shower conveniently located in the building. The shower has an unobtrusive video camera so that observers can watch as the women – who presumably will not want to put on their clothes while sweaty – shower together.

---

62 https://www.apa.org/ethics/code/.
63 Susan Folkman, "Privacy and Confidentiality", in Sales and Folkman (2000): 49–57, at 51.
64 The experiment I outline here is purely hypothetical, but for an actual experiment that raises similar issues, see the study of "personal space invasions in the lavatory" cited by James Korn (1997): 3. It should be noted that the experiment Korn mentions was done in the 1970s when ethical standards may have been more fluid. And the subjects were not debriefed, so this experiment does not conform to the current APA guidelines. (The subjects were probably happier being forever ignorant that they had been observed.)

This part of the experiment has to be kept from the subjects because they might skip the shower or fail to behave naturally if they know they are being watched. (The Problem of the Observer interfering with the experiment has to be avoided.) But to stave off the objection that, once debriefed, some subjects might suffer severe emotional stress, a careful screening is done beforehand. Prospective subjects fill out a long questionnaire about body image in which one of the questions is "How badly would you feel if you discovered that a stranger had frequently observed you naked without your previous consent?" Only those who answered "Not badly at all" could be selected. And a more thorough second screening could be done by a psychologist to try to ascertain that this answer on the questionnaire truly reflected the attitude of the subject. (This would raise the Problem of Translation Regarding the Subject Pool. If our subject group consists only of women who say they are happy to be "peeped at", can we be confident that the results from observing them apply to most, or even many, women?)

Even if it turned out that, once they were debriefed, some subjects did feel somewhat badly, the thinking of the experimenters is that, first of all, feeling somewhat badly is not "severe emotional stress". And a proper debriefing would include the scientific purpose of the experiment, including how knowledge helping us to understand body image could benefit future generations. So, even subjects who might feel some stress upon being debriefed could probably be brought to feel happy about their participation in the experiment. That, at any rate, is how the experimenters put it to the IRB. My suspicion is that the IRB would still feel queasy about the experiment. And there might be *legal* considerations that would block such an experiment. But given the ethical criteria proposed by the APA for deceptive experiments, this one seems ethically acceptable. Still, intuitively, it seems an invasion of the privacy of the women, and wrong, even if it does not produce severe emotional distress. And suppose – departing somewhat from the APA guidelines – the women are never debriefed about the "shower" aspect of the experiment. Then they do not suffer even the moderate emotional distress of knowing that they were being observed. Wouldn't that be okay? Most of us probably say "No". It is still an invasion of privacy. But why is privacy important? Or is it?

The APA code associates privacy with self-determination and many philosophers make the same connection; respecting someone's privacy is part of recognizing their autonomy. So, privacy and freedom are related. Adam D. Moore, considering the fundamental value of privacy as it might affect moral issues in neuroscience and neuro-surveillance, writes,

> Rights to privacy erect a moral boundary that allows individuals the space to order their lives as they see fit…. Privacy, autonomy, and sovereignty, it would seem, come bundled together… Arguably, any plausible account of human wellbeing or flourishing will have a strong

right to privacy as a component. Controlling who has access to us is an essential part of being a happy and free person. This may be why 'peeping Toms' are held up as moral monsters – they cross a boundary that should never be crossed without consent.[65]

If indeed people have a right to privacy (however we parse the concept of "rights"), then it is prima facie wrong to override that right. This is the case whether or not the invasion of privacy results in physical pain or severe emotional distress. If the "peeping" examples have any force, it is the invasion itself, whether or not the victims even know that their personal boundary has been breached, that wrongs them. Certainly, there might be times when other values come into play and override the person's interest in privacy, but, if privacy is important, these values would have to be significant.[66] Certainly, subjects need to be protected from serious physical and emotional harm, but if the object of study is the subject making morally significant choices, then the possibilities of moral risk and of violation of privacy need to be considered.

Harms and Wrongs to Researchers and Beyond

The subjects in a deceptive experiment are not the only people involved, of course, and there are dangers beyond the effects on subjects. One argument sometimes mentioned is that, as more and more people hear about deceptive experiments, the pool of naïve subjects will shrink, making it difficult to conduct deceptive research. But one whose criticism of deceptive experiments is focused mainly on the thought that deception wrongs the deceived by failing to respect (or overriding) his autonomy will not be unhappy with the consequence that deceptive experiments can't be done.

A different sort of worry lies in the moral damage done to researchers. This moral damage may have a harmful ripple effect throughout the profession of psychology and indeed throughout the culture as a whole. Sissela Bok writes, "The greatest harm from deceptive experimentation may be that to the investigators themselves, to the students trained in their professions, and to the professions as such."[67] Diana Baumrind notes that the costs of deceptive research include "encouraging students to lie in the

---

65 Adam D. Moore, "Privacy, Neuroscience, and Neuro-Surveillance", *Res Publica* 23 (2017): 159–77, at 166. See also, Alasdair McIntyre (1984): 104; Thomas Nagle, "Concealment and Exposure", *Philosophy and Public Affairs* 27 (1998): 3–30, at 4; Mark Tunick, "Brain Privacy and the Case of Cannibal Cop", *Res Publica* 23 (2017): 179–96, at 187–91.
66 For example, a standard argument against abortion is that, although the pregnant woman has a right to privacy, the rights, interests, or value of the unborn human being involved are significant enough to make killing him or her unjustified.
67 Bok (1978): 195.

interests of science and career advancement".[68] And that it may "undermine the commitment to truth of the researchers themselves".[69] An interesting feature of this argument, unlike the criticisms discussed above, is that there is almost no opposing position expressed in the literature. That is, no one (to my knowledge) has called into question the claim that engaging in deceptive research does (or at least could) render the researchers less trustworthy. Joan Sieber, in her contribution to *Ethics in Research with Human Participants*, notes that when an experiment is planned, risks to the experimenter should be considered, but her example involves the possibility of an experimenter doing research in a dangerous area and does not mention the sort of worries that Bok and Baumrind raise.[70] Christopher Herrera does address (briefly) the question of this sort of harm to the researchers in deceptive experiments. His response is that "research oversight is meant to protect subjects, not researchers".[71] This is a puzzling response. One assumes that when researchers and students are dealing with dangerous chemicals there are protocols in place to protect them. Perhaps most who deal with ethical questions regarding research with human participants do not see this as a problem. But perhaps they should.

The argument raised by Bok and Baumrind can be expressed as a slippery slope argument (among psychologists, "foot in the door" seems to be the term): once you engage in this small and apparently innocuous activity, you can be led (or are likely to move), small step by small step, to eventually doing something large and harmful that you never would have agreed to do at the beginning of the process. In the case of deceptive experiments, the argument would be that participating in the accepted and apparently innocuous deception of the experiments could result (over time) in students and experimenters being willing to engage in less savory deception – deception that they would have rejected had they not been involved in the original deception. The slippery slope admits of at least two species: a logical version and a psychological version. (The slippery slope is sometimes listed as a fallacy, and, of course, one might misapply the reasoning or be mistaken about the realities of human psychology and so be wrong about what will lead to what. But, whether or not Bok and Baumrind are ultimately correct, their reasoning is not fallacious.) The logical slippery slope argues that, although you may not have recognized it at first, the very reasons that justified the first small step also justify the further steps, including

---

68 Baumrind (1985): 168.
69 Baumrind (1985): 169.
70 Joan E. Sieber, "Planning Research: Basic Ethical Decisions-Making", in Sales and Folkman (2000): 13–26, at 14, 21.
71 Herrera (2001): 249. I posed the problem about this sort of harm to researchers to the woman at my university in charge of information concerning research on human subjects. It took a while for her to understand the question, and when she did, her response was exactly the same as Herrera's.

the step you would have resisted originally. The psychological version argues that the actual taking of the first step makes taking the next step easier for you – not as a matter of cold reasoning but rather of just breaking down psychological barriers – and taking that step makes the next step easier, and so on, until you find yourself psychologically comfortable with the large and harmful act that you would not have done without the small steps down the slippery slope.

The thesis that people can be led incrementally to do things they might not have done without being led on step by step is well known to psychology. It is often said that the Milgram experiments provide a powerful demonstration of this claim. The psychological version of the slippery slope argument against deceptive research thus seems to have significant power. Add the self-perception forces that lead us to continue along a chosen path, lest backtracking suggest that we have been in the wrong, and the psychological version of the slippery slope argument against deceptive experimentation gains even more force.[72] That students and experimenters may become the sort of people who are comfortable with deceiving others – perhaps in more and more significant ways – seems a serious damage to their characters. And if many students and experimenters do indeed descend that slippery slope, the discipline of psychology and the entire culture may suffer harm as a result.

What about the logical version of the slippery slope argument? The current APA code allows deception when their stated criteria can be met. Deception constitutes a cost, but if an experiment meets the criteria, the benefits can often be judged to outweigh the cost. Bruce D. Sales and Michael Lavin, in their contribution to *Ethics in Research with Human Participants*, though not fully endorsing Milgram's reasoning, offer it as an example of how one might weigh obligations. Milgram had a prima facie obligation to respect the autonomy of his subjects by telling them the truth, but "The moral principle of fidelity to science simultaneously created a prima facie obligation for Milgram to do the experiment in the most effective way possible.... Milgram viewed his actual obligation as doing the best research possible."[73]

Given this analysis of how to weight costs and benefits, the moral reasoning behind allowing deceptive experiments could also allow the experimenter to deceive his colleagues. Here is a (fabricated) example: Prof. D is

---

72 Burger appeals to these "self-perception forces" to justify his thesis that the subjects in his Milgram replication would likely have gone all the way on the shock machine ((2009): 9).
73 Bruce D. Sales and Michael Lavin, "Identifying Conflicts of Interest and Resolving Ethical Dilemmas", in Sales and Folkman (2000): 109–28, at 114. Sales and Lavin say that "questions can be raised about the ethical decisions made in this experiment and whether the actual obligations were appropriately met". They do not say that Milgram got it wrong.

interested in recreating one of the experiments discussed in Chapter 4: the experiment in which the subject is told to do some typing at a computer and, when he is done, is told that he has broken one of the keys. A confederate agrees, saying he noticed that the subject had broken the key. The subject is then likely to confabulate and agree that he did indeed break the key, perhaps even saying that he remembers doing so. The experiment was motivated by a concern that police interrogations might lead people to confabulate and confess to crimes they had not committed.[74]

Prof. D has reason to believe that false confessions are a serious problem, so it is important to gain more evidence. Moreover, he hopes to study whether or not confessions might be obtained more easily from members of one group than from members of another. He is concerned about racial, gender, economic, and educational disparities. Justice is at stake. Prof. D's colleagues on the IRB agree that the issue of false confessions is important and that the typing experiment – which can be conducted cheaply and efficiently – can shed light on the issue. But the board has recently become queasy about deceptive experiments and is dissatisfied with the standard consent form. It includes the following statement: "I may receive incomplete information about the nature and purpose of the experiment, and I may receive misleading information before and during the experiment. I will receive a full and accurate description of the experiment at its conclusion." But this statement appears at the end of the form in small print. It is unlikely that subjects read it. The IRB decides that, from now on, consent forms should include the statement in large bold print near the top. If Prof. D will not conform to the new guidance, the IRB will not pass his proposal. Prof. D is loath to include this since he fears that, seeing this advertisement for deception up front, subjects will catch on the minute they are accused of breaking the key, so the data will not reflect a subject's natural response. But he's got to pass the IRB, so Prof. D agrees to use the new consent form which relocates and emphasizes the statement about deception. The IRB reviews the proposal with the new consent form and passes the proposal.

Prof. D believes that the IRB's insistence on changing the form is ridiculous. Fidelity to science – that is, doing the important experiment in the most effective way – demands that the subjects not be actively entertaining the likelihood of deception. So, when the time comes, he sends the previous form to the office manager, who copies it and gives it to the grad student who is going to distribute it to the subjects as they arrive at the lab. It is a small deception and when his series of experiments is finished, he will (almost) "debrief" the IRB. He will tell them that the wrong form was sent, feign dismay, and blame it on his own carelessness. The experiment is very valuable. It cannot be conducted without deceiving the subjects. No one is

---

[74] Kassin and Kiechel (1996): 125.

harmed. Wouldn't the same cost/benefit justification that the APA provides for deceiving subjects justify Prof. D's deceiving his colleagues on the IRB? So, couldn't the logical slippery slope lead from deceiving subjects to deceiving colleagues? If not, why not?

In setting out the moral principle of "Fidelity and Scientific Integrity" in *Ethics in Research with Human Participants*, M. Brewster Smith writes, "Scientific integrity – truthfulness – is not open to compromise."[75] Presumably, this applies to deceiving one's colleagues. In order to block the logical slippery slope, there has to be a principled difference between one's colleagues and one's subjects that will bear the weight of making the distinction such that deceiving the former is absolutely forbidden and deceiving the latter is accepted common practice. A first thought might be that, in order for the business of psychology to proceed, psychologists must be able to trust each other. Prof. D might believe that no one will discover that he deliberately sent the wrong consent form to the office manager, but someone might suspect, trust might be broken, and – if such goings on were common practice – the whole discipline would be harmed. Even if no one ever finds out about Prof. D's ruse, he himself will know that he deliberately deceived his colleagues; in the long run, he may fear that others are deceiving him and he may become less trusting of his colleagues and harder to work with. All of this causes harm to his own work and to others in his work environment. There seems to be good reason, then, to obey the dictum to deal truthfully with colleagues.

But doesn't this point suggest a similar argument in favor of dealing truthfully with participants in experiments? Knowing that psychologists frequently deceive in the course of research might lead the lay person to suspect that they are not as generally trustworthy as they might be. And this could harm the relationship between professional psychologists and the larger society. Consideration of Milgram's descriptions and defenses of his controversial experiments provides an illustration: In her book *Behind the Shock Machine*, Gina Perry notes worrisome lacunae and even misinformation in Milgram's work. I reviewed one example above in talking about subjects' later attitude toward the experiments. Milgram writes that he instituted interviews by a psychologist with some of those subjects judged most likely to have suffered ill effects. Perry's research uncovered archival evidence that it was Yale, not Milgram, which motivated the interviews, and of the roughly 140 who were asked, the 32 subjects interviewed

---

75 M. Brewster Smith, "Moral Foundations in Research with Human Participants", in Sales and Folkman (2000): 3–10, at 8. In the paperback edition I am citing, there is what has to be a very unfortunate typo. The Fidelity Principle is the fifth principle listed, and one through four were listed by roman numerals. But instead of "Moral Principle V. Fidelity and Scientific Integrity", we read "Moral Principle Versus Fidelity and Scientific Integrity".

were the only ones who showed up.[76] Another example of suspicious "incompleteness" is Milgram's choice not to mention, in his 1974 book, the versions of the experiment he did using pairs of friends and relations as teacher and learner. Perry hypothesizes that he left these experiments out as they might be "difficult to defend".[77]

Another example is Milgram's explanation of the four prods (plus two more if the subject suggested that the learner might be hurt or that the learner wanted to quit) that the "experimenter" would deliver in a firm but polite voice. Apparently, in listening to the tapes, Perry concluded that Williams, the supposed experimenter, had sometimes gone well beyond this minimal commanding that Milgram suggested.[78] Perry notes that, in the original paper on the experiments, Milgram does not explicitly say how many times the prods should be repeated. Rather he says *both* that "If the subject refused to obey the experimenter after Prod 4, the experiment was terminated" *and* that "The sequence was begun anew on each occasion that the subject balked or showed reluctance to follow orders." The prods could apparently go on indefinitely.[79] Williams recorded that he told one woman 26 times that she had to continue.[80]

The failure to be clear that subjects were sometimes badgered at great length to continue with the experiment makes a difference to the value and interpretations of the experiment. For example, the situationist thesis is undermined if the subjects' behavior was not precipitated by a minor element in the setup. The point is this: It is possible that Milgram's incomplete and misleading report of his work does not actually represent an intent to deceive. We might hypothesize benign explanations for what look to be omissions or misinformation on Milgram's part. But knowing that Milgram was willing to intentionally deceive people makes one suspicious that his misleading and incomplete descriptions may be deliberate misinformation. This thought need not entail that Milgram was self-serving in his deception. He undoubtedly believed that deception in the interests of gaining scientific knowledge was acceptable, and one could suspect that he fibbed a bit in his record of the events in order to defend deceptive experimentation against its detractors. But the fact remains, knowing that the experimenter is willing to deceive in doing research makes one doubt his trustworthiness in other areas. And if we layfolk are suspicious of psychologists because of their conducting deceptive experiments, that can hinder the work of the profession and damage society in general.

76 Perry (2012): 216–17.
77 Perry (2012): 177.
78 Perry (2012): 115–19.
79 Perry (2012): 118. This seemingly contradictory description is repeated in Milgram's book (1974): 21.
80 Perry (2012): 116.

There is a final harm to the experimenter (and the larger society) to be mentioned here. It is closely related to the thought that the experimenter himself may become (or at least be judged to be) less trustworthy and that is that the experimenter may come to think of (and to treat) his "subjects as objects".[81] Evidence that this worry has some grounding comes from Milgram's condescending descriptions of some of his subjects. In his 1974 book, he quotes some of the notes that he took about the volunteers, people he knew only from observing them during the experiment. A 37-year-old welder "has a rough-hewn face that conveys a conspicuous lack of alertness. His over-all appearance is somewhat brutish".[82] Another subject "is about fifty years old, dressed in a jacket but no tie; he has a good-natured, if slightly dissolute, appearance. He employs working-class grammar and strikes one as a rather ordinary fellow."[83] One woman

> has an unusually casual, slow-paced way of speaking, and her tone expresses constant humility; it is as if every assertion carries the emotional message: 'I'm just a very ordinary person, don't expect a lot from me.' Physically, she resembles Shirley Booth in the film *Come Back, Little Sheba*.[84]

Perhaps this was just the style for psychologists back at the beginning of the 1960s, but in Milgram's book, the condescending descriptions seem part and parcel with his deceptive practice.

Again, the worry is a slippery slope, both psychological and logical. If the rationale for allowing deceptive experiments is that the importance of gaining scientific knowledge trumps the obligation to respect the autonomy of the subject, then (one could argue) this devalues the subject. Hence – the logical version – if gaining scientific knowledge is more important than respecting subjects' autonomy and dignity, then the subjects do seem to be objects for the experimenter to use. But there are other values the researcher might hold as important as gaining scientific knowledge. So, if it is morally permissible to run the cost/benefit analysis in a way that overrides respect for the subject while doing research, why shouldn't the experimenter judge that other important values outweigh the autonomy and dignity of other people with whom he may come in contact in other contexts? And – the psychological version – repeatedly doing research in which the subject's autonomy and dignity take second place to the researcher's goals could

---

81 This is the title of Chapter 4 of Perry's book. Diana Baumrind's 2015 review of Perry's book is entitled, "When Subjects Become Objects: The Lies Behind the Milgram Legend".
82 Milgram (1974): 45.
83 Milgram (1974): 73.
84 Milgram (1974): 77.

easily lead the experimenter to *feel* (if not to think) that his own interests are more important than the conflicting interests of others. This unwholesome effect may be magnified (the Problem of Elitism) if researchers are adamant about their principled truthfulness to one another while feeling comfortable in deceiving their subjects. They may come to see themselves as the elite, superior to the mass of mankind, so they get to do things that *hoi polloi* must avoid.[85]

There is, then, a long list of ethical problems that might occur with certain sorts of research on human subjects. Deceptive research is especially worrisome since the subject cannot give *informed* consent beforehand. But even if we take these ethical issues seriously, we need not conclude that deceptive research should be avoided. The moral calculus involves weighing the harms against the benefits. So, two questions remain: Do the possible benefits we hope to gain from our deceptive experiments justify the possible harms and wrongs that subjects, experimenters, and even the larger society may suffer? And could the expected benefits be achieved without the use of deceptive experiments?

Expected Benefits

When the costs and benefits of the experiments in question are assessed, one difficulty is that neither is easy to pin down with certainty. With deceptive experiments, one might say that experimenters do incur the certain cost of overriding the subject's autonomy and dignity, but if the subject truly does not care, then this might seem a small cost. (But that depends on how one values truth-telling. It might seem small to some and large to others. As I noted, if subjects don't care because deception is ubiquitous, that may indicate that something is amiss in society at large.) Regarding the other harms and wrongs that I suggested in the previous section, maybe many subjects and experimenters do suffer seriously, in one way and another, from participation in deceptive experiments. But maybe not. Maybe only a few suffer. Maybe for those who are harmed or wronged, the negative effects are minimal. One of the themes that should have emerged from the preceding section is that it is difficult to make an accurate assessment on the cost side of the moral equation.

The same is true for the benefit side. Presumably, the aim of research is knowledge, and knowledge is valuable in two ways: it is an intrinsically good thing to have knowledge, and knowledge can be used for benefitting humanity (and perhaps other creatures). Milgram writes, "the laboratory

---

85 Milgram defends deception (he prefers "masking", "staging", or "technical illusions"), arguing that we suspend moral rules in the practice of various professions – for example, the gynecologist may do what the man in the street may not – and so why not in social science? Milgram (1977): 20–1.

psychologist senses his work will lead to human betterment, not only because enlightenment is more dignified than ignorance, but because new knowledge is pregnant with humane consequences".[86] So, we need to discuss these two values, and (as usual) we will take the Milgram experiments as our example for the same two reasons that made them useful in discussing harms and wrongs: their morally controversial nature makes them intrinsically interesting, and a robust literature has grown up around them.

What of the intrinsic value of knowledge? Some knowledge is so trivial that it is not worth pursuing. In most circumstances, it would be silly to bother to count the number of hairs on your head "just to know". And there are some areas where people argue that it could be better not to find out the truth. For example, some hold that attempting to research cognitive differences between people on the basis of race and gender might turn up evidence that would perpetuate negative stereotypes that our society hopes to leave behind. Saul Smilansky offers an example of (what he takes to be) a truth that had better not be known: He is confident that the choices of human agents are determined, but he believes it would do terrible damage to our society if that belief were widely held.[87] But, setting aside these sorts of examples, I take it that most of us can agree that coming to understand – in however local and limited a way – how the natural universe works is a noble pursuit. Aristotle began his *Metaphysics* with the thought that the desire for theoretical knowledge is natural to human beings. We thirst to understand and rejoice when we do. So let us grant that, prima facie and bracketing certain qualifications, the mere acquisition of knowledge is a good.

Nevertheless, three initial questions regarding the acquisition of knowledge are worth asking of a deceptive experiment before we include, on the benefit side of the moral calculus, simply the "gaining of knowledge" as opposed to the further good of the practical consequences the knowledge might produce. Is the knowledge we gain new? That is, do we find out something that we did not know before? Is the knowledge we gain significant? And could the knowledge have been gained without the deceptive experiment? With the Milgram experiments, we are asking these questions in hindsight, but considering whether intrinsically valuable knowledge is gained from the Milgram experiments could help in thinking about future experiments.

Almost everyone engaged in discussing the Milgram experiments agrees that they do provide interesting information. Some reports of the experiments, such as Doris's, and Milgram's own film *Obedience* do them something of a disservice. Doris and *Obedience* include only one of many

---

86 Stanley Milgram "Issues in the Study of Obedience: A Reply to Baumrind", *American Psychologist* 19 (1964): 848–52, at 852.
87 Smilansky (2002).

experiments. A glimpse of one version of the experiments does not capture the extent of Milgram's work. His 1974 book describes 18 different versions of the basic "teacher shocking the learner" setup. For example, sometimes the confederate learner and confederate experimenter switch places. Sometimes two experimenters give different instructions. And on and on. And the simple data on the behavior of subjects in all these different cases are fascinating.

Questions arise when Milgram moves beyond the simple data to offer theoretical interpretations and conclusions. One point on which commentators do seem to agree is that the experiments offer a striking demonstration of what I have called the "psychological slippery slope" principle. Having taken the small steps of giving the learner a series of minor shocks, many of the subjects were willing to move, by small increments, up the levers on the shock machine to the point of possibly doing the learner serious harm. But history bombards us with cases of ordinary people doing terrible things.[88] And the thought that agents are subject to this small-steps process has long been known. So, we cannot give Milgram credit for introducing this bit of knowledge.[89]

Furthermore, it is not clear that he does demonstrate a slippery slope in obedience. None of the versions of his experiment includes telling the subject to administer the severe and dangerous shock right at the beginning. Everyone assumes – as do I because the small-steps principle is common knowledge and intuitively plausible – that it was the small incremental steps that enabled so many subjects to eventually act in a way that (we further assume) they would not have done originally. But the experiments themselves do not demonstrate that. In no version of the experiments were subjects commanded to deliver the extreme shock right at the beginning and then observed to refuse to do so. We have no contrast case to *show* that subjects would not have given the highest-voltage shock had they not started by giving the lower-voltage shocks.

The theory which Milgram constructs from his data proposes to explain destructive obedience by holding that people can undergo an "agentic

---

88 A glance at the French Revolution or the events following the partition of India and Pakistan or the "Great Leap Forward" in China should suffice to make this depressing case. The thought that Germans in the first half of the twentieth century were somehow uniquely monstrous could only be entertained by someone lacking in historical perspective.

89 The defender of Milgram could respond by noting that, when he asked people beforehand, few expected the results. But he asked three groups of people: psychiatrists, college students, and an audience of middle-class adults of various occupations (Milgram: 1974): 27–8). It would be interesting to know what the expectations would have been if he had asked a group of historians. This raises the question of how we should value the demonstration of knowledge that might be already available to some but is not widely appreciated.

shift" – a giving over of their wills to the authority of another – which is difficult to reverse.[90] But this theory has apparently not found many takers among psychologists.[91] And on the question of whether or not the experiments cast any light on how the Nazis were able to do what they did – which Milgram says was the original motivation for the experiments – opinion is divided.[92] Baumrind holds that the events in Milgram's lab offer little in the way of explaining the behavior of the Nazis and sees this as an illustration of a common concern in social psychology research (what I am calling the Problem of Translation Regarding the Situation): Can the information we derive from studying the behavior of subjects in a lab really be translated to the world at large?[93] Baumrind notes that deception is sometimes defended so that it is possible to conduct the experiment in the lab. The supposed benefits are that the lab allows a uniform psychological reality and a high level of certitude regarding causal inferences. But Baumrind takes issue with both claims, writing,

> The level of complexity of social phenomena and the implausibility of treating human beings as interchangeable or even as identical with themselves over time sharply limit the level of certitude that can accompany any empirical generalization in the sociobehavioral sciences.[94]

In the particular case of whether or not Milgram's experiments bear on understanding the Holocaust, there are many reasons, including the Problem of Translation Regarding the Situation in the Lab versus the outside world, to be critical of his thesis that they do. Milgram himself briefly mentions some of the differences.[95] He points out that his subjects were encouraged to think of the memory experiments as ultimately beneficial to humanity, whereas the Holocaust would have been impossible had it not been for the preceding centuries of vicious anti-Semitism in Europe. And his subjects were told that the shocks they were administering did not cause

---

90 Milgram (1974): 123–34.
91 Kaposi (2017): 385.
92 Milgram (1974): 1–2. George R. Mastroianni offers an assessment of the competing views, "Milgram and the Holocaust: A Reexamination", *Journal of Theoretical and Philosophical Psychology* 22 (2002): 158–73. His overall thesis is that uncritically applying Milgram's results to the Holocaust is a mistake.
93 Diana Baumrind (1964): 423. I will focus on the Milgram experiments, but another example which might inspire skepticism is the experiment, used as an example above, where the subject types and is then told that he has broken a key (Kassin and Kiechel (1996): 125). The real-world application of the results was intended to be interrogation by police, but the differences between the situations of the accused in the two cases, and between the lab and the police station, seem very significant.
94 Baumrind (1985): 172.
95 Milgram (1974): 176–7.

any permanent damage to the learner, whereas the organizers and perpetrators of the Final Solution knew that it was the death of millions that was the goal.

Other differences include the one-on-one and face-to-face nature of the authority in the experiments in which subjects tended toward obedience. Milgram ran other experiments in which the authority was not immediately present and in these experiments obedience fell significantly.[96] Apparently, in Milgram's lab, high rates of obedience required the immediate presence of the authority. But in the world outside the lab, including the Third Reich, it would be logistically impossible for such an arrangement between commander and commanded.[97] This is especially interesting since Milgram repeatedly associates the evidence of his experiments with Hannah Arendt's thesis about the banality of evil. Milgram frequently connects this thesis with the suggestion that what he has shown is that the modern human being often loses himself, becoming a mere cog in a great institutional machine.[98] But his experiments do not show that at all. When the immediate authority is not breathing right down the neck of the subject, disobedience is common. When the authority gives commands over the phone, the subjects often cheat.[99]

Milgram responds to the point that the situation in his lab is disanalogous to that in Nazi Germany:

> Yet the essence of obedience, as a psychological process, can be captured by studying the simple situation in which a man is told by a legitimate authority to act against a third individual. This situation confronted both our experimental subject and the German subject and evoked in each a set of parallel psychological adjustments.[100]

But the claim that the situation in his lab was a simple version of the more complex situation in Nazi Germany is difficult to accept. Milgram's argument here echoes Libet's claim that the wrist-flexing process he studied could be viewed as a simpler version of similar processes involved in more complex decisions and actions. In some disciplines – physics perhaps – one can construct the experiment with few and simple elements and then translate one's conclusions to larger systems. But if the goal is to understand human choice and behavior, it will take much more to defend the move from the lab to the outside world than just the suggestion that in the lab we

---

96 See Milgram's tables on Experiment 7 and Experiment 14 (1974): 60, 95.
97 Charles Helm and Mario Morelli, "Stanley Milgram and the Obedience Experiment: Authority, Legitimacy, and Human Action", *Political Theory* 7 (1979): 321–45, at 335–8.
98 Milgram (1974): 5–6, 11, 188.
99 Milgram (1974): 59.
100 Milgram (1974): 177.

have a simple version of what is more complex outside the lab. Regarding the Milgram experiments and the Nazis, George R. Mastroianni has (it seems to me) expressed the most reasonable view: "We should also abandon the convenient but simplistic notion that there is, from a psychological viewpoint, a single or even a small set of likely explanations for the behavior of Holocaust perpetrators among which we should choose."[101]

The results of Milgram's many versions of his experiments are striking, but it is not clear that they give us much new knowledge. The value of intrinsic knowledge gained in the Milgram experiments may well not outweigh the costs. But there are defenders of Milgram who argue that not only do Milgram's experiments give us new knowledge, but they also provide the sort of knowledge that will have significant practical benefits. Alan Elms writes that "better and wider public understanding of the conditions most likely to promote destructive obedience on a small scale could have a prophylactic effect with regard to destructive obedience on a large scale".[102] Arthur G. Miller agrees, arguing that real harm "could result from *not doing* research on destructive obedience.... If one reads Milgram's (1961) research proposal.... it is hard to imagine a more convincing presentation in terms of the usefulness of a basic research project."[103]

But – even on the supposition that Milgram's experiments do give us new knowledge –there are several responses to these endorsements of their usefulness, and these criticisms can be aimed at many deceptive experiments purporting to provide beneficial knowledge. For example, many of the "group effect" experiments may be open to the charges expressed here. First, however, I think the possibility of the Milgram experiments proving beneficial to certain individuals cannot be denied. Milgram himself quotes participants who feel that they have learned something from the experiments.[104] And many readers of his book will likely come away with the wholesome thought that they must be discerning about the appropriateness of obedience when confronted with authority. Similarly, when one learns of the evidence from the "group effect" experiments, one is likely to take note that one should carefully evaluate the group behavior that might unduly influence how one behaves oneself. So, it should be granted that some deceptive experiments have likely produced some benefits.

However, this evidence of beneficial effects is anecdotal and intuitive. To my knowledge, no comprehensive studies have been done to show that deceptive research – Milgram's, the group effect studies, or other experiments – has

101 Mastroianni (2002): 170.
102 Alan Elms, "Keeping Deception Honest: Justifying Conditions for Social Scientific Research Stratagems" in *Ethical Issues* in *Social Science Research* edited by T. Beauchamp, R.R. Faden, F.J. Wallace, Jr., and L. Wallace (Baltimore, MD: Johns Hopkins University Press, 1982): 232–5, at 239–40.
103 Miller (1986): 138.
104 Milgram (1974): 195–6.

made any significant change for the good in the way people in general behave. I believe there is no doubt that clinical psychologists have helped a great many people, and in back of their efforts stands the work of researchers in psychology, so I do not mean to question the thought that psychology as a discipline has benefited society. My concern is very specific: Is there evidence that the information gained from *deceptive* experiments has produced significant benefits for society? We are speaking about information that is genuinely new – that is, not information that historians or novelists or your mother had already imparted to the curious. And, given the moral calculus we are considering, it must be information that could not have been acquired without the deception. To my knowledge, no study addresses this specific question, but it is the question that needs to be answered if it is claimed that benefits outweigh harms with deceptive experiments.

James F. Korn disagrees. He writes,

> Research in social psychology *has* produced benefits for society; we have a better understanding of human nature and that knowledge has been used to promote human welfare. Some of the research that produced these benefits involved the use of deception.

He cites Milgram as providing knowledge, but he does not show that the knowledge has benefitted society. His key example of benefit regards equality for women. "There is a large amount of published research on gender roles, discrimination, and sexual harassment which has advanced our understanding and in doing so may have helped to change our attitudes."[105] But Korn does not cite evidence that it was these studies that helped change attitudes rather than changing attitudes that generated interest in doing the studies. (Korn is writing in the late 1990s, and popular attitudes began changing rapidly and publicly by at least the early 1970s.) So, even if some benefits are likely, I stand by the claim that no comprehensive studies have been done to demonstrate these benefits. (The example of women's equality illustrates at least two general methodological challenges: One must be able to show that it is knowledge produced by the experiments, rather than other social factors, that have led to the benefits. And one will need to be sensitive to the extent to which politicization of the issues in question may taint the assumptions, construction, and conclusions of one's experiments.) Social psychologists have been engaged in deceptive research for only about a century now.[106] Perhaps it is too early to try to mount comprehensive studies of benefits accruing to society from the research. But the fact

---

105 Korn (1997): 175. It should be noted that Korn is not trying to defend a developed case, he is just offering a quick page of possible benefits of deceptive experiments as the conclusion of his book.
106 Korn (1997): 8.

remains that one of the key criteria for allowing deceptive experiments is the possibility of the knowledge gained providing significant practical benefits to society. It seems clear that some individuals have benefitted from some deceptive experiments, as the Milgram example shows. But whether society in general has benefitted, and to what extent, is an open question.

A related and perhaps more worrisome criticism is amply illustrated by the treatment of the Milgram experiments by those who defend them as providing new knowledge about destructive obedience. They assume that the knowledge will be used for benign purposes. But knowledge concerning how to get people to obey authority looks to be easily weaponized. Perhaps some individuals may profit by thinking harder about resisting authority, but governments – history teaches – are happy to adopt whatever means serves their purposes to procure obedience. And having procured it, they have (as often as not) used it to slaughter innocent millions. Granted, the twentieth century was unusually vile in this regard, but the difference from previous centuries may be one of degree and not of kind. Defenders of Milgram from the community of psychologists are likely to be making their predictions from the perspective of those attempting to gain knowledge for the benefit of mankind. (Here, I suggest, the Problem of Perspective involves the psychologists failing to appreciate the motivations of rulers.) From the perspective of world history, it approaches bizarre to assume that the results from the Milgram experiments – experiments motivated by the example of National Socialism – would (on balance) produce more benefits than harms. In that governments from time immemorial have been brilliant at getting ordinary people willingly to do (and to suffer) dreadful harms, we may suppose that Milgram does not actually have much to teach those who wield power. But that, again, casts doubt on whether or not his experiments produced new knowledge. The bottom line here is that *if* the Milgram experiments give us new knowledge, we have no reason at all to suppose that the knowledge will produce more good than harm. The same goes for the group effect experiments and the "false confession" experiments. Perhaps what is most troubling is that the psychologists who have weighed in on the ethical issues apparently take it for granted that new knowledge about the causes of human behavior will be used only (or mainly) for benign purposes. That is not the lesson of history.

So, in our test case of the Milgram experiments, there are significant questions to be raised about whether or not the value of the knowledge they provide is worth the costs they incurred. The cost/benefit analysis regarding deceptive research involves one more point and that is whether or not the knowledge could have been gained without the deception. In the case of the Milgram experiments and the Nazis, the discussion in the literature suggests that there is a better alternative if we hope to understand how Holocaust perpetrators came to do what they did. And that is to ask them. Or, at this late date, to study the wealth of documentary evidence that we have from those terrible times. Here might be an ideal project for interdisciplinary collaboration. Historians who knew how to access, read, and understand the documents could work with psychologists sensitive to patterns in human behavior and in first- and third-person expressions and explanations of that behavior, and this methodology might be able to make some real progress. It could prove tedious and time-consuming, but (besides not deceiving subjects) it would have the significant advantage of avoiding the problem of translating from the lab to the real world.[107] Ultimately, it may be that looking for one or a few theoretical explanations for the behavior of perpetrators is a mistake. And if our team of historians and psychologists came to that conclusion, well, that would be useful knowledge.

A different sort of alternative to deceptive experiments involves role-playing, an approach that today can be made vivid through the use of virtual reality.[108] The participant can be informed at the beginning that the situation is manufactured but asked to engage with it as naturally as he can. For some people, it is possible to become immersed in role-playing, and most of us have had the experience of empathetic excitement, fear, and so on at the movies or even when we are thoroughly involved in a book. Right now, there are bugs to be worked out before the experience of virtual reality successfully mimics real reality. (For example, at present, one cannot experience one's own body in virtual reality the way one experiences it in the actual world.[109]) But we can imagine that in the future the virtual will seem as real as the real. So, if participants are asked to act as if the situation were real, it seems likely that they will be able (to some extent) to behave naturally. And virtual reality experiments will be able to tell us something about people's actual thought processes and behavior.

But we must be cautious before we assume that virtual reality will allow us to observe the whole range of human activity as if we were watching people actually going about their business. There is a dilemma here. Suppose we are concerned to study significant moral choice and hope that observing people making choices in a virtual setting will shed some light on how people make choices in the real world. If the participant knows all

---

107 Studying the possibility of false confessions and confabulation in the context of criminal interrogations might also profit from this sort of real-world approach.
108 See, for example, Mel Slater, Angus Antley, Adam Davison, David Swapp, Christoph Guger, Chris Barker, Nancy Pistrang, Maria V. Sanchez-Vives, "A Virtual Reprise of the Stanley Milgram Obedience Experiments", PLOS ONE (Dec 2006). https://doi.org/10.1371/journal.pone.0000039. With this experiment, apparently the subjects were still deceived about the nature of the test they were giving, although they were told, and could observe, that the learner was not an actual person. For present difficulties with using virtual reality in social psychology experiments, see Xueni Pan and Antonia F. de C. Hamilton, "Why and How to Use Virtual Reality to Study Human Social Interaction: The Challenges of Exploring a New Research Landscape", *British Journal of Psychology* 109 (2018): 395–417.
109 Pan and Hamilton (2018): 405.

along that the situation is a false creation of the experimenter, then the Problem of Translation arises; it is reasonable to question whether his actions and reactions reflect what his behavior would be in the real world. We do not assume that devoted players of first-person shooter video games would be so trigger-happy out on the real street. It is the problem of translating from the lab to reality in a different guise. But suppose that our virtual situation is extremely realistic and our participant is such a good "pretender" that he forgets he is in a virtual, and not a real, reality. Then many of the ethical issues raised about actual experiments might apply. If the participant is so immersed that (from his perspective) he is making ethical choices as real as those that Milgram's subjects made, then he might feel all of the stress and suffer the harm of shame and the damage of having actually made morally wrong choices. And, unless the participant was carefully informed about the possibility that he might believe the situation, he has not given his informed consent to being in the experiment as he actually experiences it.[110]

One way to avoid using deception, and to circumvent the worry that what goes on in our manufactured situation does not reflect what goes on in the actual world at large, is to observe people going about their business in settings where either the experimenter had asked permission or the people are in public such that they are inevitably observed and aware of the fact. The experimenter would not be in control of the situation but that is what makes it real and not manufactured. And the real world has a lot more going on in it than the lab, so it might take long and careful observation to address the question that the experimenter is concerned with. But many of the harms and wrongs that deceptive experiments may produce would be avoided. Diana Baumrind writes, "Most deceptive research is motivated more by convenience than necessity.... Surely, were their code of ethics to prohibit deception research, psychologists could use their ingenuity to devise non-deceptive alternatives to studying destructive obedience, and other socially significant phenomena."[111] The inconvenience attendant on alternative methods can be counted as a cost of not engaging in deception. But the costs of deception are serious, so if the beneficial knowledge can be gained without the deception, that should weigh heavily against deception in the moral calculus.

---

110 Pan and Hamilton (2018) give the example of a virtual reality experiment in which participants are told that their task is to operate an elevator and then are "shocked" when a gunman enters the elevator and starts shooting, forcing them into a situation in which they can save five people only by actively sacrificing one (a trolley-car setup). Pan and Hamilton point out that it is very important that participants know *that* they can quit, and *how* they can quit, the game.
111 Baumrind (2015): 695.

Uncharitable Interpretation

There is one more point that should be mentioned briefly in this chapter on ethical issues in research with human beings. Assuming that it is wrong to demean people without good evidence, if the experimenter offers an interpretation of his data that casts his subjects in a negative light, we should ask whether or not the data might support a more charitable interpretation equally well. In the present context, much of the experimental evidence has been taken to undermine human free will one way or another. If we embrace the connection between freedom and dignity, then the more charitable interpretation may be the one that sees the subjects as able to deliberate reasonably and able to act freely in light of their deliberations. For example, as discussed in Chapter 5, Doris reads Milgram's data as showing that many of the subjects behaved cruelly, impelled by trivial elements in the situation. That portrays Milgram's subjects in a very negative light. Milgram's own interpretation of his subjects' behavior is slightly less negative since he grants that subjects embrace the authority in question because of a shared belief in the value of scientific enquiry. But Milgram still portrays his obedient subjects as choosing destructive obedience over the morally correct option. I suggested a more charitable interpretation: the obedient subjects were torn between two perceived duties – their duty not to harm an innocent and their duty to science. I do not say that the charitable interpretation should be preferred simply because it is more charitable. But in studying human agency, when the more positive conclusion fits the data as well as the negative conclusion, that is a point that should be noted, especially if (as I have argued) the burden of proof lies with the one who would deny free will.

I take it that this principle would encourage good scientific practice. It is common knowledge that research can be biased because experimenters – like the rest of us – suffer from confirmation bias. They tend to find what they are looking for. Milgram wanted to study destructive obedience and that is what he found. Suppose his motivating question had been "Are ordinary Americans so devoted to the value of science that they can be brought to behave badly through faith in the beneficence and integrity of scientists?" A good case can be made that Milgram's data support a resounding "Yes!" in answer to that question, but since that was not the question he was asking, he does not consider that that is what his data show. Being open to the possibility of a more positive interpretation might encourage the experimenter to consider whether or not he has allowed bias to affect his reading of the data. (Alternatively, if one has arrived at a very rosy conclusion regarding some human behavior, it might be well to consider darker interpretations, especially if one grants that one was looking for good news about humanity.) This methodological prescription means that the experimenter may have to accept that the data support several different conclusions equally well, and that is less appealing (perhaps) than being able to advance a single unified theory. But if reality, especially human reality, is messier than we would like, it is we who had better rethink our approach since reality is unlikely to budge.

Another example of uncharitable interpretation is illustrated by the "false confession" experiment involving the subject who is told to type and then, when he's done, is informed that he has broken a key on the computer keyboard, an accusation that is backed up by a confederate witness who claims to have seen the subject break the key.[112] The subject has not in fact broken the key. He cannot remember actually breaking the key. And often he at first denies that he broke it. But when the experimenter and the "witness" insist, he can be brought to agree that he broke it, and even to confabulate, to generate a false memory of the event. Wegner uses this experiment as evidence of his thesis that people's actions are not caused by their consciously willing them.

As Wegner and the original experimenters understand the behavior of the supposed key-breaker, he has simply been led to misremember what he has done. And that seems like a bad thing. The suggestion is that a rational and responsible agent – such as Wegner holds to be non-existent – would stick to his guns and deny having broken the key. But the evidence with which the key-breaker is presented is this: (1) I do not remember breaking the key. (2) The experimenter – who would have no reason to lie about it – is sure I broke the key. (3) This witness – who would have no reason to lie about it – says that he witnessed my breaking the key. We who are in the know know that the experimenter and the "witness" have lied. But the Problem of Perspective arises. Consider how the situation looks from the perspective of the subject. Most people don't make a note of how hard they hit the keys on the keyboard as they type. Given his evidence, the most rational belief is that his memory is faulty and so he tries to resurrect a more accurate memory. Not only is his behavior rational, but it is epistemically virtuous. As we go about our business in the world, a moderate amount of humility regarding our memories, a willingness to change our minds in the face of powerful evidence, *and* a default attitude of trust toward our neighbors all count as virtues. We can be misled, of course, but the fact that we can be tricked into adopting, and even confabulating about, a false belief is consistent with the claim that the adoption of some false belief can be evidence of both our rationality and our epistemic virtue. It is interesting and useful to know that people can easily be led to confabulate, but the interpretation of the data that sees the subject as just a gullible dupe does not give the subject proper credit and fails to capture important information about how people assess their memories. Wegner offers the uncharitable interpretation in support of his thesis that we do not act on the basis

---

112 Kassin and Kiechel (1996): 125–8.

of our deliberate intentions, but in that this conclusion is demeaning to human beings in general, that is all the more reason to consider other, more charitable interpretations.

Rejecting uncharity entails that unless we find very powerful empirical evidence to the contrary, we should suppose that our neighbors are free, autonomous beings who have intrinsic dignity and are worthy of respect. In this chapter, I have tried to raise a host of ethical issues surrounding the study of human thought and behavior. If (in the future) scientists hope to settle the question of free will, they will have to study human beings closely. And if they plan to do so ethically (or at least to pass their proposals by their IRBs), they will have to confront the sorts of moral problems that have been discussed here. (They may have to confront new and currently un-thought-of moral problems as well, but problems that no one has thought of yet lie outside the scope of the present work.) Having looked at problems – practical and ethical – that debate over past experimentation has raised, we can turn now to the future.

Chapter 7

The Future Study of Human Freedom
Setting the Stage and Ethical Issues

Introduction

In this chapter and the next, I hope to show that the question of whether or not human agents have free will is a more difficult one to answer than is often assumed, even if the prime example of "free will" is taken to be the ability to make *libertarian* free moral choices (LFMCs). I will consider how science in the future might try to address this heretofore metaphysical question experimentally. At present, the scientific consensus is that there is indeterminacy in the physical universe. This has given aid and comfort to some of those defending a libertarian theory of free will.[1] This might change and universal causal determinism (UCD) once again become the dominate view. (Is this a likely hypothesis? My local philosopher of physics says it is "very likely" or "somewhat likely" but that ultimately it is hard to tell what the future of physics holds. On the other hand, my local particle physicist responds with an unequivocal "not likely at all".[2]) But if UCD

---

1 Robert Kane in *The Significance of Free Will* ((1996): 129–30) proposes that indeterministic subatomic events in the brain might allow for non-determined choices on the part of the agent. Mark Balaguer ((2010): 157) sketches a "neural-dependence-on-micro-indeterminacy model of neural/mental indeterminacy" in arguing that, to date, this suggestion, or something like, has not been disproven. This is a very speculative case, and I do not propose to defend it. It is worth mentioning that the defender of responsibility-grounding free will, who wants to associate free choice with quantum mechanics, had better reject the many-worlds interpretation. That theory looks to entail the curious deterministic thesis that if your choice between A and B appears indeterministic, it is because "you" exist in a super position, choosing both. But in any event, that contemporary physics allows that *anything might* behave in an indeterministic manner at least shows that it is not "unscientific" to deny universal causal determinism.
2 Alasdair MacIntyre, crediting Karl Popper, offers a charming argument for the proposition that the future of physics cannot be foretold: Theoretical changes in physics tend to be radical, involving previously unthought of ideas. Thus, such a radical change, occurring at some point in the future, cannot be foretold because the forecaster would have to be reporting the radical, new idea in the present. But if the idea exists in the present the theoretical change is not something that occurs in the future. (*After Virtue* (Notre Dame, IN: University of Notre Dame Press, 1984): 93–4.)

DOI: 10.4324/9781003258988-8

becomes popular, the compatibilist can continue to make the case that human agents are free nevertheless, and the libertarian can (as in the past) stick to the thought that, although much of the business of the physical universe is determined, some human activities, such as making moral choices, is not. UCD is a metaphysical thesis which is not empirically provable, and a sea change in its favor among scientists would leave the question of human free will more or less where it has been for the past two thousand years. The question is, can the issue of free will be settled *experimentally* in the future?

In the present chapter, I will first imagine a future in which technology has advanced far beyond where we are today. This technology, by itself, will solve some of the most difficult problems raised by the recent experiments purporting to be relevant to free will. This sets the stage for a discussion of the still numerous and weighty practical and ethical problems that will face the future scientist, even with his amazing technology. Then I will apply the discussion of ethical problems from Chapter 6 to a consideration of moral issues as they might surface in efforts to study human free will in the future. The next chapter will look at practical problems that are likely to plague the empirical study of free will, even in a scientifically advanced future. In that the practical problems are so serious, discussion of the ethical issues might seem beside the point. It is unlikely that future neuroscientists or psychologists will be able to design workable experiments which actually address the question of free will, so they probably will not get to the stage of worrying about the ethical issues involved. Nonetheless, I am aiming to produce a substantial list of problems. (I dare not say "complete" since chances are I have missed some.) It may be that one (or a few) of the practical problems are weighty enough on their own to preclude an empirical answer to the question of human free will. Still, in that so many people assume that science can answer the question, it seems worthwhile to point out the numerous difficulties in achieving that goal. Furthermore, scientists are likely to continue the study of human volition and agency. The ethical issues that arise regarding a hypothetical future attempt to settle the question of freedom may well arise for future research related to other areas of human volition and agency. Thus, a discussion of the ethical issues related to hypothetical future experiments on free will is useful.

A Possible Future: The Brainiometer

We can imagine a science of the future (perhaps a distant future) that has advanced spectacularly in its ability to study human brains and human conscious activity. If the question is responsibility-grounding free will, then brains and consciousness must be the objects of study, rather than overt behavior, since overt behavior is not where the moral action is. If there is free choice (at least as I have portrayed an LFMC), then it occurs *before* any overt deed and after the torn condition. So, let us hypothesize a scientist of the future – call him Dr. F, short for Dr. Future – who is concerned to settle the question of human freedom. We can imagine that Dr. F can, at a distance, train his Brainiometer toward some human agent, S, and observe all that is going on in S's brain. Suppose we assume that all conscious phenomena are closely correlated with brain events allowing Dr. F to discern, from observing the brain activity, what S is consciously experiencing. (This hypothesis does not rule out dualism or idealism since both can be consistent with the proposed correlation. Idealists do not deny the existence of brains; they simply hold that brains are ultimately mind-stuff.) I do not say that Dr. F can cognitively grasp *all* that is going on in S's brain and S's consciousness simultaneously. That is probably too much information at a time for any human being to assimilate. Since we are imagining, we might suppose that humans have evolved into something else that *can* assimilate that much information at a time, or perhaps we might imagine that Dr. F is a human being melded with a super computer or that he *just is* a super computer. But this sort of imagining would not be fruitful since it would project us beyond the bounds of thought experiments that we ordinary humans here and now can entertain. So, let us suppose that Dr. F could train his Brainiometer on any part (or parts) of S's brain and observe what goes on there and that, if that brain activity correlates to a conscious experience that S is having, Dr. F can know that, too. Moreover, all of these physical and mental goings-on can be recorded for Dr. F to study at his leisure.

In the next chapter, I will make three points relevant to the Brainiometer. First, I will argue that, if there were any chance of settling the question of free will empirically, such a device would offer the best (or only) hope. Second, I will propose that a working Brainiometer may simply be impossible. Third, I will try to show that, *even with* a Brainiometer, Dr. F will likely not be able to settle the question of free will. But in the current chapter, I want to address a different issue – ethical barriers to a neuroscientific study of meaningful free will – and so I assume that Dr. F has his Brainiometer up and running.

Dr. F hopes to discover whether or not human beings have meaningful freedom. He avoids the Problem of Description by understanding the freedom in question to be the ability to make LFMCs; the agent in the torn condition assesses morally significant options rationally and chooses between the options on his own *a se*. The choice is made by the agent and is not the product of causally necessitating factors. In order not to fall into the Problem of Domain, Dr. F does not assume any metaphysical theses that might color his experimental approach. To conduct his experiments using the Brainiometer, he feels justified in presupposing that there is a correlation between the mental and physical/brain events of a person's life, but he suspends judgment on UCD, physicalism, epiphenomenalism, dualism, and idealism. Any of those positions would allow for the mental/physical correlation (or something like). UCD rules out (libertarian) free will, as does epiphenomenalism if it is thought that preceding brain events determine the causally inert mental events; thus, he cannot assume UCD or epiphenomenalism without begging the question against the existence of LFMCs. Accepting one of the other metaphysical theses – physicalism, dualism, or idealism – would leave the question open of whether or not people make LFMCs since they are consistent with determinism (UCD and LCD) and with indeterminism. But Dr. F's hope is to concentrate on the actual empirical data, so he can bracket metaphysical theses for the time being.

Dr. F agrees with my argument from Chapter 1 that the burden of proof is on the one who would deny free will, and he takes the Translation Problem Regarding the Object of Study seriously. Evidence concerning "choices" or "decisions" that are distant from what a morally significant choice is thought to be should not, without more argument, count for much in the free will debate. Experiments where you "decide" to flex your wrist or push the right button rather than the left tell us little (if anything) about how human agents go about making meaningful free choices. It is not plausible that the relevant difference between these "decisions" and what look to be morally significant choices is that the former are simple and the latter are complex. Granted, there are categories of choice which seem to come much closer to the morally significant choices we care most about. The prudential choices with no moral content which I hypothesized in Chapter 2 probably come the closest. Those are choices where immediate desires conflict with one's long-term goals. One might well be in a torn condition, and judgment and will might need to be invoked in order to resist the immediate desires. I have my doubts that such choices are really devoid of moral content. There are better and worse long-term goals, and the ability to exercise self-discipline is a virtue and its opposite a vice. If these hypothesized non-moral prudential choices truly do not involve any element of value, virtue, or right and wrong, then even these sorts of choices may not resemble the LFMC enough to allow evidence to transfer, given the burden of proof. And if these non-moral choices *are* sufficiently similar, then most of the difficulties of studying morally significant choice may well apply to this other species of choice. Thus, for purposes of the present discussion, I will bracket the possibility of prudential, non-moral choices. We may imagine that Dr. F, equipped as he is with the Brainiometer, decides that the most direct and conclusive way to solve this Problem of Translation is to study human agents making (what at least appear to be) morally significant free choices.

Dr. F is in a position to look to see whether some agent, S, finds himself in the torn condition, deliberating between choosing A, the morally better option, and B, the morally worse option. Then he can observe S opting for one over the other. (Whether S's opting is done with libertarian freedom or not is the question Dr. F hopes to answer.) It is not necessary for S to provide any first-person reporting on his mental states since Dr. F can ascertain them, so the Problem of First-Person Reporting and the Problem of the (First-Person) Observer that seriously undermined the conclusions of the Libet experiments do not arise. The subject does not need to be attending to his own mental states, which introduced an unnatural situation at the outset. Nor does Dr. F need to rely on the sometimes untrustworthy first-person reports. It is not even necessary that S engage in some overt action since Dr. F can observe what goes on in S's brain and know what S is consciously experiencing throughout the process of choosing, and it is in connection with the *choice* that the responsibility-grounding freedom is found, if it is found anywhere. The Problem of Focus can be avoided since Dr. F – having carefully described what he is looking for: the LFMC – will not be tempted to shift the focus of his experiment away from the locus of freedom to happenings that occur before or after the process of choosing or to other elements which are not relevant to the nature of the actual choice.

Dr. F is in a vastly better position to study human agency than any scientist is at present or is likely to be in the near future. For example, use of the Brainiometer could settle the question of whether or not agents are choosing in accord with their reasons: If there is a process of rational deliberation going on, Dr. F can observe it, and he can tell whether the option pursued was among those under rational consideration. But even if he finds that S has deliberated before choosing, there remains the further issue of causal necessitation. Even with his marvelous technology, it will be extremely difficult for Dr. F to settle the question of whether or not human agents have libertarian freedom. But, first, there are ethical barriers in his way.

The Future Study of Human Freedom: Harms and Wrongs

We can apply the moral worries set out in the previous chapter to Dr. F's work as he attempts to design his studies of human freedom. Moral choice is an especially ethically sensitive area of research. The use of the Brainiometer can minimize some ethical concerns but it significantly amplifies others. We are assuming that Dr. F cares about morally responsible research or at least that he has to pass an institutional review board (IRB) that cares. We are further assuming that the moral questions discussed in the previous chapter are still relevant in the future. (Were our time-travelling thought experiment to take us beyond these ethical issues, our intuitions about, and understanding of, the moral concerns that might face the future researcher using human subjects would entirely lose their moorings. As I noted at the end of the previous chapter, Dr. F may confront ethical questions currently un-thought-of but those cannot be addressed in the present work.) These are large assumptions. Possibly, by the time the Brainiometer becomes functional, the whole planet, and whatever extra-terrestrial colonies there may be, might be governed by evil, totalitarian dictators who don't care a fig about the sort of moral issues involved with research on human subjects that we are concerned about now – issues involving personal autonomy, respect for the individual, and not harming people. It might appear to be the case that living in such a society, though rather dreadful on the whole, would at least facilitate conducting experiments on free will since one would not have to worry about all the red tape involved in trying to experiment ethically. However, I think this initial impression is false. Dr. F actually has a better shot at studying meaningful freedom in a society that tries to impose ethical constraints on his work.

To see this, suppose that Dr. F lives in the hypothesized society governed by evil, totalitarian dictators. In order to allow him the education and resources to conduct his experiments, we will place him in the ruling class. Being able to conduct his research without the constraints of contemporary moral worries, he can perform his experiments on whomever he pleases – outside of the ruling class – and however he pleases. He can place his subjects in whatever situations he believes will produce the best data, and he can turn the Brainiometer on them whenever he deems it useful, with or without their knowledge. Suppose he amasses solid empirical data which he plausibly interprets as showing that his subjects do not choose freely. Their choices are produced by locally causally determining factors. Has the question of free will been settled against free will and in favor of LCD? I think not. The Problem of Translation Regarding the Subject Pool renders the determinist conclusion suspect. It is reasonable to suppose that the non-ruling citizens raised in such a society, where they have absolutely no privacy and no rights at all and are objects to be used by those in power, would be so psychologically stunted by constant terror, misery, oppression, and deprivation that they might *not* have free will. They might never find themselves in the torn condition, rationally considering morally significant options, and able to choose *a se*. It may be the case that there have been (and are) people rendered unfree by the terrible situations in which they exist. Setting aside oppressive societies (North Korea comes to mind), even some of those who are in relatively benign societies but who suffer from addiction or mental disability may not be free and perhaps should not be held morally responsible for their decisions and actions. So, the evidence that Dr. F amasses in the society where he is not expected to take a moral stance toward his subjects would not show that human agents, in less extreme circumstances, are not free. We do not know what the future holds, but if Dr. F has any hope of studying the question of human free agency, including the possibility of freedom for human beings not crushed from birth by extreme circumstances, he had better be conducting his studies in a society that expects him to operate within an ethical framework. So, our assumption that Dr. F (or at least his IRB) is concerned with ethical questions regarding human subjects actually puts Dr. F in a better position to study free will than the assumption that he lives in a society where such issues do not arise.

Dr. F plans to observe agents' brains as they are making (what appear to be) LFMCs, the sorts of choices for which the agent can justifiably be held morally responsible. (Here I will often use LFMCs as a shorthand for what *appear to be* or are *ostensibly* LFMCs. His question is whether or not human agents make choices that genuinely meet the criteria for LFMCs.) That way, he can avoid the Problem of Translation Regarding the Object of Study. In observing his normal adult subject, agent S, Dr. F will look for the torn condition – S debating between morally significant options. That human agents sometimes find themselves at least *feeling* torn is not (I take it) open to question. The behavior of Milgram's subjects seems clear evidence of this phenomenon. Dr. F might find that a specific sort of brain activity precedes S's being in the torn condition. So, he might conclude that *that* condition is locally determined. On the description of an LFMC that I am working with, that conclusion does not pose a problem for the thesis that human agents have libertarian free will. The conflicting desires that set the stage for a morally significant choice may well be determined. We are free so long as we can choose between them on our own.[3] In order to address the question of meaningful free will, Dr. F must focus on whether or not he can detect activity in the brain that will allow him to conclude that the choice for *this over that* is causally necessitated by preceding factors.[4] One test of success would be for him to be able to predict, based on preceding brain activity, which of the considered options S will choose. (Note that, although finding indeterminism in the process is necessary for the conclusion that agent S has made an LFMC, it is not, by itself, sufficient for this conclusion. More on this in the next chapter.)

A first question for Dr. F to consider as he designs his experiments is whether or not to conduct them in the lab. He will have more control over what the subjects are confronted with in the lab, so let us consider that method first. Experimenting in the lab will allow him to recruit a large number of subjects and have them all face roughly the same morally significant choice. Suppose, for example, that he attempts a recreation of the Milgram experiments, except that instead of observing through one-way glass, Dr. F will (unbeknownst to his subjects) be observing them with his Brainiometer. Chances are that in a future that contains the Brainiometer

---

3 Rogers (2015): 127–41.
4 The dualist or idealist might believe, on philosophical grounds, that human choices are determined by non-physical factors such that the Brainiometer does not detect them, but since our topic is the attempt to study free will empirically, that possibility must be bracketed. We are assuming the kind of close mental/physical correlation that would ground the Brainiometer's success.

it will be difficult to find naïve subjects who are likely to believe that they are actually engaged in an experiment about the effect of punishment on learning where the punishment involves the crude method of shocking the learner. That sort of experiment would belong to the twentieth century – the distant past. But the ethical issues raised by the Milgram experiments are applicable to any deceptive experiments where the object of study is human subjects put in the position of having to make moral choices, so allow the Milgram experiments to stand in for whatever experiment Dr. F can devise that will allow him to gather a sufficient number of participants and study moral choices.

Moral worries quickly arise. Dr. F (in keeping with Milgram's methodology) will be deceiving his subjects about the nature and goal of his experiment and that in itself constitutes an overriding of respect for them and their autonomy. So, let us assume that Dr. F will have to make the case for his experiments to his IRB taking the guidelines for deceptive research of the American Psychological Association (APA) Code into consideration. He will have to think about what harms to the subject his experiment might cause. We can hope that future ethics codes could take into account not just those harms the APA is currently concerned with – physical pain and severe emotional stress – but also the further harms and wrongs discussed in Chapter 6. So, he will have to think about moderate, ongoing emotional stress that could add up to a great deal of discomfort over the years. And he will need to keep in mind the other wrongs of placing the subject at moral risk and of violating the subject's right to privacy. We can further hope that future ethics codes will take note of harm to the experimenters and their associates and students. So, he will have to be alert as to how his own behavior forms his character and what impact participation in his experiments might have on his students and the discipline at large. He will have to ask whether or not the possible value of the knowledge to be gained outweighs the costs, and he will have to consider whether or not the information he hopes to gain could have been found in other ways.

Milgram's subjects suffered severe stress during some of his experiments. Dr. F may try to circumvent this ethical difficulty by recreating Burger's recapitulation, so that subjects are stopped if they show a willingness to go beyond the 150-voltage point on the shock machine. But a possible dilemma arises from the suggestion of watering down the experiments. If Dr. F hopes to study meaningful freedom, then the moral choices his subjects are confronted with will have to have a certain minimum level of significance or seriousness. Too trivial a choice may not generate any torn condition and so no meaningful free choice could be discovered, leaving open the question of whether or not more important choices do (or do not) produce the torn condition followed by the agent opting freely. But choices important enough to make the agent seriously debate may cause stress. Simply being in the torn condition is likely to be stress-producing. In order to conduct experiments to discover what the histories of morally significant choices entail, the situation of the subjects inevitably has to be somewhat stressful and that is a problem. But perhaps Dr. F can hit upon the correct balance between the significance of the choice and the amount of stress that it is likely to produce – enough significance for the subject to be torn but not so much that the subject suffers *severe* stress during the experiment. This introduces the Problem of Perspective since the proper balance is likely to be different for different subjects. But here the Brainiometer comes to the rescue. Dr. F can design the experiment so that the Brainiometer registers information concerning the point at which each subject, supposedly giving increasingly higher levels of shocks, begins to debate about what to do and begins to feel stress. The Brainiometer will provide much better insight into what the subjects are thinking and feeling than would merely observing their external behavior. As the level of stress increases, Dr. F can stop the experiment before the point at which the stress becomes severe. As regards the question of stress during the experiment, that might satisfy his IRB.

With the original Milgram experiments and with Burger's recreations, a further question about stress arose. Might not the subjects suffer shame and embarrassment throughout the rest of their lives because of their performance in the experiments? Perhaps they would suffer fairly mild stress but over a long period of time. When one does a cost/benefit analysis, it is appropriate to consider the extent of the stress not just in immediate strength but also in duration. We don't know whether Milgram's or Burger's subjects did indeed suffer ongoing stress. With Dr. F's subjects, we might continue to observe them with the Brainiometer after their participation in the experiments to discover whether or not they did indeed continue to feel shame and embarrassment, but there are two difficulties with this proposal. First, if we find that participants do suffer noticeable stress over the years, it is too late. The experiment has already been conducted. Second, the practice of keeping someone under Brainiometer surveillance has problems of its own, as we will see. Before conducting his experiments, Dr. F cannot know the extent to which his subjects might experience stress over the years.

In regard to the original experiments, some of the shame that subjects might have felt had to do with the fact that subsequent publicity of the experiments emphasized the Nazi connection. Perhaps Dr. F could design a scenario in which he observes his subjects making morally significant choices, but in debriefing he could warn his subjects not to tell anyone what they decided and assure them that he will keep their information entirely anonymous. This could reduce the likelihood of significant, ongoing stress to some extent but not entirely. Add to this the wrong of placing the unwitting subject in a morally risky situation and there looks to be the possibility of significant harm and wrong done to the subject. (The important issue of privacy will be taken up later.)

In the face of such problems, could Dr. F tell his subjects the truth concerning the nature and purpose of the experiment in order to obtain their informed consent? No, researching free will (at least prima facie) appears to require deception to circumvent the Problem of Translation Regarding the Situation. In order to manufacture a situation in which the subject is confronted with a particular moral choice, the subject cannot know that the situation is indeed manufactured. Once recognizing that he is participating in a sort of play or performance (as Milgram liked to style his experiments), the subject will likely be unable to engage in a natural and genuine moral choice. This point would hold true for any experiment which attempts to set all the subjects up to make a similar sort of moral choice. One advantage ascribed to conducting experiments in the lab is that the experimenters can control the situation to allow for repetitions of a scenario. But if the scenario involves a specific sort of moral choice, *that* element of the experiment must be kept from the subjects.

The current APA guidelines suggest telling the participant as much about the deceptive experiment as feasible without undermining its value. Could Dr. F explain to the participants that they *might be* confronted with some sort of moral choice as they engage in the learning experiment? Probably not. Another advantage of the lab is that it can restrict the number of elements involved in the experimental situation, but the downside of this is that – given that the participant needs to attend to only a limited number of things in the lab environment – the subject who has been tipped off to his possibly having to make a moral choice is likely to recognize the moral choice as it arises, see that he himself is the subject under scrutiny, and be unable to make a natural and genuine moral choice. Dr. F could just omit the fact that the experiment involves moral choice and simply tell the subject that he might be misled. Berger included that point in his consent form and his experimental design passed his IRB. I argued that, given the possible ongoing harm, this move is insufficient to support the thought that the subjects had been sufficiently informed before giving their consent.

Moreover, simply deceiving someone at all wrongs them by violating their autonomy and hence failing to respect them. But here Dr. F may have a card to play that was not available to Milgram and Berger. Milgram, Berger, and others who defend deceptive experiments argue that the participants in such experiments, far from expressing anger or shame or embarrassment, say afterwards that they are happy to have participated. Opponents of deception, notably Diana Baumrind, argue to the contrary that subjects are not really happy about their participation but are trying to salvage some dignity after having been treated as objects.[5] Dr. F, using the Brainiometer, is in a position to find out how subjects really feel about being in deceptive experiments. Before he attempts to get his free will

5 Baumrind (1985): 169.

experiments past his IRB, he could conduct another series of experiments. Perhaps his colleagues are engaged in deceptive experimentation on innocuous topics not involving serious moral choices. As subjects in his colleagues' experiments are being debriefed, Dr. F can (with their permission) observe their brain activity with the Brainiometer to discover whether or not they are *actually* happy to have participated. If he amasses data to show that (contrary to what they say) subjects are made unhappy by having been deceived, then Dr. F will have to grant that ongoing stress should be added to the anticipated costs of his experiments. But perhaps he will find that the vast majority of these subjects did not mind being deceived. In that case, he will have some solid evidence that it is unlikely that his subjects will object to having been deceived. He can argue that perhaps his subjects will suffer a little stress and maybe they will have been wronged and disrespected in some trivial ways, but since in general people don't mind being deceived as part of scientific experimentation, it is unlikely that his subjects will object.

But even in the case where Dr. F can present this evidence to his IRB, it might be argued that people can be wronged, even if they themselves do not feel that they have been wronged or harmed. (I argued in Chapter 6 that a dilemma arose for Milgram: He consistently held that his obedient subjects had done morally wrong things under the commands of authority but subsequently accepted at face value their judgments about the moral acceptability of his experiments, insisting that these same subjects should have the last word.) It is not outside the bounds of common experience to suppose that sometimes people do not appreciate what is owed to them. Perhaps the subjects in the future who are happy to participate in deceptive experiments do not recognize their own dignity and autonomy or do not recognize when someone else has failed to respect them. Moreover, it may be more objectionable to people to be deceived concerning experiments involving moral choices than to be deceived where no moral choices are involved. Dr. F cannot discover whether or not this is the case without someone already having conducted moral choice experiments so that subjects' brain activity can be observed. So, one may still doubt that it is acceptable to conduct Milgram-type experiments on subjects who cannot give their truly informed consent.

But there is a bigger problem here and that is the use of the Brainiometer itself. Use of the Brainiometer exacerbates the Problem of the Observer and *radically* exacerbates the Problem of Privacy. Dr. F is convinced that the only way to settle the question of free will scientifically is to observe in detail what is going on in agents' brains. Millennia of philosophical debate have (already in our present) shown that the overt deeds and the introspective self-reports of human agents are insufficient. And the current empirical evidence, such as Libet's, that some brain activity precedes some felt "urge" does not connect with the question of meaningful freedom. Nothing short of very exact observations of brain activity will prove adequate. And it will have to be possible to correlate the brain activity with conscious thoughts and experiences since free will involves moral choices and moral choices are conscious events. Hence the necessity for using the Brainiometer (an argument I will make at more length in the next chapter). Should Dr. F tell his subjects that he will be observing them with the Brainiometer, having explained the purpose and capacities of the instrument? This revelation will certainly undermine the experiment in that the participants will realize that it is they who are being studied – and studied *closely*.

But if Dr. F does not tell his subjects that they are being observed through the Brainiometer, then he is guilty of the most grotesque invasion of privacy. In the previous chapter, the importance of recognizing a right to privacy and the connection between privacy and autonomy were discussed. Advancing technology has raised new issues, among them the question of brain privacy. For example, already we are wrestling with problems such as whether or not prospective employers or courts of law have a right to view your brain scans and, if so, under what circumstances.[6] The invention of the Brainiometer – with its ability to reveal thoughts and experiences from observed brain activity when simply pointed at a subject – would render questions about brain privacy very pressing indeed.

Jesper Ryberg argues that access to someone else's thoughts and feelings via observation of their brain activity may not be so very different from accessing their thoughts by observing their facial expressions or other involuntary, but publicly observable, physical evidence of inner thoughts and feelings. Thus, if "mind reading" through some sort of neural scanning is a violation of privacy when the person under scrutiny has not consented, a clear difference between such mind reading and the sort we all engage in frequently will have to be spelled out. And the significant differences are not obvious, he continues. If the main distinction is thought to lie in the fact that we have control over the external, publicly available evidence in a way that we do not have control over our brain activity, that is often false. We often have no control over physical manifestations of our thoughts and feelings. For example, we may involuntarily tremble or blush, revealing fear or shame.[7]

If we attempt to locate the difference in the fact that mind reading based on, for example, facial expressions, is indirect while mind reading based on brain observation is direct, Ryberg notes that this is not the case either. Mind reading through neurotechnology is indirect as well. First, it is mediated through the technology we are using. Second, there is a complex

---

6 A recent issue of *Res Publica* (23, 2017) was devoted entirely to the questions of neuroethics and brain privacy.
7 Jesper Ryberg, "Neuroscience, Mind Reading and Mental Privacy", *Res Publica* 23 (2017): 197–211, at 205–8.

theoretical grounding supporting our beliefs about the evidence the technology provides.[8] This point about access to someone's thoughts and experiences being indirect holds even on the hypothesis of the Brainiometer. Dr. F must trust the instrumentation to faithfully access the brain activity, and he must rely on the work it took to achieve the trustworthy correlation between brain activity and conscious thoughts and experiences. However, on the hypothesis I am envisioning, the difference between Dr. F's neural spying and our frequent observation of our fellows in public is clear. The scenario is that Dr. F plans to deceive his subjects about the very central fact that he has the Brainiometer pointed their way. Surely, there are settings where you have a right to expect that you are not being observed unless you have been informed and have consented – in your bedroom, for example. That bedrooms are generally considered private (as opposed to public) spaces is an agreed-upon social norm in our culture (and in almost all cultures). Prima facie, it seems that the space within your skull is even more private than your bedroom such that if someone should be peering into your brain (without your consent), that is obviously not the moral equivalent of someone watching you in a public place. The public versus private spaces distinction seems a wholesome one and it is certainly longstanding. Someone who wanted to deny the difference or to suggest that the space between one's ears is public (rather than private) would have a difficult case to make.

Kasper Lippert-Rasmussen proposes a different approach to the acceptability of accessing people's thoughts in the absence of their consent. He imagines a future in which brain-scanning, mind-reading devices are "cheap, portable [and] reliable".[9] This future resembles the one with the Brainiometer, except that anyone can own and use the mind-reading device. And it is the fact that everyone can have (and use) one that makes their use non-threatening, according to Lippert-Rasmussen. The thought is that the damage done by mind reading lies in the shame it causes the one whose mind is being read. But since everybody has thoughts that are wicked, nasty, embarrassing, foolish, and what have you, full transparency – everybody's brain and mind open to everybody – would not cause shame. One would see that one's own thoughts were not much worse than those of the next person, so no need to feel shame and no harm done by universal use of the cheap, portable, and reliable Brainiometers.[10] In Lippert-Rasmussen's future, we can suppose, Dr. F need have no qualms about not telling his subjects that he is using the Brainiometer. They ought to expect it anyway

---

8 Ryberg (2017): 203.
9 Kasper Lippert-Rasmussen, "Brain Privacy, Intimacy, and Authenticity: Why a Complete Lack of the Former Might Undermine Neither of the Latter!", *Res Publica* 23 (2017): 227–44, at 229.
10 Lippert-Rasmussen (2017): 238–9.

since everybody does it, but in any case, no harm is done since the subjects will not feel shame when they are debriefed and told that Dr. F has been scanning their brains and reading their minds.

This is not a very persuasive case. Even if one accepted the basic argument, one might dispute the facts. What if some people really do have much worse thoughts than others, or many more terrible thoughts than others? The argument depends upon there being a certain equality in the level of mental depravity across humanity, but why think that that is the case? Some people behave much worse than others and express sentiments that are much worse than those expressed by others, so the only hard evidence we have suggests that there is not a basic sameness in the kind or amount of nasty thoughts entertained by different people. But even if we allow a rough parity from person to person regarding vile thoughts, the argument is still weak. Why should not ubiquitous use of the brain-scanning device simply induce shame across the whole society?

Furthermore, as argued in the previous chapter, invading your privacy, even if you never know about it and so do not suffer any shame, seems to be a wrong done to you. That was the point of James Rachels's Peeping Tom example. So, the claim that full transparency would minimize the feeling of shame is not sufficient to defend covert use of the Brainiometer since one need not feel shame to have been wronged. And inducing shame is not the only harm that promiscuous use of the brain scanners could cause. There are all kinds of perfectly respectable thoughts that we might not want to share with others. We might prefer to conceal that we very much like, or very much dislike, someone. We might not want to advertise our political or religious beliefs. We might be working on an idea for which we want to reserve the credit to ourselves when we reveal it to the world. There are all sorts of thoughts that we might want to keep to ourselves in addition to the thoughts that we would be ashamed to own.

The argument that ubiquitous scanning would be acceptable since everybody would be transparent and thus not suffer shame is somewhat analogous to the argument, discussed in the previous chapter, that lying to potential subjects is acceptable because, in our society, everybody lies and expects to be lied to. One response to that argument was that, far from showing that lying is acceptable, it could show that our society is deeply corrupt. Were it the case that everyone could peer into everyone else's thoughts, via the brain scanner, then perhaps it would be considered acceptable in that society for Dr. F not to inform his subjects that he will be using the Brainiometer during the experiment. His subjects would just assume that their brain activity and their innermost thoughts are available to Dr. F and to everyone. That, in itself, would not show that such ubiquitous invasion was acceptable.

Would living in this fully transparent society facilitate Dr. F's efforts to research free will? Probably not. (Granted, a society in which everyone is reading everyone else's minds constantly would be such a radically different society from any the earth has ever seen that we cannot appeal to intuition with any confidence.) First, the Problem of the Observer arises. The object of Dr. F's studies is morally significant choice. Believing that the experimenter is reading your mind as you find yourself in the experimental situation faced with an important moral choice seems very likely to render it impossible for you to make a natural choice. You will almost certainly not face open options since you will try to choose what you believe the observer thinks to be the right choice. Moreover, if the association between privacy and autonomy that was noted in the previous chapter is genuine and important, then it is possible that citizens of the transparent society, like the citizens of the future evil dictatorships mentioned earlier, simply lack free will. Morally significant open options might be shut down for people whose inmost thoughts are constantly under scrutiny. If Dr. F finds evidence that the inhabitants of Transparent World do not make LFMCs, this will not show that human beings like us do not do so since there is a Problem of Translation with the Subject Pool. So, if Dr. F hopes to find out whether or not human beings of the usual sort have free will, he should not conduct his studies in Transparent World.

In order for Dr. F to recreate the Milgram experiments, the assumption must be that Brainiometers are few and far between, so the subjects will not assume that their brains are being scanned and their thoughts read. But the argument suggesting that mind reading through brain scanning is similar to the sort of mind reading from external evidence that we all do often is not strong – at least in the context of Dr. F's experimental design. And the thesis that ubiquitous mind reading would render the practice innocuous does not succeed, either. It appears that if Dr. F should deceive his subjects about their being observed through the Brainiometer, that would constitute a gross violation of their right to privacy.

Dr. F, moreover, needs to consider the possible harm that recreating the deceptive Milgram (or Burger) experiments using the Brainiometer does to his own character and that of his students. In the previous chapter, I raised the concern that being willing to deceive people in the experimenter/subject relationship could encourage experimenters to deceive more generally and to think of others – or at least of non-colleagues – as objects to be used. If we allow that secretly employing the Brainiometer is an extreme violation of the subject's right to privacy, then willingness to use it might well magnify these character-damaging tendencies. The experimenter, his students, and perhaps even his colleagues and society in general could be wronged and harmed if Dr. F conducts his deceptive, free will experiments in the lab with the Brainiometer. The potential for valuable knowledge gained from Dr. F's experiments must be very significant indeed if deception in this situation is to be judged permissible.

With these problems in mind, Dr. F might abandon the thought of recreating the Milgram experiments or of trying to do any experiments in the lab and opt for observation of human agents going about their normal business. This loses the advantage of being able to run numerous iterations of roughly the same scenario, but it has the moral advantage of not having to put subjects at moral risk in a manufactured situation where they are forced to make a moral choice. And it solves the Problem of Translation Regarding the Situation in the lab. Dr. F will follow various participants living their normal lives and, presumably, they will now and again have to make moral choices. The Brainiometer will just stay trained on them, or be trained on them during certain hours, and record brain activity and so catch the moments when moral choices are made. On the analysis of free choice with which I am working, it may well be that agents make moral choices only rarely and so it is likely that subjects will have to be observed for a very long time. And Dr. F (and perhaps the many grad students he has recruited) may have to wait a long while and sift through a lot of data in order to observe the record of the brain activity at the moment of choice. So, this is a less efficient way of conducting research on free will, but it may have certain advantages, including that it avoids deliberately placing subjects in morally risky situations.

Experiments that observe people in unqualifiedly public spaces and that simply record overt behavior, without attaching names to the reports, are usually not problematic morally and do not require that those observed consent. The Brainiometer, however, is an invasive instrument and its use on subjects, even – *or especially* – in their going about their normal business, requires fully informed consent. In that *real life* is where most of the important events that we actually care about happen, the question of privacy is even more important than it was in Dr. F's lab. Dr. F will need to find participants willing to conduct their lives, including making moral choices, under the observation of the Brainiometer. But outside the lab, with the experimenter at a distance, unlike in the Milgram experiments, Dr. F may hope that his subjects forget that they are being observed. This might minimize the Problem of the Observer, the problem that you cannot make natural choices if you know your brain is being scanned and your thoughts read.

But here is a related difficulty. Assume that for most people privacy is valued and important, at least sometimes. If there is indeed a close connection between privacy and autonomy, it may be that agents who understand and experience themselves as autonomous and morally responsible are the very people who are most likely to care the most about privacy. The point at which one might be engaged in making a choice with moral significance, an act for which one might be praiseworthy or blameworthy, would seem to be exactly the sort of situation when a mature, self-respecting person, who believes that he is autonomous, would insist upon privacy. Dr. F, in explaining the experiment to potential participants, so that they can be fully informed, will have to tell them that the goal is to observe their brains as they make moral choices. A case can be made that someone who would happily allow open access to his brain under these circumstances is someone who is psychologically aberrant. To conduct his experiments ethically, Dr. F must get informed consent, but this limits his pool of participants to people who apparently don't care about privacy and who do not feel the need of any space to call their own. Thus, the Problem of Translation Regarding the Subject Pool arises again.

Moreover, allowing someone to use the Brainiometer on you gives that person enormous power over you. On the assumption that human beings in the future are similar to human beings today, and from the perspective of the twenty-first century, having just emerged from a terrible century of human-against-human violence, it appears to be madness to put yourself at the mercy of a stranger in that way. (Presumably, Dr. F cannot just use his nearest and dearest as subjects. Given the nature of human relationships, it might be better for all concerned if his nearest and dearest were never under the gaze of his Brainiometer.) If many potential subjects recognize the danger of giving a stranger free access to your brain and mind, then not only would the pool of subjects be limited to those who do not care about privacy, but it would be further limited to those who are unreasonably trusting of strangers or at least of strangers who are scientists.[11] So informing participants, which limits the pool in these ways, undermines the value of the information gained from the experiments. But failing to inform them is a gross violation of their privacy and hence a very significant cost. If Dr. F is very persuasive, he might be able to recruit people who are appropriately concerned about being observed with the Brainiometer but care so deeply about scientific progress that they overcome their worries. But people who are so committed to the experiment that they will overcome their concern for privacy and open their brains to the experimenter might have a difficult time forgetting that they are being observed, and the Problem of the Observer arises again. Perhaps Dr. F will be able to find a pool of representative participants willing to go about their daily lives under the gaze of the Brainiometer in a way that allows them to make natural moral choices – but it will not be easy.

The Future Study of Human Freedom: Benefits

To his IRB and to would-be participants, Dr. F needs to make the case that the knowledge to be gained by the experiments will be so valuable as to outweigh the costs. Is the good aimed at by the experiments so significant

---

11 Perhaps in the distant future they will stop teaching history and so potential subjects will not appreciate their danger. But a pool of such ill-informed subjects may render skewed data.

that people *ought* to agree to participate, even though they are deeply uncomfortable about the severe invasion of privacy the experiments involve, in addition to other possible harms? Could it be that the good is so significant that it would even justify deceiving participants about the goals and methods of the experiments, such that Dr. F can conduct them inside or outside the lab and omit informing subjects about the detail of the Brainiometer?

Dr. F's experiments can come to one of three possible conclusions: (1) Human agents make LFMCs; (2) human agents do not make LFMCs; (3) the experiments were not able to provide sufficient evidence for (1) or (2) and so, from the perspective of empirical enquiry, it remains an open question whether or not human agents make LFMCs. Each of these conclusions, even the third, would contribute something to the overall knowledge contained within the human community. If knowledge per se, regardless of further value or usefulness, is a good, then we can put that in the plus column. But it is not clear that the acquisition of knowledge for its own sake could justify the costs of conducting the experiments. This is especially the case if Dr. F insists that he cannot inform his participants about the goals and methods of the experiments.

What about the usefulness or consequentialist value of his conclusions? If Dr. F provides strong scientific evidence that human agents apparently do make LFMCs, that would (in my view) be a happy day for the human community. (Chapter 1 discussed some empirical evidence that belief in free will is beneficial and belief in determinism harmful.) If we assume that, in the future, belief in robust freedom is associated with belief in human dignity and with the requirement that we respect our fellow human beings, then it appears to be the case that scientific evidence of freedom would promote wholesome human relations. However, the die-hard determinist (believing either UCD or LCD) need not abandon his position. He can hold onto the hope that even the Brainiometer may have missed the preceding, necessitating cause. That being the case, the anticipated beneficial social consequences of strong evidence for freedom are likely to be diluted.

On the other hand, suppose the evidence should point toward the view that what human agents experience as free choices are in fact determined? Saul Smilansky, believing on philosophical grounds that determinism regarding human agency is true, nonetheless insists that this is a truth which should not be publicized. He grants that much that is most valuable and benign in human dealings operates within the (in his view, false) assumption that human agents have robust freedom. He holds that a great deal that is good and beneficial to human society would be lost if determinism became the common view.[12] In Chapter 1, I discussed the current movement to downplay the negative effects of denying human freedom and to

---

12 Smilansky (2002): 489–505.

point to some positive consequences, such as encouraging more lenient punishments for wrongdoers. I argued that their case is not persuasive. For one thing, the defender of human free will is likely to be interested in more than justifying punishment. I proposed that it is the connection between freedom and dignity that is the most fundamental issue and that those who see little harm in denying free will seem to miss this connection. I suspect that if Dr. F were to provide strong scientific evidence for local causal determinism of human agency, the temptation would be for society – those in power anyway – to judge that human beings need not be treated with respect and may be used as objects. And this might be the *correct* way to view human beings, on a determinist hypothesis, but it is unlikely to *benefit* those human beings. The compatibilist will point out that evidence of determinism (UCD or LCD) need not undermine belief in human free will so long as free will is understood properly, but compatibilism is a more subtle view than determinism or libertarianism and it seems unlikely that the general public would embrace it if told explicitly that their choices are determined and they cannot choose other than they choose.

Of course, we do not know how things would shake out in the human community of Dr. F's distant future. We can judge only by how our observations, intuitions, and arguments, past and present, have gone. I think it likely that if most people believed that human agents do not have free will, things would go badly for us overall. The die-hard defender of libertarian free will can raise various objections to the conclusiveness of the evidence and insist that sometimes some of us do make free choices. So, perhaps, even if the experiments support LCD, the harmful consequences would be somewhat mitigated. But this skeptical libertarian move undermines the value of the supposed knowledge gained.

The third, inconclusive, conclusion might have some use in that, given that Dr. F cannot settle the question of free will empirically, even using the marvelous Brainiometer, it might be widely accepted that it is a question that cannot be settled by scientific experiment. That might save future scientists from wasting their time with empirical experiments trying to prove or disprove free will. Moreover, in the previous chapter, I argued that one aspect of treating subjects with respect entailed making a point of considering a charitable interpretation of the data if it is just as viable as other interpretations. Given his failure to find solid evidence for either side in the debate, Dr. F should publish the fact that, as far as science is concerned, libertarian free will is at least as likely as LCD. Thus, for those who are not persuaded of the likelihood of determinism (UCD or LCD) on philosophical grounds and who find the burden of proof argument from Chapter 1 persuasive, admitting that science cannot answer the question should lead them to commit to belief in free will, even libertarian free will.[13] We have to

---

13 Who knows what the dispute between libertarian incompatibilists and compatibilists will look like in the distant future?

act in the world, and judge the actions of others, so we cannot sit on the fence on the question of free will. And we should not demean our fellow human beings in the absence of powerful evidence that they are not worthy of the sort of respect that attaches to robust freedom. So, this third conclusion should encourage the people of the future to accept (possibly libertarian) free will, which would be a good thing for their society in general. But since we cannot foreknow how many actually would accept the burden of proof argument, it is hard to project whether or not this third conclusion would produce significant value.

All of this leaves Dr. F with a difficult case to make to his IRB. He is hoping to settle the free will question empirically. There are large and certain costs involved. If he discovers strong evidence that human agents do indeed have free will, that is likely to benefit society, but how much cannot be foreseen. If he discovers strong evidence that human agents do not have free will, that is likely to harm society, but how much cannot be foreseen. If he should come to the third conclusion – that his experiments leave the question of free will as open as ever – that might be of some benefit to society, but, again, how much cannot be foreseen. And he cannot anticipate beforehand which conclusion he will come to.

Considering these three possibilities, the IRB must weigh the certain costs against merely possible benefits. In the next chapter, I will argue that the third conclusion – science cannot settle the free will question – is *by far* the most likely conclusion because of serious practical problems that will likely prevent Dr. F, even with the Brainiometer, from coming to a well-supported conclusion for or against meaningful freedom. That means that if my arguments in the next chapter are persuasive, the third conclusion could be arrived at without engaging in the experiments on human beings that raised so many ethical difficulties.

Alternative Methods and Charitable Interpretation

The Brainiometer allowed Dr. F to get around the very difficult Problem of Translation Regarding the Object of Study, but attempting to study actual morally significant choices raises a host of ethical difficulties. Could Dr. F avoid them by studying subjects as they make other sorts of choices? One suggestion mentioned in the previous chapter is placing subjects in a virtual, rather than a real, situation. But that produced what appears to be an intractable dilemma. Either the subjects maintain the virtual stance, in which case their choices are not made naturally and do not reflect genuine moral decisions, or they become so immersed that they are indeed making moral choices, in which case all, or most, of the ethical problems that pertained in the experiments conducted in the "real world" apply in the virtual situation. Dr. F may move to research choices that are not moral but perhaps closely resemble moral choices (e.g., the prudential choice with no moral content). But even if the object of research is not moral choices, many of the problems noted above still arise. This is especially true of questions about privacy when the Brainiometer is employed. These problems may be somewhat less severe if the decisions involved are not as deeply personal and important as moral choices. Nevertheless, the wrongs and harms cannot entirely be avoided.

If Dr. F concludes that ethical concerns require that he study only choices of indifference – choices for which a mental or literal coin flip is a proper way to decide – he will confront the added difficulty of having to make the case that the evidence translates appropriately to conclusions concerning human freedom. And here the burden-of-proof principle and the emphasis on charitable interpretation of the results of experiments dovetail. In the previous chapter, I suggested that when interpreting the data from experiments, if conclusions that respect the subject are as well supported as conclusions that do not, then, at the very least, one should not prefer the less respectful interpretation of the data. And, since to deny that someone possesses free will is to demean them, the burden of proof lies with the one who would claim that human beings lack freedom. So, suppose Dr. F intends to study non-moral choices and manages to get his experimental design past his IRB. And suppose he finds some evidence that when an agent chooses, the preference for this over that was causally produced by determining factors. First, even in the face of some evidence, he will have to be very cautious before he concludes that his subjects were not free when they made their non-moral choices. Probabilistic conclusions leave open the possibility of freedom. Second, he will have to give very powerful arguments to show that the evidence should be applied to the case of morally significant choice.

Respect for the subject raises serious ethical problems with attempting to study human freedom empirically. Doing the moral calculus, Dr. F's IRB may well reject his proposal. But that is just the beginning of Dr. F's difficulties. In the next chapter, I will argue first that any hope of settling the question of human freedom will necessitate use of the Brainiometer or something very like it. Then I will try to show that it will never be possible for humanity to produce such an instrument. Lastly, I will make the case that, even with the Brainiometer, the question of human freedom probably cannot be settled experimentally.

Chapter 8

The Future Study of Human Freedom

Practical Problems

Introduction

In the previous chapter, I hypothesized a future scientist, Dr. F, who hopes to settle the question of whether or not human beings have responsibility-grounding, libertarian freedom. He is equipped with a Brainiometer, which, by hypothesis, is capable of allowing a researcher to observe what goes on in a subject's brain and translate that data into information concerning what the subject is thinking and experiencing. In the present chapter, I will argue, first, that Dr. F cannot possibly conduct his research without a Brainiometer. Sadly for Dr. F, as I will argue next, it is likely impossible for human beings to construct a Brainiometer. Finally, I will show that even if we allow Dr. F his Brainiometer, he faces further problems which are probably insuperable.

The Need for a Brainiometer

Dr. F agrees that the free will debate is mainly about morally significant choice. If we are concerned with the sort of freedom that can ground moral responsibility and that is associated with human dignity, then it is choice with a moral dimension that is at issue. Dr. F also agrees that the most perspicuous – or perhaps the *only* – way to empirically study the possibility of meaningful freedom is to attempt to observe the very act which is or appears most like or seems to the agent to be a morally significant free choice. (Of course, we cannot just ask Dr. F to observe a libertarian free moral choice [LFMC] since his question is whether or not such things exist.) Other sorts of decisions, like the choices of indifference where it is reasonable to do a mental coin flip or hypothetical academic exercises where one is to decide what course would be the best for someone to take, do not meet the criteria of a morally significant choice. There may be ethical advantages for Dr. F to study only non-moral decisions. But if he does limit himself to observing decisions occurring outside of a moral context, he will have to make the further case that these choices are sufficiently similar to moral choices. Perhaps he will be able to make this further case but this adds an extra step to his research program. And, should he discover evidence of local causal determinism, the committed libertarian can exploit the loophole and insist that the evidence does not, in fact, translate from one sort of choice to another. (This is true even if one allows the possibility of prudential choices that are devoid of moral content.) Furthermore, many of the difficulties to be raised with attempting to study moral choices apply equally to studying other sorts of choices. So, it is reasonable for Dr. F to attempt to observe the very phenomenon his research question is about: morally significant free choices – or what look most like or seem to the agent to be morally significant choices.

In Chapter 2, I offered a rough description of what might constitute an LFMC which, I believe, captures what most libertarians look for in a theory of free choice. Sketching a portrait of a free choice helps get clear on what we mean by human free will and so avoids the Problem of Description. It is also useful to have a concrete example to work with. For instance, setting out the criteria for an LFMC allows us to see when an experiment has focused on some element not actually relevant to free will. To see what Dr. F hopes to study, we can review the description of an LFMC very briefly: The subject, Agent S, must be in the torn condition. That involves pursuing at least two robust desires ("desires" understood broadly) with moral content and hence debating between what at least appear to S to be morally significant, conflicting, and genuinely open options. (Or perhaps it is enough that Dr. F, or most people, consider the options morally significant. In Chapter 2, I allowed that S might not be perfectly clear on the import of his options.) S must then opt to pursue one or the other of his desires. In that we are operating with a libertarian theory, the question will be: Was it up to S alone, as the agent, to choose one option in such a way that, given everything about his history preceding the choice, he could have opted for the other? Dr. F will be searching for a preceding cause of the preference, a cause that is outside of the agent's control. He will be looking for some type of brain event occurring before the choice is made, the presence of which allows him to predict with great accuracy which option S will choose.

Dr. F cannot do without a Brainiometer since the information about what S is thinking and experiencing must be very specific. For one thing, Dr. F must be sure that S is in the process of making a morally significant choice as opposed to all the other choice-y actions he might be engaged in. As the discussion of the Libet experiments in Chapter 3 made clear, a rough and general picture of S's brain activity before S chooses is insufficient. Libet took the brain activity which preceded the "urge" to flex as a preconscious cause of the urge, leading some to conclude that the urge and the subsequent flexing were determined by brain events over which the subject had no control. (Daniel Wegner, as discussed in Chapter 4, comes to an even more radical conclusion: Our conscious choices are not the causes of our actions; the brain activity caused the flexing of the wrist and the epiphenomenal urge.) But, as commentators have noted, the preceding brain activity may not have caused the urge. It might have represented any number of things – for example, a conscious "buildup" preceding the subject's manufacturing the urge. (Perhaps the subject was thinking to himself something like "I really must feel that urge soon!") Were science to find – in the imprecise way that contemporary brain mapping allows – that a particular sort of brain event usually preceded what appeared to be (or what the subject took to be) a morally significant free choice, the libertarian could happily consider that event to be the neural representation of the torn condition which must precede a free choice. Assuming that the brain activity causes the subsequent mental activity, simply because the former temporally precedes the latter, commits the post hoc fallacy.

This is not to denigrate contemporary brain mapping. It is truly awe inspiring, and enormous strides are being made with amazing speed. The point is that to study morally significant free choice for some agent, S, it is vital that Dr. F be able to actually read exactly what is going on in S's mind. Is S considering at least two morally significant conflicting options, and does S end up pursuing one of them? This means that Dr. F must be able to see just what S is thinking. It will probably not be sufficient for Dr. F to appreciate that S is thinking about some basically Xish sort of thing and some other basically Yish sort of thing because Dr. F needs to feel confident that – at least from S's perspective – the options involve moral significance (or something similar) and that they actually conflict. Observing S's desires such that they appear vague leaves open the possibility that they did not have the requisite moral content or that they did not truly conflict. In order to conduct his experiments effectively, Dr. F had better be looking for S to be debating between a specific desire X and a specific desire Y.

Note that Dr. F cannot settle for observing that S is simply "thinking about" a specific X or Y. The Brainiometer must allow Dr. F to read that S *wants* both X and Y and that both desires are truly viable. It is easy to imagine a situation in which an agent has a desire for something, where the desire is such that the agent will not pursue it. Perhaps it is a fleeting desire or a weak desire. In any case, it is one that, while the agent can entertain it, does not contribute to the agent's being in the torn condition. Mark Balaguer suggests that if science should settle the question of libertarian freedom in favor of the libertarian, then it ought to be possible to assess the strengths of opposing desires, assign weights to them (taking into account relevant non-conscious factors), and thus determine with mathematical precision the probability of each option being chosen.[1] I have argued elsewhere that I do not find this a plausible picture.[2] In order to decide Dr. F's question

---

1 Balaguer (2010): 76–83.
2 Rogers (2015): 182–93.

about freedom, we need not ask the Brainiometer to generate mathematically precise probabilities regarding the options. It will be enough if the Brainiometer can allow Dr. F to grasp what S is thinking and experiencing, but it will have to do so with great specificity and accuracy, both in terms of what S is thinking about and in terms of what S is desiring.

Problems with Developing the Brainiometer

There are several conceptual problems to note at the outset. The assumption behind the Brainiometer is that a particular brain event is correlated with a particular mental event, placing the Problem of Mereology front and center. I shall continue to use the term "brain event" since (as of now) we cannot be precise about just what these events are, nor about the size, location, and mereological nature of the "parts" of the brain where these "events" occur. Even determining what different parts of the brain there are is not as obvious as it might seem. Marco Viola and Elia Zanin note that the "standard ontological framework of cognitive neuroscience" has it that "each mental entity should correspond to a single neural entity" – roughly the assumption behind the Brainiometer.[3] However, they point out that if this analysis can be sustained at all, it requires significant qualification.[4] There are various approaches to the job of mapping the brain. One might focus on some contiguous "chunk" of brain at some spatial location and think of that as a particular "part" or system. Should it be discovered that that "part" serves a number of purposes, as most neural systems do, one can label it "pluripotent". Alternatively, one might attempt to isolate a "part" based on function such that if various places in the brain seem to contribute to that function, one might think of the "part" as a network.[5] And the brain "object" under study will not be an inert part or system but an event or process. But determining the outlines which constitute a particular event, and which distinguish it from "nearby" events, is extremely difficult even at the macro level.

How we are to isolate a particular *mental* event seems an even harder problem than attempting to isolate a particular brain event. At least what goes on in the brain is in principle publicly observable. There is no reason

---

3 Among philosophers, one popular theory is Functionalism, which attempts to deal with the mind/body problem by holding that mental states are constituted by the role they play in a cognitive system. But this looks to entail that a particular mental state may be realized by different physical processes.
4 Marco Viola and Elia Zanin, "The Standard Ontological Framework of Cognitive Neuroscience: Some Lessons from Broca's Area", *Philosophical Psychology* 30 (2017): 945–69.
5 Viola and Zanin note that many cognitive functions are subserved by two or more structurally distinct neural systems. This phenomenon bears the unwholesome title of "degeneracy".

to think that the public/private distinction between the physical and the mental will ever be bridged, meaning that attempting to isolate particular mental events, in a way that will be useful scientifically, will depend upon accepting first-person reporting, trusting that your subjects are correctly understanding and following instructions, and/or making assumptions from their behavior. This adds a level of difficulty to the bare conceptual issue of what constitutes a particular mental event. (One imagines that generations of scientists working toward building a Brainiometer will be constantly plagued by the Problem of First-person Reporting and the Problem of the Observer.) The construction of the Brainiometer depends upon being able to correlate the particular public brain event and the particular private mental event, so there are deep mereological questions to be addressed. Even if the metaphysicians of the future, in partnership with the neuroscientists, succeed in answering these questions, a serious problem with the mental/physical correspondence remains. If it turns out that a number of mental events are correlated with a single brain event, then the Brainiometer (as I have envisioned it) is not a possibility. A less exact instrument might be constructed which can detect all that is going on in the brain. But if a single brain event could represent any of several different mental events, then, from the data provided by this instrument, Dr. F can hypothesize only that his subject, Agent S, is thinking or experiencing one (or some) of a number of thoughts and experiences. This will not be exact enough to allow him to study meaningful freedom.[6] Furthermore, given the public/private distinction, someone of a skeptical bent might argue against the Brainiometer in principle on the grounds that we can never be *sure* that it has correctly rendered the subject's private experiences from the (in principle) publicly observable events in his brain.

Suppose that the metaphysicians and neuroscientists of the future are able to settle the mereological questions about brain events and mental events. Suppose that they have good reason to deny the claim that a single brain event may correlate with several different mental events. And suppose that they, like the rest of us, do not allow the privacy of other minds to make us doubt their existence or make us deny that we could ever know what someone else is thinking. There are other difficulties to be confronted. The extreme complexity of the conscious life of the human being will make it very hard or impossible to successfully map mental events onto brain events with the exactitude that Dr. F's research into human freedom requires.

---

6 There is not a similar problem with the converse scenario. I take it that if a single type of idea or experience can be correlated with several different types of brain event, the Brainiometer, upon observing any of these types of event in S's brain, could report what type of idea or experience S is having.

But given the enormous strides that have been made in brain scanning in the last few decades, is this too pessimistic an assessment? The headline of an article about a recent experiment conducted at Carnegie Mellon University reads, "Scientists Can Now Read Your Thoughts with a Brain Scan".[7] If scientists can do that *now*, then is a fully functional Brainiometer coming in the near future? It will be useful to take a look at the experiment in question. It seems quite an exciting advance in understanding correlations between mind and brain. But considering this experiment – its methods and conclusions – will demonstrate the extreme difficulty (or, more likely, impossibility) of constructing a Brainiometer. The experiment was conducted by Jing Wang, Vladimir L. Cherkassky, and Marcel Adam Just. Their report, published in 2017, is entitled "Predicting the Brain Activation Pattern Associated with the Propositional Content of a Sentence: Modeling Neural Representations of Events and States".[8] Here is the abstract in full:

> Even though much has recently been learned about the neural representation of individual concepts and categories, neuroimaging research is only beginning to reveal how more complex thoughts, such as event and state descriptions, are neurally represented. We present a predictive computational theory of the neural representations of individual events and states as they are described in 240 sentences. Regression models were trained to determine the mapping between 42 neurally plausible semantic features (NPSFs) and thematic roles of the concepts of a proposition and the fMRI [functional magnetic resonance imaging] activation patterns of various cortical regions that process different types of information. Given a semantic characterization of the content of a sentence that is new to the model, the model can reliably predict the resulting neural signature, or, given an observed neural signature of a new sentence, the model can predict its semantic content. The models were also reliably generalizable across participants. This computational model provides an account of the brain representation of a complex yet fundamental unit of thought, namely, the conceptual content of a proposition. In addition to characterizing a sentence representation at the level of the semantic and thematic features of its component concepts, factor analysis was used to develop a higher level characterization of a sentence, specifying the general type of event representation that the sentence evokes

---

7 https://www.popularmechanics.com/science/health/a27102/read-thoughts-with-brain-scan/.
8 Jing Wang, Vladimir L. Cherkassky, and Marcel Adam Just, "Predicting the Brain Activation Pattern Associated with the Propositional Content of a Sentence: Modeling Neural Representations of Events and States", *Human Brain Mapping* 38 (2017): 4865–81.

(e.g., a social interaction versus a change of physical state) and the voxel locations most strongly associated with each of the factors.[9]

Someone reading that the "model provides an account of the brain representation of ... the conceptual content of a proposition" might suppose that the headline – "Scientists Can Now Read Your Thoughts with a Brain Scan" – does not represent incautious hyperbole. But the description of the experiment confirms that the Brainiometer is not on the horizon. The experiment is ingenious and the conclusions are quite exciting, but it is important to appreciate what the experiment does and does not capture. Wang et al. explain that they took a list of simple sentences which describe events and states. The "concepts" in the sentences were rated according to 42 "neurally plausible semantic features" (NPSFs). ("Concepts" here seems to mean the main terms in the sentences. A "semantic" feature is a general category under which the term could fall.) Past experiments using fMRI have shown where the brain is most active – judging by the blood flow – as the subject entertains various sorts of ideas. So, we already know where in the brain to look for activity correlated with certain general kinds of cognitive objects. The NPSFs, then, are the semantic (using the term as Wang et al. are understanding it) properties associated with a term, where we have an idea of what the neural signature (brain activity) looks like for that property. For example, the word "walk" is coded according to the NPSFs "physical action" and "change of location"; the word "judge" is coded according to the NPSFs "Social norms", "Knowledge", "Communication", and "Person"; the word "cellphone" is coded according to the NPSFs "Social action", "Communication", "Man-made", and "Inanimate".[10] An fMRI of a subject concentrating on the word "judge", for instance, should show elevated brain activity in the areas associated with thinking about social norms, knowledge, communication, and persons. "The general assumption was that individual NPSFs could be related to activation levels in particular clusters of voxels [cubes of brain tissue]."[11]

Wang et al. had their seven subjects read simple sentences such as "The witness shouted during the trial" and "The jury listened to the famous businessman."[12] All of the main words in the sentences were rated in terms of what NPSFs were applicable to that word. There were 240 sentences. The subjects read them slowly, concentrating on each word as it was added to the sentence. The key datum was the fMRI image showing the brain

9 Wang et al. (2017): 4865.
10 Wang et al. (2017): 4870.
11 Wang et al. (2017): 4866.
12 Note that this is a very quick sketch of the experiment. Seven does not sound like many participants, but, given the nature of the experiment, this does not appear to be a problem.

activation pattern from shortly after the subject had finished reading the sentence. The subject, at this point, was considering the whole sentence, consisting of the series of terms which had been rated according to their NPSFs and were now unified into a proposition. For example, the NPSFs assigned to "The witness shouted during the trial" were "Social norms" (i.e., related to laws and authority structure), "High affective arousal", "Negative affective valence" (I take it that this means that the event is likely to be perceived as a bad one), "Communication", "Person", "Social interaction", and "Perceptual action".[13] A computer model was trained on the brain images from subjects reading 239 sentences to associate particular brain activation patterns with sentences containing certain sets of NPSFs. One sentence was omitted as the test sentence. The goal was to see whether the brain activation pattern the model *predicted* for the test sentence with its set of NPSFs would match the *observed* pattern for that sentence. The experiment ran iterations of the training and test for all 240 sentences, and the model's ability to predict brain activity patterns from the set of NPSFs was well above chance.[14] Moreover, the model was able to make the correlation in the other direction, predicting with an accuracy well above chance what set of NPSFs (or roughly what set) corresponded to a new image of a brain activation pattern of the subject reading a sentence to which those NPSFs had been assigned. That is, by looking at the brain image, the model could very often predict certain semantic elements of the sentence the subject had read.[15] Furthermore, there was significant similarity in the activation patterns across the individuals in the study. The model trained on the images from six of the seven participants could predict, at a well above chance rate, the correlation between brain activation pattern and semantic elements of a sentence for the seventh subject.[16]

This is deeply impressive, but it does not justify the headline "Scientists Can Now Read Your Thoughts with a Brain Scan". (This criticism of the *headline* is not a critique of the experiment itself which, as far as this philosopher can tell, is groundbreaking.) From the brain scan, the model – at best – predicts a rather general set of NPSFs. For example, any number of sentences could have the same set of NPSFs as those listed for "The witness shouted during the trial." For example, "The judge shouted during the trial", "The juror shouted during the trial", "The prosecutor shouted during the trial", "The defendant shouted during the trial", and so on. The set of NPSFs does not entail that the sentence be about an event that occurs

---

13 Wang et al. (2017): 4873, Figure 2.
14 Wang et al. (2017): 4872. Page 4873, Figure 2, presents a striking visual showing the similarities of the predicted activation patterns to the observed activation patterns for two sentences. One evidence of the model's ability to assess the "semantics" of a sentence was the fact that it predicted similar activation patterns for similar sentences (4874).
15 Wang et al. (2017): 4874.
16 Wang et al. (2017): 4876.

at a trial, so long as some aspect of law or authority structure is included: "The professor shouted during the class", "The policeman shouted during the interrogation", or "The Pope shouted during the audience." Nor is "shouting" entailed, so long as the verb connotes high affective arousal and communication and the sentence would strike most people as describing something bad (negative affective valence). "The professor gesticulated wildly during the class", "The policeman scribbled during the interrogation", "The prisoner applauded during the execution." One could go on almost indefinitely, multiplying sentences which fit the NPSFs for "The witness shouted during the trial" but which mean something very different. The same point can be made for any of the 240 sentences used in the experiment. So, although the model may predict the subject's understanding of a sentence in terms of some *very* general categories, it cannot be said that the brain scan allows the scientist to know what the subject is thinking.

But given some time, couldn't the process be more fine-tuned? Suppose, for example, that further experiment revealed the neural signature of someone thinking "witness" and "shouted" and "trial" such that a computer model could look at a brain activation pattern and correctly conclude that the subject had just read the *specific* sentence "The witness shouted during the trial." Note, first, that this seems to be a very large supposition. In that brains are not identical, the possibility of pinpointing a neural signature for "witness" as opposed to, say, "juror" or "lawyer", which was the same across individuals, seems very unlikely. The same goes for "shouting" and "trial" (even setting aside worries about "before", "during", and "after" … or "long after" … or "very long after", etc.). So, the supposition that a model could be trained to recognize the brain activation pattern for a sentence as specific as "The witness shouted during the trial" is (and is likely to remain) science fiction.

But for the sake of argument, suppose that a computer model, from looking at the brain image, could read off that the subject has read the sentence "The witness shouted during the trial." Can the scientist now know what the subject is thinking? Not really. Without a context, the sentence "The witness shouted during the trial" conveys very little information. Is the trial in question that of St. Thomas More? A Soviet show trial from the 1930s? One of the Nuremberg trials? A trial presided over by a judge who is notoriously hard of hearing or prone to falling asleep? Perhaps it is a fictional trial? But then it makes a difference if it is the trial of Dmitri from *The Brothers Karamazov* or the trial of Chicolini from *Duck Soup*. People reading "The witness shouted during the trial" might be thinking about so many, varied events that it defeats the thesis about brain scanning if a single neural signature correlates with each and every one of them.

This is not the end of the difficulty with trying to fine-tune the correspondence between brain scanning and mind reading. For the sake of argument, allow this (pretty clearly impossible) supposition: From the brain image, the computer model can read off not only that the subject is reading "The witness shouted during the trial" but information that begins to genuinely describe the event; for example, the sentence is embedded in a text describing one of the Nuremberg trials. *Now* can the scientist know what the subject is thinking? No. A version of the Problem of Perspective arises. Is the subject a Holocaust survivor? Perhaps the subject is the granddaughter of an officer in the SS, and she has always been bitter about the trials, believing that Grandfather really was just following orders. Or perhaps the subject is a college student who is poorly educated and so cares nothing for history and is bored with reading about the aftermath of the Second World War. Even if *per impossibile* the scientist could read off from the brain scan *that* the subject is reading "The witness shouted at one of the Nuremberg trials", the scientist does not thus gain access to what the subject is thinking. Perhaps with the survivor and the granddaughter, the scientist can see that they are interested or angry in a way that the ignoramus is not, but the brain scan alone will not explain why this is the case. The scientist will not understand what these different subjects are thinking and experiencing unless he talks to them about their history and attitudes. People are different, and if the finely tuned brain scan should produce the same neural representation for all of them as they direct their concentration to the same object – for example, "The witness shouted at one of the Nuremberg trials" – that would demonstrate that the brain scan had failed to capture (except in the vaguest way) what they are actually thinking. One might believe that that would still be a notable achievement (and it *would*) but the argument here is that, even if we allow the *almost certainly impossible* claim that science could develop a system so finely tuned as to be able to tell, from a brain scan, that a subject is thinking about an event at one of the Nuremberg trials, the scientist still cannot access what the subject is actually thinking and experiencing.

This point about different people's perspectives raises a question about the experiment which is especially relevant to the construction of the Brainiometer. For Dr. F's purposes, as he attempts to settle the question of human free will, it is not enough that the Brainiometer provide information about the bare content of the beliefs of a subject, S. Dr. F must be able to read off S's *desires* and in such a way as to appreciate whether or not a desire is currently viable so as to be able to constitute one of a pair of conflicting desires. Only with this information can Dr. F conclude that S is in the torn condition, debating which way to go. Wang et al. include a value aspect in their experiment. Two of the NPSFs that can be assigned to a term or sentence are "negative affective valence" and "positive affective valence". Wang et al. say that these terms are self-explanatory. I take it that the former means that the term or sentence is likely to be perceived as referring to or describing a bad thing and that the latter means that the term or sentence is likely to be perceived as referring to or describing a good thing.[17] In assigning NPSFs to terms, "the coding was performed by two raters with disagreements adjudicated by a third rater".[18] The NPSFs of a sentence as a whole are derived from the NPSFs of its constituent terms. In the report of the experiment, Wang et al. tell us nothing about the "raters" beyond their number. What was their expertise in categorizing the terms in question?[19] This is especially relevant with the assignment of the value "valences". Two of the sentences which the model – rightly in the view of Wang et al. – took to be very similar were "The witness shouted during the trial" and "The jury listened to the famous businessman." A difference between the two is that one of the NPSFs listed for the former is "negative affective valence" whereas for the latter "positive affective valence" is listed. But this is puzzling. Did the two or three raters simply consider shouting bad and listening good? Clearly, it is easy to imagine cases where that witness did everyone a favor by shouting during the trial. And I know many academics who would immediately judge it a bad thing that the jury should listen to certain famous businessmen. The discussion above about the myriad trials (and sorts of trials) one might read about makes it clear that judgments about how a subject is likely to perceive the value of a described event cannot be made accurately in the absence of more information about the context. And the point about the myriad responses different people might have to reading about the *same* trial makes it clear that judgments about how different subjects are likely to perceive the value of the same described event cannot be made accurately in the absence of more information about the subject's history and attitudes and possibly not even then. One might present subjects with examples and ask them how they feel about them, while taking brain scans, and so correlate how these subjects felt about these particular examples (assuming their first-person reports are accurate) with their brain activation patterns. But people are not fungible. It cannot be assumed that appreciating how *these* subjects think and feel, and what goes on in their brains, gives us evidence for how the next person will think and feel and what will go on in his brain.[20]

---

17 Wang et al. (2017): 4868, Table II.
18 Wang et al. (2017): 4869.
19 One example of the NPSF coding is so odd that perhaps it is a typo in the report: "Hurricane" is assigned the NPSF of "Health", while "Walk" is not (Wang et al. (2017): 4870, Figure III). Perhaps the raters were thinking about health issues that can follow in the aftermath of hurricanes? But are those issues foremost in most people's minds when they think about hurricanes?
20 Michael Gazzaniga makes the useful point that brains are just different, too. In criticizing the use of brain scans in court to demonstrate brain abnormalities, he notes that the image of the "normal" brain that is often used is simply an average of various brain images (Gazzaniga (2011): 195–7). This may not affect the very course-grained correlation that the model discerns in the Wang et al. experiment, but it becomes a difficulty if we hope to focus down on specific brain patterns corresponding to specific thoughts and experiences that will apply across individuals.

Wang et al. do note the model's success in generalizing across individuals. Given that the sentences in the experiment are so thin on content, that is a puzzling phenomenon. Is the suggestion that all the seven participants have roughly the same understanding when they read "The witness shouted during the trial" or "The jury listened to the famous businessman"? All were in their 20s and 30s and all were from the Pittsburgh area, but still one would have to believe that they had not all had the same life experiences. They could not all be imagining the same person when reading "witness" or the same event when reading "shouting" and so on. But the NPSFs are very general, and the areas in the brain associated with them are quite large, and so perhaps on that very large and general scale there is likely to be rough similarity between people (or people with fairly similar backgrounds?) entertaining somewhat similar thoughts. As I have argued, it is the fine-tuning that is the problem and without it the Brainiometer cannot come to be.

There is a further difficulty which this experiment raises regarding invention of the Brainiometer. It is a version of the Translation Problem Regarding the Situation in the lab versus a natural setting.[21] In the experiment by Wang et al., the participants are lying quietly in the scanner slowly reading and concentrating on each word in a simple sentence.[22] The Brainiometer, on the other hand, can simply be pointed at an agent, S, and allow Dr. F to read S's mind as he is going about his business in the world. That it will be possible in the future to do brain scanning at a distance does not seem wildly improbable. The intuitive picture of the progress in instrumentation over the last century is that (in general) as devices have gotten more powerful, they have gotten smaller and able to produce their effects at longer and longer distances. So, the worry is not that it will always be impossible to scan someone's brain without enticing them into a bulky scanner. The worry is that Dr. F's research must go beyond studying subjects carefully concentrating on a few simple concepts in an artificial environment. He hopes to observe S in the act of making what appears to be a morally significant choice. Even if S is sitting in the lab and Dr. F has deceived him in some variant of the Milgram experiments, S must be genuinely engaged in considering what to do under the circumstances or Dr. F cannot observe the phenomena which will allow him to gather evidence concerning free will. But the swirl of thoughts and feelings

---

21 This is an issue that has been raised concerning the use of fMRI scans as lie detection devices. Francis Shen points out that a deliberate lie in the lab is a different phenomenon from a "real life" lie and so the two may involve different brain activity. Francis X. Shen, "Neuroscience, Mental Privacy, and the Law", *Harvard Journal of Law and Public Policy* 36 (2013): 653–713, at 680–1.

22 I presume the subjects were lying down since the experiment used Siemens Verio 3T MRI scanners (Wang et al. (2017): 4869) and the visuals for these scanners on the Siemens web page show several (and only) scanners on which the subject would have to lie down.

that S must be entertaining in the torn condition and the (one assumes) tumultuous brain activity that accompanies his inner debate about what to do would both be far, far more complex than the simple concepts and correlating brain activity in the controlled experiment by Wang et al. One might propose, as Libet does in defending the relevance of his experiments to free will, that the distinction between the simple and the complex does not denote a difference in kind; evidence derived from study of the simple process can be plausibly applied to the complex process. But in this case the complex process does not just add more of the same sort of elements to the proceedings. Making a significant decision is not the same sort of activity as reading a sentence. Above I argued that fine-tuning the scanning process so as to be able to tell what someone is thinking and experiencing – except in the vaguest and most general way – would be impossible given how specific and subjective actual thoughts and experiences are. Add to that the point that, unless they are artificially controlled, thoughts and experiences are wildly complex. Add to *that* the point that there is additional complexity involved in deciding how to act, which is something other than quietly contemplating a sentence. The conclusion must be that, although brain scanning has made tremendous progress and will undoubtedly make much more in the future, the Brainiometer will almost certainly remain science fiction.

Studying Free Will

In this section, I hope to show that even a scientist armed with a Brainiometer cannot settle the question of whether or not human agents have meaningful freedom. First, what is the current view of indeterminism in the brain? At present, according to Bryce Gessell, the best models for predicting brain activity are those that take that activity to be indeterministic. Gessell refers to this as "weak indeterminism" whereas "strong indeterminism" would apply not to the *model* but to the actual state of affairs in the brain. Gessell argues that (at least for now) it is impossible to discover empirically whether or not the model reflects the reality. He notes that we might run an experiment, take careful observational measurements, and then try running the experiment again, making the new conditions as identical as possible to the original. But if the new experiment produces different measurements, that can be explained by pointing to the difficulty in recreating the original rather than taking the difference as evidence of indeterminism. If the measurements are the same, that is consistent with at least four different interpretations, including that if we measured more finely, we would see that the results differ, so *determinism* is likely since we could not have recreated the experiment exactly, and also, if we measured more finely, we would see that the results differ, so *indeterminism* is likely since we may have succeeded in our attempt to recreate the original experiment. Gessell concludes that "[e]xperimentation simply does not provide the right kind of evidence.... The unfortunate truth is that its complexity makes the brain a bad place to look for instances of strong indeterminism. So many factors influence action that we cannot be sure we are accounting for them all."[23] Adina Roskies expresses a similar conclusion:

> The picture that neuroscience has yielded so far is one of mechanisms infused with indeterministic or stochastic (random or probabilistic) processes.... However, whether the unpredictability we perceive is really due to fundamentally indeterministic processes or to complex deterministic ones beyond our present understanding is something neuroscience cannot tell us.[24]

Brain indeterminism by itself would not entail that human agents can make LFMCs. That would require that the human agent be able to deliberate rationally and choose *a se* (from himself) between morally significant options. As I have argued, Dr. F, who hopes to find empirical evidence regarding free will, would probably do best to attempt to observe the very phenomenon which is the intended object of his study. A recent, provocative headline from 2018 reads "Scientists Think They Have Found the Anatomy of Free Will in Our Brain".[25] But the experiment in question is not aimed at studying free will; it is aimed at studying the human *perception* of free will by looking at people with an impaired sense of agency due to lesions in the brain. One sort of case was the "alien limb syndrome" (discussed in connection with Wegner and Gazzaniga in Chapter 4), where there is a disconnect between people's bodily motions and their sense of what they are doing as agents. The authors of the study note that the long-standing philosophical debate over whether or not free will exists has not been settled, but (they continue) it is evident that we *perceive* ourselves to be free agents and so recent research has focused on that perception. The experimenters were able to use neuroimaging to identify brain regions which correlate with feelings of volition and agency in normal and abnormal patients.[26] This is certainly an interesting study, but (as the experimenters make clear) it does not address the question of whether or not human agents actually have meaningful freedom. My impression is that these

---

23 Bryce Gessell, "Indeterminism in the Brain", *Biology and Philosophy* 32 (2017): 1205–23, at 1210, 1220.
24 Adina Roskies, "Neuroscientific Challenges to Free Will and Responsibility", *Trends in Cognitive Sciences* 10 (2006): 419–23, at 420.
25 https://www.sciencealert.com/lesion-network-mapping-brain-behind-free-will-agency-volition.
26 P. Ryan Darby, Juho Joutsa, Matthew J. Burke, and Michael D. Fox, "Lesion Network Localization of Free Will", *Proceedings of the National Academy of Sciences* 115, vol. 42, (2018): 10792–7.

researchers are correct in their assessment that contemporary neuroscience is not focused on trying to settle the question of the existence of free will and so we have no basis for predicting whether or not it will be a topic of research in the future.

Although many philosophers, even those defending libertarian freedom, seem to assume that science *could* and possibly *will* settle the question of the existence of meaningful freedom, very little has been written regarding just how this empirical research is to be conducted. Marcelo Fischborn attempts to make the case that neuroscience could (in principle) discover evidence for the sort of local determinism that would conflict with libertarian free will. He writes,

> We can imagine a similar law that would prevent an individual from choosing otherwise given the occurrence of some previous event whose occurrence was not within the individual's control:
> LD1. For any event x, and any subject s, if an x that is a pattern of neural activity of type B occurs in s's brain, then s will decide to push a given button.
> Here, whenever a specific pattern of neural activity happens in a subject's brain, a specific decision results, namely, a decision to push a given button.

He then generalizes this "law", proposing a statement of the "deterministic nature of choices":

> (DNC): For any subject s, any choice x, and any course of action X, if s chooses to do X, then there is a previous event y of a type Y in s's brain, such that whenever an event of type Y occurs in someone's brain, then this subject will choose for the course of action X.[27]

In that this principle applies to any choice made by any subject and in that the "previous event" from which the specific choice must follow is something over which the agent has no control, this seems an adequate statement of the sort of local causal determinism that would indeed conflict with humans having libertarian free will.

LD1, says Fischborn, is patterned after the experiments of Soon et al. (2008). This, in his view, provides reason to believe that neuroscience and psychology could in principle provide evidence to support such statements of local causal determinism.[28] The Soon experiments were discussed in Chapter 3. They purported to show that whether an agent would push the

---

27 Marcelo Fischborn, "Libet-Style Experiments, Neuroscience, and Libertarian Free Will", *Philosophical Psychology* 29 (2016): 494–502, at 497–8.
28 Fischborn (2016): 498.

button on the right or the button on the left could be predicted 10 seconds ahead of the actual push on the basis of neural imaging. I argued that the interpretation of the conclusions of the experiments was dubious. Even if one were to accept the interpretation, the "decision" to push the right or the left button is so distant from a morally significant choice that it would make little difference to the debate over meaningful free will to allow that this sort of choice of indifference is determined. Of the more sweeping statement of the deterministic nature of choices in general (DNC), Fischborn writes, "neuroscience and psychology should also be able to support it, since it is just a generalization about statements of local determination and choices".[29] Fischborn goes on to note that the Libet experiments have not demonstrated that some (or all) choices are determined. He allows that it will be difficult for neuroscience and psychology to demonstrate that some (or all) choices are determined since "much remains to be discovered on these matters".[30] But the implication is that future science may or will be able to settle the question empirically.[31]

Fischborn does not go into detail on *how* the empirical studies might go. He suggests that "[o]ne possibility would be to add some form of intervention to Libet-style experiments that induced RPs [readiness potentials] whose effects could then be analyzed".[32] Libet, as discussed in Chapter 3, purportedly found a particular sort of brain activity, the readiness potential, to precede the subject's desire to flex the wrist. It is not clear what Fischborn means by "inducing" readiness potentials, but the image it raises is one of the scientist "reaching in" to the subject's brain, perhaps by mechanical or electronic or magnetic means or perhaps simply by suggestion, to alter the goings-on therein. But this proposal points to one of the standard difficulties involved in much scientific research, the Problem of the Observer; the presence and activity of the observer can have an impact on the progress of the experiment such that it becomes impossible to see how things would have gone on had not the observer interfered.

This point is especially relevant to brain science. Suppose, as some have suggested, that the physical substrate correlated with the conscious phenomena is ultimately to be located at the quantum level. Danko Georgiev writes,

---

29 Fischborn (2016): 498.
30 Fischborn (2016): 498.
31 In a subsequent response to a critical article by Roskies and Nahmias, Fischborn puts more emphasis on the "in principle" aspect of his argument and says that he doubts whether neuroscience will ever show DNC to be true; Marcelo Fischborn, "Neuroscience and the possibility of locally determined choices: Response to Adina Roskies and Eddy Nahmias" in *Philosophical Psychology* 30 (2017): 198–201, at 201.
32 Fischborn (2016): 500.

if one's mental states are quantum states then no external agent would be capable to observe or monitor the mental (quantum) state of a quantum coherent system, because any measurement itself will alter the state of the observed quantum system.[33]

Suppose we move up from the quantum level and attempt to answer the question about determinism in the brain by observing widespread neuronal activity. A related problem remains. Adina Roskies writes, "no conceivable technology could provide the relevant information without radically disrupting the system it was meant to measure".[34] At an even more "macro" level, subjects in experiments related to making LFMCs may need to be kept in the dark about the goals and methods of the experiments because if they know they are being observed, they may not behave naturally. The image of the scientist inducing a particular brain activity in order to study its effects raises (again) the problem that the presence and interference of the observer may undermine the value of the information gained from the experiment. This underscores the importance of the Brainiometer since it can observe at a distance without worrying the observed subject or disrupting the subject's natural brain activity.

Another defender of the usefulness of neuroscience in the study of free will is Robyn Repko Waller. She writes, "testing the efficacy of conscious proximal intentions in producing what are typically held to be free and morally appraisable actions is not a far-off goal of neuroscience but rather is feasible given existing neuroscience technology and knowledge".[35] Waller notes that what I label the Problem of Translation Regarding the Object of Study is often raised against neuroscientific attempts to study free will through the sorts of experiments conducted by Libet and by Soon et al. I have emphasized this problem. Waller attempts to defend the role of neuroscience by suggesting a variant on the Soon et al. experiments where the choice of the left or the right button involves a moral dimension. A review of Waller's proposal will further my argument that use of the Brainiometer will be necessary (but probably will not be sufficient) to settle the question of human freedom empirically. Waller does not say that her proposed experiment is the sort that could settle the question. Rather she is, more modestly, hoping to provide "examples of how neuroscience can collect

---

33 Danko Georgiev, "Quantum No-Go Theorems and Consciousness", *Axiomathes* 23 (2013): 683–95, at 692. The role of the observer in quantum mechanics is a notorious puzzle for theorists; David Hodgson, "Quantum Physics, Consciousness, and Free Will", in Kane (2011): 57–83.
34 Roskies (2014): 116.
35 Robyn Repko Waller, "Beyond Button Presses: The Neuroscience of Free and Morally Appraisable Actions", *The Monist* 95 (2012): 441–62, at 451–2.

better evidence about the processes ... associated with free will and moral responsibility".[36] I will argue that even this more modest claim is dubious.

In the experiment conducted by Soon et al., the brain of subjects deciding whether to push the right or the left button was scanned. The sensational takeaway from the experiments was that an observer could tell, from looking at the image of brain activity 10 seconds ahead of the decision to push, whether the subject would decide to push the left button or the right button. As discussed in Chapter 3, there were difficulties with the experiment (e.g., timing questions and the fact that the model's predictive accuracy was barely above chance). But setting those aside, there was the fundamental problem that a button push (right or left) involves nothing like the sort of free will that people care about. Were there strong empirical evidence that mere right-versus-left choices were indeed determined by previous brain activity outside the control of the agent, that would be interesting. Indeed, it might go some small distance to undermining the introspective argument for libertarian free will if the agents in question had a strong but demonstrably mistaken feeling that it was up to them to decide on right or left and that they could have decided otherwise. But I allowed in Chapter 1 that the introspective argument is weak. The more powerful reason to commit to belief in free will is that it grounds the traditional view that human beings can be responsible moral agents with the special dignity that involves. Only very powerful reasons should budge us from that view, and empirical evidence from choices that are quite unlike morally significant choices (if it were discovered) would not be sufficient.

Waller's suggestion to rectify this problem is to modify experiments such as the Soon et al. experiment by adding that which button the subject pushes will determine whether some amount of money is given to a charity of the subject's choosing or goes into their own account. "This kind of experiment focuses on a moral choice, one that involves uncertainty about what to do and deliberation, and an action with morally praiseworthy or blameworthy consequences."[37] Thus, her claim that "testing the efficacy of conscious proximal intentions in producing what are typically held to be free and morally appraisable actions is not a far-off goal of neuroscience but rather is feasible given existing neuroscience technology and knowledge".[38] Suppose that the goal of what we will call the "Waller experiments" was to find empirical evidence for or against LFMCs. The researchers, lacking a Brainiometer (Waller's suggestion is that we need not locate this research in the far future), are taking fMRI images of the subject's brain, over a series of iterations, as the subject debates which button to push – the "charity" button or the "self" button – and then pushes the button. Note first that,

---

36 Waller (2012): 459, note 13.
37 Waller (2012): 455–7.
38 Waller (2012): 451–2.

although there is no ethical problem of deception here, there is still an ethical worry, and that is that the researchers' intent is to study a morally significant choice. I argued in Chapter 6 (and again in Chapter 7) that it may be unacceptable to deliberately place people in a situation involving moral risk to their own characters for the purpose of studying the process of moral choice. In the Waller experiment, the subjects have agreed to be put in that position, but they may not have realized the risk; moreover, even if they do, it may be wrong for someone to put themselves at risk in that way. Of course, the ethical concern needs to be weighed against the possible benefits of running such an experiment. As discussed in the previous chapter, even if these experiments could settle the question of whether or not human agents have meaningful freedom, it is not a foregone conclusion that the benefits would outweigh the risks.

A second issue is that, as it stands, it is not clear that the choice the subject makes in the Waller experiment is a morally significant choice. First, there is the difficulty mentioned above that the presence of the observer may influence the behavior of the subject in a way that undermines the goal of the experiment. This won't be a problem when the choice the subject is to make is simply to push either the right or the left button. But when the setup is that the subject is to do something for which he is to be held morally praiseworthy or blameworthy, it is difficult to imagine that the presence of the observer will not affect how the agent chooses. (I believe this is true even if the researcher is not obviously present but the subject simply realizes that the observer must know which button he pushed.) Waller includes that the subject is told that he must push each button at least once and that he must not form distal decisions about following a preset pattern. But when it comes down to it, the presence of the observer might provide so much incentive to appear praiseworthy in the eyes of the scientist that the subject might never find himself in the torn condition with both options being really viable. The subject might push the "self" button once or twice to show that he's following instructions and then stick to the "charity" button the rest of the time.

The Problem of Perspective comes up again with assessing whether or not the subject actually makes a morally significant choice. In the discussions of the Milgram experiments in Chapters 5 and 6, one of the central points was that it is possible that the experimenter's understanding of the sort of choice he is asking the subject to make is different from the subject's understanding of that choice. Milgram thought his subjects were choosing between being obedient and doing the right thing, but a case can be made that some of them assessed the situation as one where both causing pain to someone and stopping the experiment were equally bad options. Some of them apparently just did not believe that they were really inflicting pain (or much pain) and so it was not a serious moral choice. Similar points can be made for the Waller experiment. The way Waller describes it, the choice for giving money to the charity is supposed to be the praiseworthy action and giving the money to oneself is supposed to be blameworthy. Suppose the subject is well off himself and is confident that the charity has plenty of money. So, it doesn't make much difference which button he pushes, and he is thinking of the process simply as participating in an experiment and not as making a real moral choice. In that case, he may never experience the torn condition and may just push right or left at random.

Or perhaps the subject has good moral reasons for thinking that giving the money to himself is at least as praiseworthy as giving it to charity. Perhaps the vehicle that he needs to keep his job to support his family has to be repaired and this is the best (or only) way for him to get the money for the job. Or suppose he knows a family member is desperately in need of some extra money, whereas the charity is very well off, so he gives the money to himself to give to the family member. To the external observer, it might look like the subject has chosen the blameworthy option when giving to himself, but the subject himself might plausibly believe that giving to himself is the right thing to do under the circumstances, or he might hold that his options are morally equivalent. Choices of indifference – even if there is a value dimension to them (i.e., they appear equally harmful or equally beneficial) – are not the same phenomena as morally significant choices where the choice is between the praiseworthy and blameworthy actions.

One might attempt to circumvent this issue by conducting extensive interviews with potential subjects before the experiments and selecting only those who are likely to see the choice before them as morally significant. Or one might interview subjects extensively after the experiment and then take the data only from those who believe in hindsight that they made morally significant choices. But this process is likely to be extremely time-consuming. And it may fail in producing the necessary information. It might be hard for subjects to provide enough of their concerns and life histories beforehand to predict whether or not they will consider the choice before them in the experiment to be a morally significant one. And it may be hard for subjects (after the fact) to assess just how they were thinking when they made their choices. Or, as in the case of the Milgram experiments, one might have to grant the possibility that the subjects were attempting to defend their choices. Those who frequently gave money to themselves out of selfishness might portray their choices as morally virtuous under the circumstances.

Finally, we could not be sure that the information provided by subjects before or after the choice genuinely allowed us to assess their situation just before (and as) they were making the choice. We couldn't be sure that subjects were really in the torn condition, reasonably debating between what they themselves considered to be morally significant, mutually conflicting, open options. This is why (back to the future) if Dr. F hopes to study the brain activity which correlates with ostensibly free choice, he really cannot do without the Brainiometer. The process of making a morally significant choice is so involved and so personal that he needs to be able to see (with great specificity) just what is going on in the agent's brain and mind. I argued above that, given the complexity of brain processes and given the point that people (including their brains) are just different from one another, it will never be possible to construct an instrument or process capable of the specificity required for genuine mind reading– in other words, the Brainiometer will never be built.

But even if Dr. F has a Brainiometer, he will not succeed in producing experimental evidence for or against the existence of LFMCs. Let us say that Dr. F (having thrown ethics to the winds) trains the Brainiometer on a passerby, S. He mind-reads that S is debating between conflicting desires to give some money to charity (call that action C) or to keep it for himself (call that action K). The Brainiometer is so accurate that Dr. F can tell that S considers the former to be the morally better option and that is why he has the desire to do it, while he considers keeping the money the morally worse option, yet he'd really like to keep that money. Dr. F, then, is able to tell that S is in the torn condition. Then he observes that S chooses to give the money to charity. Dr. F is able to review all the brain activity that preceded S's choice for C since the Brainiometer records it all.

Dr. F's first thought might be to approach the question of LFMCs from the standpoint that it is libertarianism that is to be confirmed or disconfirmed and so he should look to see whether he can detect the sorts of processes that libertarians posit. But this is probably not a fruitful approach. One core commitment of libertarians is an agent's ability to choose otherwise. On libertarianism, the agent, S, having chosen C, could nonetheless have chosen K. But it is difficult to see what brain activity would correlate with, or provide any empirical evidence for, an actual ability to do otherwise. All we can ever *observe* is things as they are. Even with quantum mechanics, once a particle is observed, it is in a certain state and not otherwise. On the macro level, we do not detect traces of might-have-been-ness. So, there seems to be nothing for Dr. F to look to find or fail to find if he attempts to confirm or disconfirm that the agent could have chosen otherwise.

Another criterion of an LFMC is that it is the agent himself that is the cause of his choice.[39] So, Dr. F may be looking for some "trace" of aseity. On standard agent-causal theories, there does look to be a sui generis cause at work, but what this sui generis cause should look like empirically as brain activity is not a question that can be answered, it seems to me. What, exactly, should Dr. F be looking for? Dr. F might detect what appears to be sudden, anomalous brain activity, before what the agent takes to be a free

---

39 Although Robert Kane is an event-causal libertarian, I do not think he would disagree here. It must be the agent who bears the ultimate responsibility for his choice.

choice, but correlating that with the agent's agent-causing the free choice looks to be a leap of faith.[40] Furthermore (the Problem of Focus), it could be argued that it is the *whole* agent qua person that chooses and so Dr. F should not expect to find some isolated brain activity to be uniquely associated with the free choice. Even though standard agent-causation posits a sui generis cause, there is no reason to think that Dr. F could locate it in the record of S's brain activity; thus, if Dr. F does not find evidence of some unique sort of cause, that doesn't mean it wasn't at work. On the theory of parsimonious agent-causation that I mentioned in Chapter 2, there is even less hope for Dr. F to locate some special sort of cause at work in a free choice. What Dr. F would observe is the brain activity correlating with S desiring C and K, and then S desiring C, and the desire for K ceasing to be viable. Dr. F's approach of looking to find positive evidence – or the lack of same – for the sort of cause entailed by an *a se* choice is not likely to yield useful results.

Prima facie, one would expect that looking for evidence of local causal determinism is the more obvious way for Dr. F to proceed. So, he should be looking for a brain event, preceding S's opting for C, that can plausibly be held to explain or determine or causally necessitate S's opting for C over K. S's finding himself in the torn condition might be determined. It is the opting for C over K that constitutes the choice which, to be an LFMC, must not be determined and must be *a se*. So, suppose, for the sake of argument, Dr. F detects some brain event of type Y that occurs before S opts for C in the area of the brain associated with volition. He suspects that type Y events may cause people to choose C and so (following Fischborn's pattern) he forms the hypothesis he wishes to test:

> For any subject s, and any morally significant choice C, if s chooses to do C, then there is a previous event y of a type Y in s's brain, such that whenever an event of type Y occurs in someone's brain, then this subject will choose for the course of action C.
> (Assuming that the previous event of type Y is not something over which s has any control.)

The way to test the hypothesis is to observe many subjects making the same choice as S, or to study S making the same choice repeatedly, and to see whether an event of type Y does indeed precede the choosing of C over K. Unfortunately for Dr. F's project, this is impossible. What Dr. F is concerned

---

40 This finding would, however, *fit well* with standard agent-causation, so if this sudden, anomalous brain activity is what Dr. F discovers over repeated observations of different people making what they take to be morally significant choices, perhaps this should be considered some evidence of standard agent-causal libertarianism. The diehard determinist would not be convinced.

with is "any subject" choosing C. But – to reiterate a point which was made above but which bears repeating since sometimes it seems to be forgotten in the literature about experimenting on free will – *people are not fungible*. Dr. F's hypothesis to be tested seems modelled on looking at people as if they were electrons. In physics, one can devise coherent hypotheses "for any x", but the same is not true in the study of human beings. There is only one person S; moreover, there is only one instance of S being in the torn condition and then choosing C over K. There is no other S in the actual world, and S makes the choice in question only once. Yes, he may choose between keeping his money and giving to charity repeatedly, and so he is choosing between roughly similar actions, but with all the complexities that go into making a choice, two choices at different times cannot be the same. Waller's proposed experiments make this clear since she includes as part of what is being studied, the fact that at each iteration of the experiment, different motives will come into play. For example, after giving money to himself, the subject might feel a little guilty and so choose to give money to the charity on the next go-round.[41] Each time he chooses, his motivations and reasons (and digestion and posture and temperature and level of fatigue, etc.) will be different.[42]

Suppose Dr. F is studying S in the lab in a Waller experiment. S chooses to give to charity on the first pass and to give to charity again on the second pass. The second choice is not the same choice as the first. It is one thing to give some money to charity and it is another to give *even more* money to charity. Studying the preceding brain activity, Dr. F will note that either it is the same before each time S chooses to give to charity or it is different. If it is the same, an event of type Y, let's say, Dr. F might take that as evidence that type Y does not causally determine a choice since it preceded two different choices: to give and to give more. But that would not show that the choices were *not* determined, just that Y, in and of itself, is probably not a causally necessitating factor. If Y precedes X and Y precedes Z, there appears to be more to the picture than just that Y causes X. If the brain activity is different, which will almost certainly be the case since brains are not static and a lot has gone on in S's brain and mind since the first choice to give to charity, then Dr. F is left with the unsurprising observation that different brain activity precedes different choices, telling us roughly nothing about free will.

What if Dr. F were to erase S's memory of having made the choice for C and return him to the torn condition? What if Dr. F were to do this over and over? Could he then study repeated instances of the same choice? No. By erasing S's memory, Dr. F has interfered with the workings of S's brain.

---

41 Waller (2012): 457.
42 Richard Swinburne makes a similar point; "Dualism and the Determination of Action" in Swinburne (2011): 63–83, at 76–7.

A choice made by someone whose memory is intact is not the same thing as a choice made by someone part of whose memory has been erased. And a choice made by someone whose memory has been erased once is not the same as a choice made by someone whose memory has been erased twice. Moreover, a brain suffering such interference cannot be supposed to function just the way a normal brain would. The Problem of the Observer would certainly arise if Dr. F were to step in and interfere with his subjects by erasing their memories.

Each choice is unique and if we assume there is a neural correlate of each choice, that too is unique. Adina Roskies and Eddy Nahmias write,

> the complexity of the human brain suggests that any complex decision will involve such a wide disjunction of neural processes that there will be no pattern of neural activity of a given type that can be picked out as the cause of that decision. Assuming physicalism and *universal* determinism, there will be a *token* set of neural activity *just prior* to the decision that ensures that it occurs. But that exact (token) set of neural activity will likely never happen again, nor will it ever happen in another agent.[43]

The complexity of brain and mind make the Brainiometer an impossible dream, and even with the Brainiometer, the uniqueness of human choices and the complexity of corresponding brain activity make it impossible to settle the question of free will empirically.

There is one qualifier to this claim but it is of no use to Dr. F no matter how far in the future he finds himself. Suppose Dr. D is almost divine. She is almost omnipotent and almost omniscient. One of the few things she does not know, but would like to find out, is whether or not human agents have libertarian, morally significant free will. So, being almost omnipotent, she is able to either rewind the universe to its identical situation at a given point in time any number of times or create multiple identical copies of the universe at a given point in time any number of times. Then she can observe multiple iterations of the same human agents (in the rewind scenario), or identical human agents (in the copying scenario), in just the same torn conditions and then making their choices. Being almost omniscient, she knows all that goes on in their brains and in their consciousness and she is able to tell from the great number of rewinds or copies whether or not it is likely that the same pattern of brain activity produces the choice for *this* over *that* in a morally charged situation. So, the question of human free

---

43 Adina Roskies and Eddy Nahmias, "'Local Determination', Even If We Could Find It, Does Not Challenge Free Will: Commentary on Marcelo Fischborn", *Philosophical Psychology* 30 (2017): 185–97, at 193.

will *is* open to empirical investigation but just not by anyone who is not almost omnipotent and omniscient.

Conclusion

For mere mortals, the old debate over human freedom will probably never be settled by science. Even if we assume that the future scientist is in possession of a Brainiometer and that he is looking for evidence for or against freedom under a libertarian description, that being the harder task since compatibilism would be easier to square with determinism (universal or local), he cannot succeed. That being the case, I return to the claim from Chapter 1: The most important reason for committing to belief in free will – arguably robust, libertarian free will – is that it entails understanding our fellow human beings as morally responsible creatures of great dignity. To deny free will is to demean ourselves and our neighbors. We ought not to do that without powerful evidence. Over the millennia, many philosophers (for philosophical reasons) have decided the question to their own satisfaction for and against human freedom. But in that they have not been able to convince their opponents, it is appropriate to hold that the philosophical arguments are not *ultimately convincing*. They are unlikely to command a consensus. Science, however, has not settled (and cannot settle) the question of free will. Someone might try to sit on the fence but that is not doable in practice. We think of and treat ourselves and our neighbors as responsible beings with dignity, or we do not. One might be convinced that human agents do not bear moral responsibility and do not possess the associated dignity and still think of them and treat them as if they do. Cognitive dissonance, however, is uncomfortable and undesirable. Recently, free will skeptics have attempted to look on the bright side of denying free will but (as I discussed in Chapter 1) their arguments seem to derive from the thought that the importance of belief in free will has to do mainly with justifying punishment. In the Western tradition, going back at least to St. Augustine, the more fundamental reason to value free will is rooted in the connection between freedom and dignity. In the absence of decisive evidence, the situation demands a sort of Pascalian wager, and the best bet – best because it grounds the duty to respect our fellow human beings and ourselves – is on robust free will.

Appendix

Problems with the Experimental Approach to Human Freedom

Here I list problems raised in this book as they are illustrated in the philosophical debate over the free will experiments. This gives the reader a quick reference. I divide the list into practical problems and ethical problems. I have tried to choose labels that are informative and sort difficulties by the label that fits best, but often difficulties could fall under more than one problem as I list them and often problems are closely related or intertwined. Some of the problems are more serious than others or more amenable to solutions now or in the future. Some problems are so obvious and universal that I have not included them in the list. For example, the problems that experimenters – being human – may suffer from confirmation bias or that experimental data are subject to multiple interpretations are mentioned in the book, but I do not include these general points under my list since they could apply to almost any experiment. And when I say that an experiment or an interpretation raises a problem, I do not mean that the problem is intractable – only that it is an issue that needs to be considered. I list the problems in alphabetical order.

Problems: Practical

Description: Terms and concepts are not adequately defined or explained.

Domain: Controversial metaphysical assumptions relevant to the free will question are not clearly labelled as metaphysical assumptions and are allowed to color interpretation of experimental data.

First-person reporting: The reports offered by subjects of their own mental states can be open to doubt, and they are difficult to verify, since the mental states themselves are private to the subjects.

Focus: In attempting to study human freedom, experimenters may be concerned with events and behaviors that are not directly relevant to free will in the mistaken belief that such events and behaviors constitute free will or are necessary for free will.

Generalization: The simple move from "*some* Xs are Y" to the claim that "*all* Xs are Y" without a justification. This is especially problematic when we have experiential reason to believe that, although some Xs are Y, it is not the case that all Xs are Y.

Mereology: It is extremely difficult to determine what constitutes a particular, individual mental event, brain event, or part of the brain.

Observer: As experiments are being carried out, the presence of the observer affects the process or system being monitored.

Perspective: The researcher has not taken into account how elements of the experiment may appear to the subject. This can also relate to ethical problems.

Post hoc fallacy: That one thing happens after another is not, by itself, sufficient evidence that the earlier is the cause of the later.

Probabilities: In the context of experimenting on free will, evidence that some preceding event allows predictability with "more than chance" probability is not evidence of local causal determinism. That agents may lean toward one option, yet still confront genuinely open options, is a standard view for most libertarian theories.

Self-refutation: The conclusions or theories that researchers advance would, if true, render impossible their ability to conduct the experiments that produced those conclusions and supported those theories.

Translation: Doubt arises over whether the information gained through the experiment can be applied to meaningful freedom and in the natural setting. There are several sorts of problems of translation:
- with regard to the object of study: Many experiments study decisions, intentions, and actions. The question is: Are the human behaviors studied in the lab so similar to the kind of choice that the free will issue cares about that the data gained from the experiment can translate into information that is useful regarding human freedom?
- with regard to the situation: Is the situation in the lab so removed from the natural environment that the behavior of subjects likely reflects the odd and manufactured setting?
- with regard to the subject pool: Is the pool of subjects in an experiment too small, or too unrepresentative, to provide data that can translate meaningfully to the larger population?

Problems: Ethical

(These problems arise mainly in connection with deceptive experiments.)

Deception: Psychological experiments often depend on deceiving the subjects, which suggests a lack of respect and should be counted as a cost. But it is a cost that may be outweighed by the benefits gained from the deceptive experiment.

Elitism: Researchers come to see themselves as superior to their subjects and to the mass of humankind. This could justify treating the "inferiors" as objects.

Expected benefits: When the costs of an experiment are weighed against the expected benefits, it is difficult to assess what the benefits will actually be, and it may be possible to achieve the benefits without the costs of the experiment.

Harms to subjects: Experiments may cause physical harm or psychological and emotional harm. Ongoing harm to subjects after the experiments are over is important to consider.

Harms (and wrongs) to researchers: Engaging in deceptive research may encourage researchers and their students to be less trustworthy. This constitutes harm to their characters and may also harm the profession in general.

Moral risk: Putting people in a position where they will have to make a moral choice puts them at moral risk. They may choose badly. This is especially worrisome on theories of free will that hold that one constructs one's character by one's choices.

Privacy: Invasion of privacy is a cost requiring justification even if the victim does not suffer physical or psychological and emotional harm.

Uncharitable interpretations: If data from an experiment can be interpreted equally plausibly in a number of ways, interpretations that demean the subject should not be preferred. The researcher may have to settle for noting that there are several equally adequate interpretations.

Wrongs to subjects: Possibly, one can wrong someone without causing them physical or psychological and emotional harm. Putting someone at moral risk and violating someone's privacy are examples.

Bibliography

Annas, Julia, Darcia Narvaez, and Nancy E. Snow (editors) *Developing the Virtues: Integrating Perspectives* (Oxford: Oxford University Press, 2016): 34–68.

Athanassoulis, Nafsika, "A Response to Harman: Virtue Ethics and Character Traits", *Proceedings of the Aristotelian Society* 100 (2000): 215–221.

Baer, John, James C. Kaufman, and Roy F. Baumeister, "Introduction: Psychology and Free Will." In *Are We Free? Psychology and Free Will* edited by John Baer James C. Kaufman, and Roy F. Baumeister (editors) (Oxford: Oxford University Press, 2008a): 3–9.

Baer, John, James C. Kaufman, and Roy F. Baumeister (editors) *Are We Free? Psychology and Free Will* (Oxford: Oxford University Press, 2008b).

Balaguer, Mark, *Free Will as an Open Scientific Problem* (Cambridge, MA: MIT Press, 2010).

Banja, John, "Could Have Chosen Otherwise Under Identical Conditions: An Evolutionary Perspective on Free Will", *AJOB Neuroscience* 6(2) (2015): 3–11.

Banks, William P., and Susan Pockett, "Benjamin Libet's Work on the Neuroscience of Free Will." In *The Blackwell Companion to Consciousness* edited by Max Velmans and Susan Schneider (Oxford: Blackwell Publishing, 2007): 657–670.

Banks, William P., and Eve A. Isham, "Do We Really Know What We are Doing?: Implications of Reported Time of Decision for Theories of Volition." In *Conscious Will and Responsibility* edited by Walter Sinnott-Armstrong and Lynn Nadel (Oxford: Oxford University Press, 2011): 47–60.

Bargh, John A., "Bypassing the Will: Toward Demystifying the Nonconscious Control of Social Behavior." In *The New Unconscious* edited by Ron R. Hassin, James S. Uleman, and John A. Bargh (New York: Oxford University Press, 2005): 37–58.

Bargh, J.A., M. Chen, and L. Burrows, "Automaticity of Social Behavior: Direct Effects of Trait Construct and Stereotype Activation on Action", *Journal of Personality and Social Psychology* (1996): 230–244.

Baumeister, Roy F., "Free Will, Consciousness, and Cultural Animals." In *Are We Free? Psychology and Free Will* edited by John Baer, James C. Kaufman, and Roy F. Baumeister (Oxford: Oxford University Press, 2008): 65–85.

Baumeister, Roy F., Cory Clark, and Janie Luguri, "Free Will: Belief and Reality." In *Surrounding Free Will: Philosophy, Psychology, Neuroscience* edited by Alfred R. Mele (Oxford: Oxford University Press, 2015): 49–71.

Baumrind, Diana, "Some Thoughts on Ethics of Research: After Reading Milgram's 'Behavioral Study of Obedience", *American Psycyhologist* 19 (1964): 421–423.

Baumrind, Diana, "Research Using Intentional Deception: Ethical Issues Revisited", *American Psychologist* 40 (1985): 165–174.

Baumrind, Diana, "Is Milgram's Deceptive Research Ethically Acceptable?" *Theoretical and Applied Ethics* 2 (2013): 1–18.

Baumrind, Diana, "When Subjects Become Objects: The Lies Behind the Milgram Legend", *Theory and Psychology* 25 (2015): 690–696.

Bayne, Timothy, "Phenomenology and the Feeling of Doing: Wegner on the Conscious Will." In *Does Consciousness Cause Behavior?* edited by Susan Pockett, William P. Banks, and Shaun Gallagher (Cambridge, MA: MIT Press, 2006): 169–183.

Beauchamp, T., R.R. Faden, F.J. Wallace, and L. Wallace, editors, *Ethical Issues in Social Science Research* (Baltimore, Maryland: Johns Hopkins University Press, 1982).

Benham, Bryan, "The Ubiquity of Deception and the Ethics of Deceptive Research", *Bioethics* 22 (2008): 147–156.

Berthoz, A., "Neural Basis of Decision in Perception and in the Control of Movement." In *Neurobiology of Decision-Making* edited by Antonio R. Damasio, Hanna Damasio, and Yves Christen (Berlin: Springer, 1996): 83–100.

Bittner, Thomas, "Consciousness and the Act of Will", *Philosophical Studies* 81 (1996): 331–341.

Blass, Thomas, *The Man Who Shocked the World: The Life and Legacy of Stanley Milgram* (New York: Basic Books, 2004).

Blass, Thomas, "From New Haven to Santa Clara: A Historical Perspective on the Milgram Obedience Experiments", *American Psychologist* 64 (2009): 37–45.

Bleidorn, Wiebke, "Moving Character Beyond the Person-Situation Debate: The Stable and Dynamic Nature of Virtue in Everyday Life." In *Character: New Directions from Philosophy, Psychology, and Theology* edited by Christian B. Miller, R. Michael Furr, Angela Knobel, William Fleeson (Oxford: Oxford University Press, 2015): 129–150.

Bok, Sissela, *Lying: Moral Choice in Public and Private Life* (New York: Pantheon Books, 1978).

Breitmeyer, Bruno G., "Problems with the Psychophysics of Intention", *Behavioral and Brain Science* 8 (1985): 539–540.

Burger, Jerry M., "Replicating Milgram: Would People Still Obey Today?" *American Psychologist* 64 (2009): 1–11.

Caruso, Gregg D., Elizabeth Shaw, and Derk Pereboom, "Free Will Skepticism in Law and Society: An Overview." In *Free Will Skepticism in Law and Society: Challenging Retributive Justice* edited by Elizabeth Shaw, Derk Pereboom, and Gregg D. Caruso (Cambridge: Cambridge University Press, 2019).

Chalmers, David, "The Hard Problem of Consciousness." In *The Blackwell Companion to Consciousness*, 2nd Edition, edited by Susan Schneider and Max Velmans (Hoboken, NJ: Wiley-Blackwell Publishers, 2017): 32–44.

Chisholm, Roderick, "'Human Freedom and the Self', the Lindley Lecture, 1964, University of Kansas." In *Free Will* edited by Gary Watson (Oxford: Oxford University Press, 1982): 24–45.

Christensen, L., "Deception in Psychological Research: When Is its Use Justified?" *Personality and Social Psychology Bulletin* 14 (1988): 664–675.

Churchland, Patricia S., "Feeling Reasons." In *Neurobiology of Decision-Making* Damasio, Antonio R., Hanna Damasio, and Yves Christen (editors) (Berlin: Springer, 1996): 181–199.

Crick, Francis, *The Astonishing Hypothesis: The Scientific Search for the Soul* (New York: Charles Scribner's Sons, 1994).

Damasio, Antonio R., Hanna Damasio, and Yves Christen (editors) *Neurobiology of Decision-Making* (Berlin: Springer, 1996).

Darby, Ryan P., Juho Joutsa, Matthew J. Burke, and Michael D. Fox, "Lesion Network Localization of Free Will", *Proceedings of the National Academy of Sciences* 115(42) (2018): 10792–10797.

Darley, J.M., and C.D. Batson, "From Jerusalem to Jericho: A Study of Situational and Dispositional Variables in Helping Behavior", *Journal of Personality and Social Psychology* 27(1973): 100–108.

Davies, Paul Sheldon, "What Kind of Agent Are We? A Naturalistic Framework for the Study of Human Agency." In *Distributed Cognition and the Will: Individual Volition and Social Context* edited by Don Ross, David Spurrett, Harold Kincaid, and G. Lynn Stephens (Cambridge, MA: MIT Press, 2007): 39–60.

Deery, O., T. Davis, and J. Carey, "The Free-Will Intuitions Scale and the Question of Natural Compatibilism." *Philosophical Psychology* 28 (6) (2015): 776–801.

Dennett, Daniel, *Brainstorms* (Ann Arbor, MI: Bradford Books, 1978).

Doris, John M., *Lack of Character: Personality and Moral Behavior* (Cambridge: Cambridge University Press, 2002).

Dweck, Carol S., and Daniel C. Molden, "Self-Theories: The Construction of Free Will." In *Are We Free? Psychology and Free Will* edited by John Baer, James C. Kaufman, and Roy F. Baumeister (Oxford: Oxford University Press, 2008): 44–64.

Elms, Alan, "Keeping Deception Honest: Justifying Conditions for Social Scientific Research Strategems." In *Ethical Issues in Social Science Research* edited by T. Beauchamp, R.R. Faden, F.J. Wallace Jr, and L. Wallace (Baltimore, Maryland: Johns Hopkins University Press, 1982): 232–245.

Ewusi-Boisvert, Esthelle and Eric Racine, "A Critical Review of Methodologies and Results in Recent Research on Belief in Free Will", *Neuroethics* 11 (2018): 97–110.

Eyde, Lorraine D., "Other Responsibilities to Participants." In *Ethics in Research With Human Participants* edited by Bruce D. Sales and Susan Folkman (Washington, DC: American Psychological Association, 2000): 61–73.

Farah, Martha J., and Paul Root Wolpe, "Monitoring and Manipulating Brain Function, New Neuroscience Technologies and Their Ethical Implications", *The Hastings Center Report* 34(3) (2004): 35–45.

Fischborn, Marcelo, "Libet-Style Experiments, Neuroscience, and Libertarian Free Will", *Philosophical Psychology* 29 (2016): 494–502.

Fischborn, Marcelo, "Neuroscience and the possibility of locally determined choices: Response to Adina Roskies and Eddy Nahmias", *Philosophical Psychology* 30 (2017): 198–201

Fischer, John Martin and S.J. Mark Ravizza, *Responsibility and Control: A Theory of Moral Responsibility* (Cambridge: Cambridge University Press, 1998).

Fischman, Marian W., "Informed Consent." In *Ethics in Research With Human Participants* edited by Bruce D. Sales and Susan Folkman (Washington, DC: American Psychological Association, 2000): 35–48.

Flanagan, Owen, "Moral Science? Still Metaphysical After All These Years." In *Personality, Identity, and Character* edited by Darcia Narvaez and Daniel K. Lapsley (New York: Cambridge University Press, 2009): 52–78.

Folkman, Susan, "Privacy and Confidentiality." In *Ethics in Research With Human Participants* edited by Bruce D. Sales and Susan Folkman (Washington, DC: American Psychological Association, 2000): 49–57.

Frankfurt, Harry, "Freedom of the Will and the Concept of a Person", *Journal of Philosophy* 68 (1971): 5–20.

Fried, I., R. Mukamel, and G. Kreiman, "Internally Generated Preactivation of Single Neurons in Human Medial Frontal Cortex Predicts Volition", *Neuron* 69 (2011): 548–562.

Gazzaniga, Michael, *Who's in Charge? Free Will and the Science of the Brain* (New York: Harper Collins, 2011).

Gessell, Bryce, "Indeterminism in the Brain", *Biology and Philosophy* 32 (2017): 1205–1223.

Georgiev, Danko, "Quantum No-Go Theorems and Consciousness", *Axiomathes* 23 (2013): 683–695.

Gollwitzer, Peter M., Ute C. Bayer, and Kathleen C. McCulloch, "The Control of the Unwanted." In *The New Unconscious* edited by Ron R. Hassin, James S. Uleman, and John A. Bargh (New York: Oxford University Press, 2005): 485–515.

Gollwitzer, P.M., and P. Sheeran, "Implementation Intentions and Goal Achievement: A Meta-Analysis of Effects and Processes", *Advances in Experimental Social Psychology* 38 (2006): 69–119.

Gomes, Gilberto, "The Interpretation of Libet's Results on the Timing of Conscious Events: A Commentary", *Consciousness and Cognition* 11 (2002): 221–230.

Greene, Joshua D., R. Brian Sommerville, Leigh E. Nystrom, John M. Darley, Jonathan D. Cohen, "An fMRI Investigation of Emotional Engagement in Moral Judgment", *Science* 293 (2001): 2105–2108.

Greene, J.D., and J.D. Cohen, "For the Law, Neuroscience Changes Nothing and Everything", *Philosophical Transactions of the Royal Society of London B* 359 (2004): 1775–85.

Haggard, P., and M. Eimer, "On the Relation between Brain Potentials and the Awareness of Voluntary Movements", *Experimental Brain Research* 126 (1999): 128–133.

Haggard, Patrick, "Conscious Awareness of Intention and of Action." In *Agency and Self-Awareness* edited by Johannes Roessler and Naomi Eilan (Oxford: Clarendon Press, 2003): 111–127.

Haggard, Patrick, "Human Volition: Towards a Neuroscience of Will", *Nature Reviews Neuroscience* 9(12) (2008): 934–946.

Haggard, Patrick, "The Sources of Human Volition", *Science* 324 (2009): 731–733.

Haggard, Patrick, "Does Brain Science Change Our View of Free Will?" In *Free Will and Modern Science* edited by Richard Swinburne (Oxford: Oxford University Press, 2011a): 7–24.

Haggard, Patrick, "Decision Time for Free Will", *Neuron* 69 (2011b): 404–406.
Haggard, Patrick, "'Free Will': Components and Processes." In *Surrounding Free Will* edited by Alfred R. Mele (Oxford: Oxford University Press, 2015): 145–164.
Harman, Gilbert, "Moral Philosophy Meets Social Psychology: Virtue Ethics and the Fundamental Attribution Error", *Proceedings of the Aristotelian Society* 99 (1999): 315–332.
Harris, Sam, *Free Will* (New York: Free Press, 2012).
Harris, Sam, *The Moral Landscape: How Science Can Determine Human Values* (New York: Free Press, 2011).
Hassin, Ron R., James S. Uleman, and John A. Bargh (editors) *The New Unconscious* (New York: Oxford University Press, 2005)
Helm, Charles and Mario Morelli, "Stanley Milgram and the Obedience Experiment: Authority, Legitimacy, and Human Action," *Political Theory* 7 (1979): 321–345.
Herdova, Marcela and Stepen Kearns, "This is a Tricky Situation: Situationism and Reasons-Responsiveness", *Journal of Ethics* 21 (2017): 151–183.
Herrera, Christopher D., "Ethics, Deception, and 'Those Milgram Experiments'", *Journal of Applied Philosophy* 18 (2001): 245–256
Hodgson, David, "Quantum Physics, Consciousness, and Free Will." In *The Oxford Handbook of Free Will*, edited by Robert Kane (Oxford: Oxford University Press, 2011): 57–83.
Isen, A.M., and P.F. Levin, "Effect of Feeling Good on Helping: Cookies and Kindness", *Journal of Personality and Social Psychology* 21 (1972): 384–388.
Jayawickreme, Eranda, Peter Meindl, Erik G. Helzer, R. Michael Furr, and William Fleeson, "Virtuous States and Virtuous Traits: How the Empirical Evidence Regarding the Existence of Broad Traits Saves Virtue Ethics from the Situationist Critique", *Theory and Research in Education* 12 (2014): 283–308.
Johansson, Petter, Lars Hall, Sverker Sikstrom, and Andreas Okson, "Failure to Detect Mismatches between Intention and Outcome in a Simple Decision Task", *Science* 310 (2005): 116–119.
Kane, Robert, *The Significance of Free Will* (New York: Oxford University Press, 1996).
Kane, Robert (editor) *The Oxford Handbook of Free Will*, 1st Edition (Oxford: Oxford University Press, 2002).
Kane, Robert (editor) *The Oxford Handbook of Free Will*, 2nd Edition (Oxford: Oxford University Press, 2011).
Kane, Robert, "Free Will, Bound and Unbound: Reflections on Shaun Nichols' *Bound*", *Philosophical Studies* 174 (2017): 2479–2488.
Kaposi, David, "The Resistance Experiments: Morality, Authority and Obedience in Stanley Milgram's Account", *Journal for the Theory of Social Behaviour* 47 (2017): 382–401.
Kassin, Saul M., and Katherine L. Kiechel, "The Social Psychology of False Confessions: Compliance, Internalization, and Confabulation," *Psychological Science* 7 (1996): 125–128.
Klein, Colin, "Philosophical Issues in Neuroimaging", *Philosophy Compass* 5(2) (2010): 186–198.

Klein, Stanley, "Libet's Research on the Timing of Conscious Intentions to Act: A Commentary", *Consciousness and Cognition* 11(2) (2002): 273–279.

Klemm, W.R., "Free Will Debates: Simple Experiments are not so Simple", *Advances in Cognitive Psychology* 6 (2010): 47–65.

Korn, James H., *Illusions of Reality: A History of Deception in Social Psychology* (Albany, New York: State University of New York Press, 1997).

Lagas, Martin and Katarzyna Jaworska, "How Predictable Are "Spontaneous Decisions" and "Hidden Intentions"? Comparing Classification Results Based on Previous Responses with Multivariate Pattern Analysis of fMRI BOLD Signals", *Frontiers in Psychology* 3 (2012): 56.

Lapsley, Daniel, "Moral Self-Identity and the Social-Cognitive Theory of Virtue." In *Developing the Virtues: Integrating Perspectives* edited by Julia Annas, Darcia Narvaez, and Nancy E. Snow (Oxford: Oxford University Press, 2016): 34–68.

Lapsley, Daniel, "Situationism and the Pyrrhic Defense of Character Education." In *Moral Psychology: Volume 5: Virtue and Character* edited by Walter Sinnott-Armstrong and Christian B. Miller (Cambridge, Massachusetts: MIT Press, 2017): 171–183.

Latane, B., and J. Rodin, "A Lady in Distress: Inhibiting Effects of Friends and Strangers on Bystander Intervention", *Journal of Experimental social Psychology* 5 (1969): 189–202.

Latane, B., and J.M. Darley, *The Unresponsive Bystander: Why Doesn't He Help?* (New York: Appleton-Century-Crofts, 1970).

Lewis, C.S., "The Humanitarian Theory of Punishment", *Res Judicatae* 30 (1954): 224–230.

Libet, Benjamin, C.A. Gleason, E.W. Wright, and D.K. Pearl, "Time of Conscious Intention to Act in Relation to Onset of Cerebral Activities (Readiness-Potential): The Unconscious Initiation of a Freely Voluntary Act", *Brain* 106 (1983): 623–642.

Libet, Benjamin, "Unconscious Cerebral Initiative and the Role of Conscious Will in Voluntary Action", *Behavioral and Brain Science* 8 (1985a): 529–539.

Libet, Benjamin, "Author's Response: Theory and Evidence Relating Cerebral Processes to Conscious Will", *Behavioral and Brain Science* 8 (1985b): 558–566.

Libet, Benjamin, A. Freeman, and K. Sutherland. *Towards a Neuroscience of Free Will* (Exeter, UK: Imprint Academics, 1999).

Libet, Benjamin, "Do We Have Free Will?" In *The Oxford Handbook of Free Will*, 1st Edition, edited by Robert Kane (Oxford: Oxford University Press, 2002): 551–564.

Libet, Benjamin, *Mind Time* (Cambridge, MA: Harvard University Press, 2004).

Lippert-Rasmussen, Kasper, "Brain Privacy, Intimacy, and Authenticity: Why a Complete Lack of the Former Might Undermine Neither of the Latter!" *Res Publica* 23 (2017): 227–244.

Lott, Micah, "Situationism, Skill, and the Rarity of Virtue", *Journal of Value Inquiry* 48 (2014): 387–401.

Lowe, E.J., "Self, Agency and Mental Causation", *Journal of Consciousness Studies* 6 (1999): 225–39.

Lowe, E.J., *Personal Agency: The Metaphysics of Mind and Action* (Oxford: Oxford University Press, 2008).

MacIntyre, Alasdair, *After Virtue* (Notre Dame, Indiana: University of Notre Dame Press, 1984).
Malle, Bertram E., "Of Windmills and Straw Men: Folk Assumptions of Mind and Action." In *Does Consciousness Cause Behavior?* edited by Susan Pockett, William P. Banks, and Shaun Gallagher (Cambridge, MA: MIT Press, 2006): 207–231.
Maoz, Uri, Liad Mudrik, Ram Rivlin, Ian Ross, Adam Mamelak, and Gideon Yaffe, "On Reporting the Onset of the Intention to Move." In *Surrounding Free Will* edited by Alfred Mele (Oxford: Oxford University Press, 2015): 184–202.
Mastroianni, George R., "Milgram and the Holocaust: A Reexamination", *Journal of Theoretical and Philosophical Psychology* 22 (2002): 158–173.
McGinn, Colin, *The Mysterious Flame* (New York: Basic Books, 1999).
McKenna, Michael and Brandon Warmke, "Does Situationism Threaten Free Will and Moral Responsibility?" *Journal of Moral Philosophy* 14 (2017): 698–733.
Mele, Alfred, *Autonomous Agents* (Oxford: Oxford University Press, 1995).
Mele, Alfred, *Free Will and Luck* (Oxford: Oxford University Press, 2006a).
Mele, Alfred, "Free Will: Theories, Analysis, and Data." In *Does Consciousness Cause Behavior?* edited by Susan Pockett, William P. Banks, and Shaun Gallagher (Cambridge, MA: MIT Press, 2006b): 187–205.
Mele, Alfred, *Effective Intentions: The Power of Conscious Will* (New York: Oxford University Press, 2009).
Mele, Alfred, "Testing Free Will", *Neuroethics* 3 (2010): 161–172.
Mele, Alfred, "Another Scientific Threat to Free Will?" *The Monist* 95 (2012): 422–440.
Mele, Alfred R. (editor) *Surrounding Free Will: Philosophy, Psychology, Neuroscience* (Oxford: Oxford University Press, 2015).
Milgram, Stanley, "Behavioral Study of Obedience", *Journal of Abnormal and Social Psychology* 67 (1963): 371–378.
Milgram, Stanley, "Issues in the Study of Obedience: A Reply to Baumrind", *American Psychologist* 19 (1964): 848–852.
Milgram, Stanley, *Obedience to Authority* (New York: Harper and Row, 1974).
Milgram, Stanley, "Subject Reaction: The Neglected Factor in the Ethics of Experimentation", *The Hastings Center Report* 7 (1977): 19–23.
Miller, Arthur G., *The Obedience Experiments: A Case Study of Controversy in Social Science* (New York: Praeger, 1986).
Miller, Christian, "Social Psychology, Mood, and Helping: Mixed Results for Virtue Ethics", *Journal of Ethics* 13 (2009): 145–173.
Miller, Christian, *Character and Moral Psychology* (Oxford: Oxford University Press, 2014).
Miller, Christian B., R. Michael Furr, Angela Knobel, and William Fleeson, "Introduction." In *Character: New Directions from Philosophy, Psychology, and Theology* edited by Christian B. Miller, R. Michael Furr, Angela Knobel, William Fleeson (Oxford: Oxford University Press, 2015a): 1–16.
Miller, Christian B., R. Michael Furr, Angela Knobel, William Fleeson (editors) *Character: New Directions from Philosophy, Psychology, and Theology* (Oxford: Oxford University Press, 2015b).
Miller, J., P. Shepherdson, and J. Trevena, "Effects of Clock Monitoring on Electroencephalographic Activity: Is Unconscious Movement Initiation an Artifact of the Clock?" *Psychological Science* 22(1) (2011): 103–109.

Monroe, Andrew E., and Bertram F. Malle, "Free Will Without Metaphysics." In *Surrounding Free Will: Philosophy, Psychology, Neuroscience* edited by Alfred R. Mele (Oxford: Oxford University Press, 2015): 25–28.
Montague, P. Read, "Free Will", *Current Biology* 18(14) (2008): R584 under "Quick Guide."
Moore, Adam D., "Privacy, Neuroscience, and Neuro-Surveillance", *Res Publica* 23 (2017): 159–177.
Morelli, Mario F., "Milgram's Dilemma of Obedience", *Metaphilosophy* 14 (1983): 183–189.
Murray, Dylan, "Situationism, Going Mental, and Modal Akrasia", *Philosophical Studies* 172 (2015): 711–736.
Mylopoulos, Myrto I., and Hakwan Lau, "Naturalizing Free Will: Paths and Pitfalls." In *Surrounding Free Will: Philosophy, Psychology, Neuroscience* edited by Alfred R. Mele (Oxford: Oxford University Press, 2015): 123–144.
Nagle, Thomas, "Concealment and Exposure", *Philosophy and Public Affairs* 27 (1998): 3–30.
Nagel, Thomas, *Mind and Cosmos* (Oxford: Oxford University Press, 2012).
Nahmias, Eddy, "When Consciousness Matters: A Critical Review of Daniel Wegner's *The Illusion of Conscious Will*", *Philosophical Psychology* 15 (2002): 527–541.
Nahmias, Eddy, "Agency, Authorship, and Illusions", *Consciousness and Cognition* 14 (2005): 771–785.
Nahmias, Eddy, S. Morris, T. Nadelhoffer, and J. Turner, "Surveying Freedom: Folk Intuitiions About Free Will and Moral Responsibility", *Philosophical Psychology* 18(5) (2005): 561–584.
Nahmias, Eddy, "Why 'Willusionism' Leads to 'Bad Results': Comments on Baumeister, Crescioni, and Alquist", *Neuroethics* 4 (2011): 17–24
Nahmias, Eddy, J. Shepard, and S. Reuter, "It's OK if 'My Brain Made Me Do It': People's Intuitions about Free Will and Neuroscientific Prediction", *Cognition* 133(2) (2014): 502–516.
Narvaez, Darcia and Daniel K. Lapsley (editors) *Personality, Identity, and Character* (New York: Cambridge University Press, 2009).
Nelkin, Dana, "Freedom, Responsibility, and the Challenge of Situationism", *Midwest Studies in Philosophy* 29 (2005): 181–206.
Nichols, Shaun, "How Can Psychology Contribute to the Free Will Debate?" In *Are We Free? Psychology and Free Will* edited by John Baer James C. Kaufman, and Roy F. Baumeister (Oxford: Oxford University Press, 2008): 10–31.
Nichols, Shaun, *Bound: Essays on Free Will and Responsibility* (Oxford: Oxford University Press, 2015).
Ocampo, Brenda, "Unconscious Manipulation of Free Choice by Novel Primes", *Consciousness and Cognition* 34 (2015): 4–9.
O'Connor, Timothy, *Persons and Causes* (New York: Oxford University Press, 2000).
O'Connor, Timothy, "Freedom with a Human Face", *Midwest Studies in Philosophy* 24 (2005): 207–227.
Pacherie, Elisabeth, "Toward a Dynamic Theory of Intentions." In *Does Consciousness Cause Behavior?* edited by Susan Pockett, William P. Banks, and Shaun Gallagher (Cambridge, MA: MIT Press, 2006): 145–167.

Pan, Xueni and Antonia F. de C. Hamilton, "Why and How to Use Virtual Reality to Study Human Social Interaction: The Challenges of Exploring a New Research Landscape", *British Journal of Psychology* 109 (2018): 395–417.

Paris, Panos, "Scepticism about Virtue and the Five-Factor Model of Personality", *Utilitas* 29 (2017): 423–452.

Patten, Steven, "The Case that Milgram makes", *Philosophical Review* 86 (1977): 350–364.

Pereboom, Derk, *Living Without Free Will* (Cambridge: Cambridge University Press, 2001).

Pereboom, Derk, *Free Will, Agency, and Meaning in Life* (Oxford: Oxford University Press, 2014).

Perry, Gina, *Behind the Shock Machine: The Untold Story of the Notorious Milgram Psychology Experiments* (New York, NY: The New Press, 2013).

Pinker, Steven, "The Fear of Determinism." In *Are We Free? Psychology and Free Will* edited by John Baer, James C. Kaufman, and Roy F. Baumeister (Oxford: Oxford University Press, 2008): 311–324.

Pockett, Susan, William P. Banks, and Shaun Gallagher (editors) *Does Consciousness Cause Behavior?* (Cambridge, MA: MIT Press, 2006)

Polger, Thomas W., and Lawrence Shapiro, *The Multiple Realization Book* (Oxford: Oxford University Press, 2016).

Rachels, James, *Elements of Moral Philosophy*, 4th Edition (New York: McGraw-Hill, 2003).

Radder, H., and G. Meynen, "Does the Brain 'Initiate' Freely Willed Processes? A Philosophy of Science Critique of Libet-type Experiments and Their Interpretation", *Theory and Psychology* 23(1) (2013): 3–21.

Ravven, Heidi M., "Putting Free Will in Context and Beyond", *AJOB Neuroscience* 6(2) (2015): 1–2.

Rigioni, Davide and Marcel Brass, "From Intentions to Neurons: Social and Neural Consequences of Disbelieving in Free Will", *Topoi* 33 (2014): 5–12.

Ringo, James L., "Timing volition: Questions of what and when about W", *Behavioral and Brain Sciences* 8 (1985): 550–551.

Roessler, Johannes and Naomi Eilan (editors) *Agency and Self-Awareness* (Oxford: Clarendon Press, 2003).

Rogers, Katherin, "What's Wrong with Occasionalism?" *American Catholic Philosophical Quarterly* 75 (2001): 345–69.

Rogers, Katherin, "Retribution, Forgiveness, and the Character Creation Theory of Punishment", *Social Theory and Practice* 33 (2007): 75–103.

Rogers, Katherin, *Freedom and Self-creation: Anselmian Libertarianism* (Oxford: Oxford University Press, 2015).

Roskies, Adina, "Neuroscientific challenges to free will and responsibility", *Trends in Cognitive Sciences* 10 (2006): 419–423.

Roskies, Adina, "How does neuroscience affect our conception of volition?" *Annual Review of Neuroscience* 33 (2010): 109–130.

Roskies, Adina, "Why Libet's Studies Don't Pose a Threat to Free Will." In *Conscious Will and Responsibility* edited by Walter Sinnott-Armstrong and Lynn Nadel (Oxford: Oxford University Press, 2011): 11–22.

Roskies, Adina, "Can Neuroscience Resolve Issues about Free Will?" In *Moral Psychology, Volume 4: Free Will and Moral Responsibility* edited by Walter Sinnott-Armstrong (Cambridge, MA: MIT Press, 2014): 103–126.

Roskies, Adina and Eddy Nahmias, "'Local determination', Even If We Could Find It, Does Not Challenge Free Will: Commentary on Marcelo Fischborn", *Philosophical Psychology* 30 (2017): 185–197

Ross, Don, "Introduction: Science Catches the Will." In *Distributed Cognition and the Will: Individual Volition and Social Context* edited by Don Ross, David Spurrett, Harold Kincaid, and G. Lynn Stephens (Cambridge, MA: MIT Press, 2007): 1–16.

Ross, Don, David Spurrett, Harold Kincaid, and G. Lynn Stephens (editors) *Distributed Cognition and the Will: Individual Volition and Social Context* (Cambridge, MA: MIT Press, 2007).

Ross, Peter W., "Empirical Constraints on the Problem of Free Will." In *Does Consciousness Cause Behavior?* edited by Susan Pockett, William P. Banks, and Shaun Gallagher (Cambridge, MA: MIT Press, 2006): 125–144.

Russell, Paul, "Free Will, Art and Morality", *The Journal of Ethics* 12 (3–4) (2008): 307–325.

Ryberg, Jesper, "Neuroscience, Mind reading and Mental Privacy", *Res Publica* 23 (2017): 197–211.

Sabini, John and Maury Silver, "Lack of Character? Situationism Critiqued", *Ethics* 115 (2005): 535–562

Saigle, Victoria, Veljko Dubljević, and Eric Racine, "The Impact of a Landmark Neuroscience Study on Free Will: A Qualitative Analysis of Articles Using Libet and Colleagues' Methods", *AJOB Neuroscience* 9(1) (2018): 29–41.

Sales, Bruce D., and Susan Folkman (editors) *Ethics in Research With Human Participants* (Washington, DC: American Psychological Association, 2000).

Sales, Bruce D., and Michael Lavin, "Identifying Conflicts of Interest and Resolving Ethical Dilemmas", in *Ethics in Research With Human Participants* edited by Bruce D. Sales and Susan Folkman (Washington, DC: American Psychological Association, 2000): 109–128.

Saxe, Rebecca, "The Neural Evidence for Simulation is Weaker than I Think You Think it is", *Philosophical Studies* 144 (2009): 447–456.

Schlosser, Markus E., "Free Will and the Unconscious Precursors of Choice", *Philosophical Psychology* 25 (2012): 365–384.

Schlosser, Markus E., "Conscious Will, Reason-Responsiveness, and Moral Responsibility", *Journal of Ethics* 17 (2013): 205–232.

Schlosser, Markus E., "The Neuroscientific Study of Free Will: A Diagnosis of the Controversy", *Synthese* 191 (2014): 245–262.

Schneider, Susan and Max Velmans, editors, *The Blackwell Companion to Consciousness*, 2nd Edition (Hoboken, NJ: Wiley-Blackwell Publishers, 2017).

Schooler, Jonathan, Thomas Nadelhoffer, Eddy Nahmias, and Kathleen D. Vohs, "Measuring and Manipulating Beliefs and Behaviors Associated with Free Will." In *Surrounding Free Will: Philosophy, Psychology, Neuroscience* edited by Alfred R. Mele (Oxford: Oxford University Press, 2015): 72–94.

Searle, John, *Freedom and Neurobiology* (New York: Columbia University Press, 2007).

Sehon, Scott, *Free Will and Action Explanation: A Non-Causal, Compatibilist Account* (Oxford: Oxford University Press, 2016).

Shariff, Azim F., Jonathan Schooler, and Kathleen D. Vohs, "The Hazards of Claiming to Have Solved the Hard Problem of Free Will." In *Are We Free? Psychology and Free Will* edited by John Baer, James C. Kaufman and Roy F. Baumeister (Oxford: Oxford University Press, 2002): 181–204.

Shariff, A.F., J.D. Greene, J.C. Karremans, J. Luguri, C.J. Clark, J.W. Schooler, R.F. Baumeister, K.D. Vohs, "Free Will and Punishment: A Mechanistic View of Human Nature Reduces Retribution", *Psychological Science* 25(8) (2014): 1563–1567.

Shaw, Elizabeth, Derk Pereboom, and Gregg D. Caruso (editors) *Free Will Skepticism in Law and Society: Challenging Retributive Justice* (Cambridge: Cambridge University Press, 2019).

Shen, Francis X., "Neuroscience, Mental Privacy, and the Law", *Harvard Journal of Law and Public Policy* 36 (2013): 653–713.

Shepard, Jason and Shane Reuter, "Neuroscience, Choice and the Free Will Debate", *AJOB Neuroscience* 3 (3) (2012): 7–11.

Sieber, Joan E., "Planning Research: Basic Ethical Decisions-Making." In *Ethics in Research With Human Participants* edited by Bruce D. Sales and Susan Folkman (Washington, DC: American Psychological Association, 2000): 13–26.

Simkulet, William, "On Free Will and Evolution", *AJOB Neuroscience* 6(2) (2015): 12–13.

Simmons, Joseph P., Leif D. Nelson, and Uri Simonsohn, "False-Positive Psychology: Undisclosed Flexibility in Data Collection and Analysis Allows Presenting Anything as Significant", *Psychological Science* 22(2011): 1359–1366.

Simons, Peter, "Forward." In *Free Will and Modern Science* edited by Richard Swinburne (Oxford: Oxford University Press, 2011): vii–xv.

Sinnott-Armstrong, Walter and Lynn Nadel (editors) *Conscious Will and Responsibility* (Oxford: Oxford University Press, 2011).

Sinnott-Armstrong, Walter (editor) *Moral Psychology, Volume 4: Free Will and Moral Responsibility* (Cambridge, MA: MIT Press, 2014).

Sinnott-Armstrong, Walter and Christian B. Miller (editors) *Moral Psychology: Volume 5: Virtue and Character* (Cambridge, MA: MIT Press, 2017).

Slater, Mel, Angus Antley, Adam Davison, David Swapp, Christoph Guger, Chris Barker, Nancy Pistrang, Maria V. Sanchez-Vives, "A Virtual Reprise of the Stanley Milgram Obedience Experiments", *PLOS ONE* (2006). https://doi.org/10.1371/journal.pone.0000039.

Smilansky, Saul, "Free Will, Fundamental Dualism, and the Centrality of Illusion." In *The Oxford Handbook of Free Will*, 1st Edition, edited by Robert Kane (Oxford: Oxford University Press, 2002): 489–505.

Smilansky, Saul, "Free Will and Respect for Persons", *Midwest Studies* 29 (2005): 248–261.

Smith, M. Brewster, "Moral Foundations in Research with Human Participants." In *Ethics in Research with Human Participants* edited by Bruce D. Sales and Susan Folkman (Washington, DC: American Psychological Association, 2000): 3–10.

Smithdeal, Matthew, "Belief in Free Will as an Adaptive, Ungrounded Belief", *Philosophical Psychology* 29(8) (2016): 1241–1252.

Soon, Chun Siong, Marcel Brass, Hans-Jochen Heinze, and John-Dylan Haynes, "Unconscious Determinants of Free Decisions in the Human Brain", *Nature Neuroscience* 11 (2008): 543–545.

Soon, C.S., A.H. He, S. Bode, and J.D. Haynes, "Predicting Free Choices for Abstract Intentions", *Proceedings of the National Academy of Sciences of the United States of America* 110(15) (2013): 6217–6222.

Spence, Sean, *The Actor's Brain: Exploring the cognitive neuroscience of free will* (Oxford: Oxford UP, 2009).
Stamm, John S., "The Uncertainty Principle in Psychology", *Behavioral and Brain Sciences* 8 (1985): 553–554.
Stapp, Henry, *Quantum Theory and Free Will: How Mental Intentions Translate into Bodily Actions* (Cham, Switzerland: Springer Nature, 2017).
Sternberg, Eliezer, *My Brain Made Me Do It* (Amherst, NY: Prometheus Books, 2010).
Steward, Helen, *A Metaphysics for Freedom* (Oxford: Oxford University Press, 2012).
Strawson, Galen, "The Bounds of Freedom." In *The Oxford Handbook of Free Will*, 1st Edition, edited by Robert Kane (Oxford: Oxford University Press, 2002): 441–460.
Strawson, Galen, "The Impossibility of Ultimate Responsibility?" In *Free Will and Modern Science* edited by Richard Swinburne (Oxford: Oxford University Press, 2011): 126–140.
Swinburne, Richard (editor) *Free Will and Modern Science* (Oxford: Oxford University Press, 2011a).
Swinburne, Richard, "Dualism and the Determination of Action." In *Free Will and Modern Science* edited by Richard Swinburne (Oxford: Oxford University Press, 2011b): 63–83.
Trevena, J., and J. Miller, "Cortical Movement Preparation Before and After a Conscious Decision to Move", *Consciousness and Cognition* 11(2) (2002): 162–190.
Trevena, J., and J. Miller, "Brain Preparation before a Voluntary Action: Evidence Against Unconscious Movement Initiation", *Consciousness and Cognition* 19(1) (2010): 447–456.
Trope, Yaacov and Ayelet Fishback, "Going Beyond the Motivation Given: Self-Control and Situational Control Over Behavior." In *The New Unconscious* edited by Ron R. Hassin, James S. Uleman, and John A. Bargh (New York: Oxford University Press, 2005): 537–565.
Tunick, Mark, "Brain Privacy and the Case of Cannibal Cop", *Res Publica* 23 (2017): 179–196.
Vinding, M.C., M. Jensen, and M. Overgaard, "Distinct Electrophysiological Potentials for Intention in Action and Prior Intention for Action", *Cortex* 50 (2014): 86–99.
Viola, Marco and Elia Zanin, "The Standard Ontological Framework of Cognitive Neuroscience: Some Lessons from Broca's Area", *Philosophical Psychology* 30 (2017): 945–969.
Vohs, Kathleen D., and Jonathan W. Schooler, "The Value of Believing in Free Will: Encouraging a Belief in Determinism Increases Cheating", *Psychological Sciences* 19 (2008): 49–54.
Waller, Robyn Repko, "Beyond Button Presses: The Neuroscience of Free and Morally Appraisable Actions", *The Monist* 95 (2012): 441–462.
Walsh, E., S. Kuhn, M. Brass, D. Wenke, and P. Haggard, "EEG Activations During Intentional Inhibition of Voluntary Action: An Electrophysiological Correlate of Self-Control?" *Neuropsychologia* 48(2) (2010): 619–626.
Walter, Sven, "Willusionism, Epiphenomenalism, and the Feeling of Conscious Will", *Synthese* 191 (2014): 2215–2238.

Wang, Jing, Vladimir L. Cherkassky, and Marcel Adam Just, "Predicting the Brain Activiation Pattern Associated With the Propositional Content of a Sentence: Modeling Neural Representations of Events and States", *Human Brain Mapping* 38 (2017): 4865–4881.

Watson, Gary (editor) *Free Will* (Oxford: Oxford University Press, 1982).

Webb, T.L., and P. Sheeran, "Does Changing Behavioral Intentions Engender Behavior Change? A Meta-Analysis of the Experimental Evidence", *Psychological Bulletin* 132(2) (2006): 249–268.

Wegner, Daniel, *The Illusion of Conscious Will* (Cambridge, MA: MIT Press, 2002).

Wegner, Daniel, "Who is the Controller of Controlled Processes?" In *The New Unconscious* edited by Ron R. Hassin, James S. Uleman, and John A. Bargh (New York: Oxford University Press, 2005): 19–36.

Wegner, Daniel, "Self is Magic." In *Are We Free? Psychology and Free Will* edited by John Baer, James C. Kaufman, and Roy F. Baumeister (Oxford: Oxford University Press, 2008): 226–247.

Wegner, Daniel M., and Thalia Wheatley, "Apparent Mental Causation: Sources of the Experience of Will", *American Psychologist* 54 (1999): 480–491.

Wielenberg, E.J., "Saving Character", *Ethical Theory and Moral Practice* 9 (2006): 461–491.

Wolpe, N., and J.B. Rowe, "Beyond the "Urge to Move": Objective Measures for the Study of Agency in the Post-Libet Era", *Frontiers in Human Neuroscience* 8 (2014): Article 450.

Index

Pages followed by n refers notes.

action projection 84–96, 100–101
agent-causation 86, 224–225;
  parsimonious 51, 225
agentic shift 121–124, 156, 172–173
American Psychological Association,
  Code of Ethics 15–16, 142–143,
  145–147, 150, 158, 160–161, 190, 192
animal experiments 55–56
Anselm, St. of Canterbury 51
apparent mental causation 82, 85, 88;
  see also Wegner, D.
Arendt, H. 174
Aristotle 108–109, 132–135, 138, 171
artistic choice 58–59
Augustine, St. of Hippo 13–14, 228
automatisms 83, 90–91, 99
autonomy 8, 103, 106, 142–143,
  162–163

Balaguer, M. 2, 16, 24, 183n1
Banja, J. 28
Banks, W. 68
Bargh, J.A. 91
Baumeister, R. 35
Baumrind, D. 146, 149n26, 155,
  163–164, 173, 179, 192
Bayne, T. 97
benefits of deceptive research 141,
  154, 165, 170–178; see also expected
  benefits, problem of
Benham, B. 156–157
Berthoz, A. 55
Bok, S. 142n2, 143, 163–164
brain in a vat 80–81
Brainiometer 11, 184–187, 191–216,
  220–221, 223–224, 227–228

brain mapping 206–216
Brass, M. 21
burden of proof 7, 12–13, 16–20, 48,
  50–51, 54–56, 59–60, 66, 75, 128,
  138n76, 143, 180–181, 186, 201–203,
  228
Burger, J. see Milgram experiments,
  recreations
Buridan's ass 46–47
Burrows, L. 91

Caruso, G. 18n17, 38
Causal Closure, Principle of 38
causation 40, 71–73, 97; probabilistic
  32, 34n59, 35, 49n6, 72n31, 77, 203,
  206–207, 217
Chalmers, D. 36–37
character-building 48, 52–53, 107–108,
  131–139, 157–159, 231
character-determined choice 52–53,
  117–118
character traits 107–110, 131–139
charitable interpretation see
  uncharitable interpretation,
  problem of
Chen, M. 91
Chisholm, R. 29
Christian tradition 13–14
Churchland, P. 29
Clever Hans 95, 100
A Clockwork Orange 23
Cohen, J.D. 33
compassion 10, 22, 109–110, 131,
  133–134, 136–138
compatibilism 3–6, 13n1, 184, 201
confabulation 93–95, 101, 166, 181

confirmation bias 180–181, 229
consequence argument 4–5
consequentialism 160
Crick, F. 28, 35–36

Darby, P. 217–218
deception, problem of 140–179, 190–197, 230
deceptive experiments *see* deception, problem of
Dennett, D. 29
description, problem of 26–31, 64, 70, 74–75, 82–87, 115–118, 127, 185, 205, 229
determinism 4–5, 31–35, 74, 200–201; local causal 4–5, 32, 99, 115, 201, 218, 225–226, 230; universal causal 4, 12, 31, 183–186
dignity 1–4, 7–8, 12–16, 18–20, 23, 26, 29, 45, 50, 52, 107, 138n76, 142–144, 160–161, 169, 201, 221, 228
dime experiment 114–115, 118–119, 138
domain, problem of 31, 40–41, 84, 98–99, 185, 229
Doris, J. 108–115, 119–121, 131–134, 135n67, 171–172, 180
dualism 37, 185–186, 189n4

Eichmann, A. 126n50, 151
Einstein, A. 87
Elitism, problem of 103, 170, 231
Elms, A. 175
epiphenomenalism 39–40, 82–83, 185–186
epistemic humility 130–131, 181
evaluation of choice 53–54, 101
expected benefits, problem of 170–179, 199–202, 231

facilitated communication 95–96, 99–100
first-person reporting, problem of 67–71, 96, 102, 187, 208, 229; *see also* introspection
Fischborn, M. 218, 225
Fischer, J.M. 80, 107
focus, problem of 87, 99–101, 122–123, 137–139, 187, 225, 229
folk view of free will 6–7
forgiveness 22
free will defense 14

free will theodicy 14
functionalism 37, 207n3

Gazzaniga, M. 9, 27, 79–80, 88–90, 93–103, 214n20, 217
generalization, problem of 97–98, 230
Genovese, Catherine 109–110
Georgiev, D. 219–220
Gessell, B. 216
Gestapo *see* National Socialism
Good Samaritan experiment 112–113, 116–119, 129, 136–137
Greene, J.D. 33, 56
group effect experiments 113–114, 129–131, 136–137, 175

Haggard, P. 34–36, 41
Harmon, G. 108, 121, 131, 134
harms and wrongs to researchers 163–170, 190, 197, 231
harms to subjects 146–157, 190–193, 231
Harris, S. 22
Herdova, M. 116
Herrera, C. 164
Holmes, O.W. 18–19
homunculus 27–28
Huckleberry Finn situation 45
Hume, D. 83

idealism 38, 185–186, 189n4
ideomotor effects 83, 91
illusion thesis *see* Wegner, D.
incompatibilism 5
indeterminism 32–34, 115, 186, 189, 216–217; *see also* open options
indifference, choice of 46–48, 57, 59, 65, 75–76, 126–128, 203–204, 219, 223
informed consent *see* deception, problem of
introspection 23–26, 54, 69, 82, 86–87, 221; *see also* first-person reporting, problem of
Isham, E. 68
I Spy experiment 92, 99, 102

Jaworska, K. 76
Jayawickreme, E. 135

Kane, R. 14, 24, 29–30, 32, 43, 51–52, 59, 183n1, 224n39

Kant, I. 13n1
Kaposi, D. 123, 125–126
Kassin, S. 92–93
Kearns, S. 116
Kiechel, K. 92–93
Klein, C. 68n21
Klemm, W.R. 23
knowledge, value of 170–171, 200
Korn, J. 161n64, 176

Lagas, M. 76
Lapsley, D. 104–105
Lavin, M. 165
Lewis, C.S. 19
libertarian free moral choice (LFMC), described 31, 44–55, 205
libertarianism 2–6, 12, 14–17, 22, 24–26, 29, 31–34, 39–41, 43, 49–51, 58, 64, 77, 80, 98, 103, 106–107, 183–184, 189, 201–202, 205–206, 218, 221, 224, 228, 230; *see also* libertarian free moral choice (LFMC), described
Libet, B. 9, 37, 60–73, 97, 101, 174, 205, 216
Libet experiments 9, 60–73, 83, 89, 98, 119, 122, 187, 193, 205, 219–220; veto experiments 63–64, 66–67
Lippert-Rasmussen, K. 195
Lott, M. 138–139
Lowe, E.J. 33, 37
luck problem 26, 98

MacIntyre, A. 183n2
Maoz, U. 68–69
Mastroianni, G. 175
McGinn, C. 37
Mele, A. 50, 64, 67, 86–87
memory of choice 54
mereology, problem of 68–69, 76–78, 207–208, 230
Milgram experiments 10–11, 105, 110–112, 119–129, 135–137, 141, 143–159, 171–178, 191, 222–223; recreations 105–106, 125n48, 152–154, 159, 165n72, 180, 189–192, 197, 215
Milgram, S. 10–11, 110, 119, 121–124, 126–128, 141, 144–159, 165, 167–171, 173–177, 192–193, 222
Miller, A. 147n20, 175
Miller, C. 138n73

moment of choice 51, 68–69
Moore, A. 162–163
moral laxity 20–21
moral luck 50, 58n23
moral objectivity 45–46
moral responsibility 1, 3, 5–6, 8, 13–14, 16–19, 22–23, 36, 39, 43, 45, 47, 50, 52–53, 57, 80, 85, 101, 107, 114–117, 119, 129, 183n1, 184, 187, 204, 221, 224n39, 228
moral risk, problem of 10, 157–159, 190–191, 198, 222, 231
moral status of a deed 51–52, 65–66, 80–81, 184
Murray, D. 129n53

Nagel, T. 33
Nahmias, E. 80, 97, 227
National Socialism 110, 121, 133, 142, 144, 150–151, 154, 173–175, 177–178, 191
Nazis *see* National Socialism
Nelkin, D. 106–107
Nichols, S. 24

observer, problem of 69, 162, 187, 194, 198–199, 208, 219, 222, 227, 230
occasionalism 39–40
O'Connor, T. 14, 30, 51
open options 6, 25, 32, 46, 48–51, 98, 189–190, 197, 205, 223–224, 230

parallelism 39–40
Pascalian wager 228
Peeping Tom 160, 163, 196
perceptual judgments 42, 56, 58
Pereboom, D. 14–15, 17, 18n17, 22n25, 34n59
Perry, G. 123, 148n21, 151n30, 155, 167–168
personal identity 36
perspective, problem of 10, 70, 119–131, 137, 148, 177, 181, 191, 213, 222–223, 230
physicalism 35–39, 98, 185–186
Pinker, S. 17, 26, 36
placebos 144
Pockett, S. 68
political implications 23
post hoc fallacy 9, 71–73, 76–78, 206, 230
practical wisdom 133–134

priming experiments 91, 98
privacy, problem of 10–11, 16, 159–163, 190, 194–198, 231
probabilities, problem of 34n59, 49n6, 77, 203, 230; *see also* causation, probabilistic
prudence 59
prudential decisions 3, 43–44, 59, 186, 202–203, 205
punishment 16–20, 22–23, 45, 121, 200–201

Rachels, J. 159–160, 196
Ravizza, M. 80, 107
Ravven, H.M. 6
readiness potential 62–63, 67, 72–73, 205–206, 219
reasons-responsiveness 62, 80, 89, 106–107, 115–131
respect *see* dignity
responsibility *see* moral responsibility
responsibility-grounding freedom *see* moral responsibility
rewind scenario 226–227
Rigioni, D. 21
Ringo, J. 66
role-playing 178–179, 202
Roskies, A. 55–56, 217, 220, 227
Ross, D. 15
Ross, P. 24
Russell, P. 58
Ryberg, J. 194

Saigle, V. 72–73
Sales, B. 165
Schlosser, M.E. 65, 116
Schooler, J. 20–21, 61
scientific advancement, value of 120–122, 125, 165, 169
Searle, J. 24
Sehon, S. 17
self-refutation, problem of 101–103, 128–129, 230
semi-compatibilism 17n14
Shariff, A. 61
Shen, F. 215n21
Sieber, J. 164
Simons, P. 3–4
situationism 10, 44, 62, 104–139, 168

skepticism, free will 17, 19, 22n25, 50–51, 228
slippery slope 164–170, 172
Smilansky, S. 15, 171, 200
Smith, M. 142
Soon experiment 9, 73–78, 89, 218–221
Sophie's choice situation 47, 126
Spence, S. 61–62
split-brain experiments *see* Gazzaniga, M.
Stamm, J. 69
Stapp, H. 38
Sternberg, E. 46n4
Strawson, G. 29, 50

timing problem 67–71, 76–78
torn condition *see* open options
tracing 26n35, 52–53
translation, problem of 9, 40, 230; regarding object of study 40, 44–49, 54–56, 59–60, 64–67, 69, 75–76, 96, 105, 112, 127–128, 186, 189, 202–205, 219–221, 230; regarding the situation 56, 66, 69, 96–97, 112, 173, 178–179, 192, 198, 215–216, 230; regarding the subject pool 56, 96–97, 101, 112, 129, 149–150, 162, 188–189, 197, 199, 230
trolley car intuitions 56

uncharitable interpretation, problem of 180–182, 203, 231
uniqueness of choice 11, 49, 225–227

van Inwagen, P. 4
Viola, M. 207
virtual reality *see* role-playing
Vohs, K. 20–21, 61

Waller, R. 220–223, 226
Wang, J. 209–216
Wegner, D. 9, 28, 34, 75n40, 79–103, 122, 128, 181–182, 205–206, 217; *see also* Gazzaniga, M.
will power 48, 56–57, 59, 86
willusionism *see* Wegner, D.
wrongs to subjects 157–163, 190, 193, 231

Zanin, E. 207